The Translator and Editor

ILAN STAVANS is Lewis-Sebring Professor in Latin American and Latino Culture at Amherst College. He is the author of many books, including *The Hispanic Condition, On Borrowed Words, Spanglish, Dictionary Days, Love and Language*, and *Quixote*. He is the editor of *The Norton Anthology of Latino Literature, The Oxford Book of Jewish Stories*, and *The FSG Book of Twentieth-Century Latin American Poetry*. He has translated Jorge Luis Borges, Pablo Neruda, Juan Rulfo, and Mariano Azuela from the Spanish; Isaac Bashevis Singer from the Yiddish; Yehuda Halevi from the Hebrew; William Shakespeare, Herman Melville, and Emily Dickinson from the English; and *Don Quixote of La Mancha* into Spanglish. He has also written for radio, movies, and TV and is the author of several children's books and graphic novels. He is the publisher of Restless Books and cofounder of the Great Books Summer Program.

Norton Critical Editions
Renaissance

For a complete list of Norton Critical Editions, visit
wwnorton.com/nortoncriticals

A NORTON CRITICAL EDITION

THE LIFE OF LAZARILLO DE TORMES, HIS FORTUNES AND ADVERSITIES

A NEW TRANSLATION
CONTEXTS
CRITICISM

Translated and Edited by

ILAN STAVANS
AMHERST COLLEGE

W · W · NORTON & COMPANY · *New York* · *London*

W. W. Norton & Company has been independent since its founding in 1923, when William Warder Norton and Mary D. Herter Norton first published lectures delivered at the People's Institute, the adult education division of New York City's Cooper Union. The Nortons soon expanded their program beyond the Institute, publishing books by celebrated academics from America and abroad. By mid-century, the two major pillars of Norton's publishing program—trade books and college texts—were firmly established. In the 1950s, the Norton family transferred control of the company to its employees, and today—with a staff of four hundred and a comparable number of trade, college, and professional titles published each year—W. W. Norton & Company stands as the largest and oldest publishing house owned wholly by its employees.

Manufacturing by Maple Press
Book design by Antonina Krass
Production manager: Vanessa Nuttry

Library of Congress Cataloging-in-Publication Data

Lazarillo de Tormes. English
    The life of Lazarillo de Tormes, his fortunes and adversities : a new translation, contexts, criticism / translated and edited by Ilan Stavans, Amherst College. —First edition.
        pages cm.—(A Norton Critical Edition)
    Includes bibliographical references.

  ISBN 978-0-393-93805-0 (pbk.)

  1. Lazarillo de Tormes.   2. Picaresque literature, Spanish—History and criticism.   I. Stavans, Ilan, translator.
    PQ6408.E5 2015
    863'.3—dc23

                                                                2015034608

W. W. Norton & Company, Inc., 500 Fifth Avenue, New York, N.Y. 10110
www.wwnorton.com

W. W. Norton & Company Ltd., Castle House, 75/76 Wells Street,
London W1T 3QT

1 2 3 4 5 6 7 8 9 0

Contents

List of Illustrations

Introduction

In the First Part, Chapter XXII of *Don Quixote of La Mancha* (1605), the knight-errant converses with a prisoner. We learn he is Ginés de Pasamonte, who will reappear in the Second Part, released a decade later, as the puppeteer Maese Pedro. In their dialogue, Don Quixote is told that Ginés is writing his autobiography. "Is it good?" he asks. Ginés responds that it's so good, "it means trouble for Lazarillo de Tormes and for all other books of that type that have been or will be written." While brief, the exchange allows us to appreciate the standing *Lazarillo de Tormes* had in early-seventeenth-century Spain. Released anonymously exactly half a century before the publication of the First Part of Cervantes's novel, the novella had achieved by then the status of a literary landmark.

Not much has changed in the following centuries. It remains a centerpiece of Renaissance literature and is arguably the most popular example of the so-called picaresque novel, in which a rogue first-person narrator, often a rambunctious boy of illegitimate birth and with a troubled poor family background, described the abuse and corruption of Spain at the time.

Its full title is *La vida de Lazarillo de Tormes y de sus fortunas y adversidades*. Although it appears that the first edition came out in 1552 or 1554, four contemporary editions were printed in 1554, and those are the only extant ones: one in Alcalá de Henares, a second in Burgos, a third in Antwerp, and a fourth in Medina del Campo. The first of them includes some additional episodes that are probably written by another hand. While there is abundant speculation on the identity of its original author, nothing has ever been proven. It seems obvious that such a critique of the Catholic Church and other social types might be done only under a veil of secrecy.

As a result of its strong anticlerical views, the novella was listed by the Holy Inquisition in its *Index Librorum Prohibitorum* (*Index of Forbidden Books*), promulgated by Pope Paul IV in 1559. In 1573, a censored edition (without the Fourth and Fifth Chapters, along with other modifications) was allowed to circulate. It wasn't until the nineteenth century that the unabridged edition reached the hands of Spanish readers. Translations of it into French (1560), English (1576), German (1617), and Italian (1622), all based on the Belgian edition, which escaped censorship, made the book popular in Europe.

The *Lazarillo de Tormes* prompted a couple of sequels, none nearly as engaging as the original. The first was published, also anonymously, in 1555, just a year after the original, and the protagonist in it is a tuna. Its author probably lived in Flanders. It was twice reprinted in Milan, in 1587 and 1615. The second sequel was written by Juan de Luna, a Protestant from Toledo, and was released in Paris in 1620. In spirit it is much closer to the original.

The impact of *Lazarillo de Tormes* is felt not only in Spanish literature but throughout the Western canon. Jean-Jacques Rousseau's *Emile* is in debt to it. Likewise, the first novel written in the New World, José Joaquín Fernández de Lizardi's *El periquillo sarniento* (*The itching parrot*; written in 1816, published in 1831), is a confessed adaptation. After it, the *pícaro* as a character acquired a ubiquitous presence in Latin American literature. Charles Dickens's *Oliver Twist* and Mark Twain's *Adventures of Huckleberry Finn*, which have children as protagonists, are also acknowledged inheritors.

This is a notoriously raw, unfinished, difficult text. The author is no stylist. The Spanish of the sixteenth century has aged substantially. Embarking on a new translation has been an exhilarating endeavor. My Ur-text was the popular edition prepared by Amparo Medina-Bocos (Madrid: Cátedra, 2006), used in universities throughout the Hispanic world.

For reference, I used as my primary source the authoritative *Lazarillo de Tormes*, edited and annotated by the first-rate scholar Francisco Rico (Madrid: Cátedra, 1992; reprinted, Barcelona: Galaxia Gutemberg–Círculo de Lectores, 2011). However, Rico doesn't break the narrative into chapters, as I do. I consulted and often depended on the previous renditions of the book into English, starting with J. Gerald Markley (1954) and moving to Harriet de Onís (1959), W. S. Merwin (1962), Michael Alpert (1969), and Stanley Appelbaum (2001). Where I found a fortunate word choice or turn of phrase that was better than mine, I embraced it. Translating a classic is about making it freshly accessible to new audiences; it is also about acknowledging and even depending on one's precursors.

I have acquired this philosophy after years of translating works, historical and contemporary. Classics need to be rendered anew, in part because language ages. Today, for example, it is easier to understand *Lazarillo de Tormes* in English than in the original, sixteenth-century Spanish. And every generation is eager to give its own reading to a classic. Translation, thus, is synonymous with interpretation.

Yet the view that every translation needs to be radically different from the earlier ones is absurd. Language changes, yes, but not dizzily. Every translator walks through the doors opened by those who came before. A comparative study of the previous translations and of other partial works made available by scholars enabled me to decipher obtuse passages and, when appropriate, to be playful.

I also drew from a wealth of lexicographic volumes, particularly Antonio de Nebrija's *Gramática de la lengua española* (1492), Sebastián de Covarrubias's *Tesoro de la lengua castellana o española* (1611), and *Diccionario de Autoridades* (1726–39). I have kept appellative expressions such as *Tío* and *Sobrino* in Spanish to season the translation with contextual flavor. In doing so, I have taken advantage of the growing population of bilingual readers in the United States, for whom code-switching is a natural act.

The supporting materials of this Norton Critical Edition are divided into two parts. In the first, "Context," I have included the complete Chapter XXII of the First Part of *Don Quixote*. Although *Lazarillo de Tormes* gets only the one fleeting reference in it, this chapter gives a taste of the affinities that defined various social classes in Renaissance Spain. Also included are Chapters II and III of Juan de Luna's sequel, in which Lazarillo is involved in a shipwreck, almost drowns, and is accidentally rescued by sailors who think he is a fish.

"The Night Serene," an ode by Fray Luis de León (1527–1591), is a window into contemplative Christian life; it serves as contrast to the criticism of the Church by the anonymous author of *Lazarillo de Tormes*. *The Way of Perfection*, a manual to achieve enlightenment by the Carmelite mystic Teresa de Ávila (also known as Santa Teresa de Jesús, 1515–1582), follows along these lines. These pieces help to illuminate the complexities of the sixteenth century. I have added to them the *testimonio* by Miguel de Piedrola, a tinker, a globe-trotting soldier (he was in Granada, Flanders, North Africa, Naples, Florence, Rome, and perhaps even Istanbul), and a prominent victim of the Inquisition—Piedrola was arrested by the Holy Office in 1587—who paraded himself as a prophet.

The second part of the scholarly portion, "Criticism," consists of eight insightful studies. Howard Mancing offers a reading of Lázaro as both an innocent boy and a repulsive creature. Edward H. Friedman uses *Lazarillo de Tormes* as an example to appreciate future novels. T. Anthony Perry believes that this is not a psychological novel but a work in which the characters become figures reminiscent of heroes from the Hebrew and Christian Bibles, such as the Creator, Satan, and an angel. Louis C. Pérez proposes that the novella is really about the lack of laughter and about Lázaro's arrested emotion. David Gitlitz puts the novella in the context of the ordeal of *conversos* and the plight of those persecuted by the Holy Inquisition. Gabriel H. Lovett and E. Herman Hespelt deal with the vicissitudes of *Lazarillo de Tormes* in translation, specifically into Russian and German. Jane W. Albrecht focuses on the mother–son dynamic. Together these articles offer a variety of tools to access this fascinating text. For those wishing to go beyond this volume, a list of selected readings appears in the end matter.

My wholehearted gratitude to Carol Bemis at Norton for commissioning the translation and to her wonderful assistant editor, Thea Goodrich, a Kenyon graduate with whom I worked for years at the Amherst College campus of the Great Books Summer Program before she entered the publishing industry. Gracias to Alane Mason, my trade editor at Norton, whose friendship and encouragement over the years have been invaluable. My student assistant Rebecca Pol was diligent in all manners related to the manuscript. Candace Levy did a remarkable copyediting job. I am also in debt to my colleagues Dwayne Carpenter, William Childers, James Maraniss, and Gonzalo Sobejano.

One last comment: in Hispanic lore, in part due to the influence of this novella, the Spanish word *lazarillo* means "a handicapped person's guide."

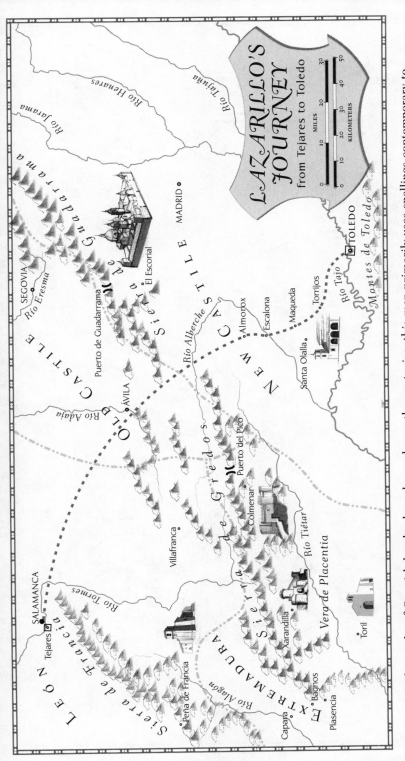

Orthography of Spanish locales has changed over the centuries; this map primarily uses spellings contemporary to Lazarillo's time. Some locations for the sites of his journey are unknown or approximations.

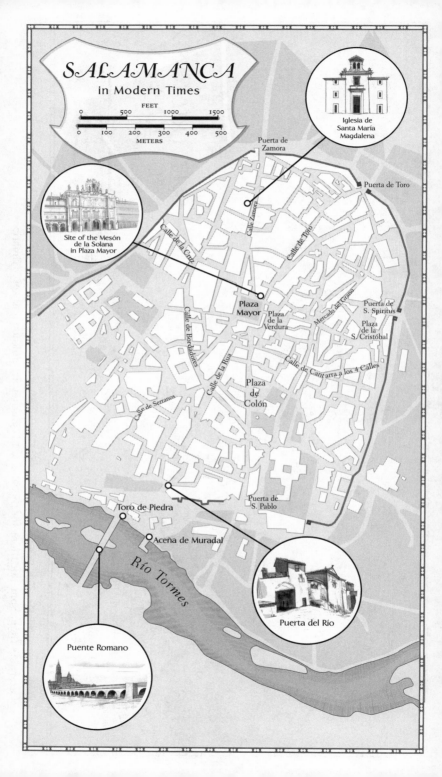

SALAMANCA
in Modern Times

FEET
0   500   1000   1500

0   100   200   300   400   500
METERS

Iglesia de
Santa María
Magdalena

Site of the Mesón
de la Solana
in Plaza Mayor

Puerta de
Zamora

Puerta de Toro

Calle Zamora

Calle de la Cruz

Calle de Toro

Plaza
Mayor

Plaza
de la
Verdura

Mercado del Grano

Puerta de
S. Spiritus

Plaza
de la
S. Cristóbal

Calle de Bordadores

Calle de la Rúa

Calle de Cantarra a los 4 Calles

Plaza
de
Colón

Calle de Serranos

Puerta de
S. Pablo

Toro de Piedra

Aceña de Muradal

Puerta del Río

Río Tormes

Puente Romano

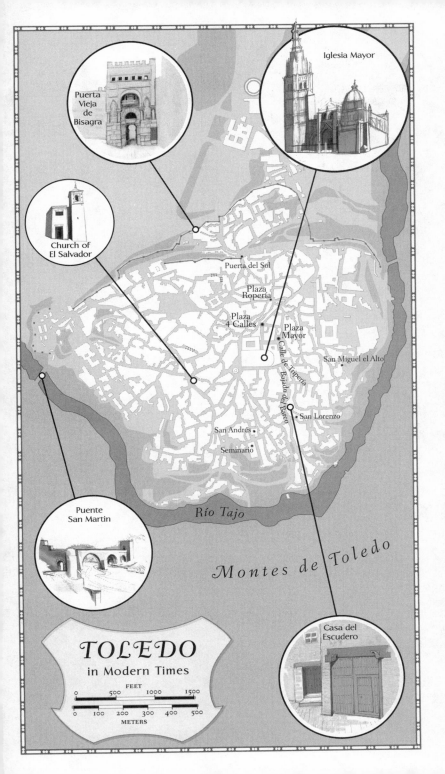

Puerta Vieja de Bisagra

Iglesia Mayor

Church of El Salvador

Puerta del Sol

Plaza Roperia

Plaza 4 Calles

Plaza Mayor

San Miguel el Alto

Calle de Imperia

Bajada del Barco

San Lorenzo

San Andrés

Seminario

Puente San Martin

Río Tajo

Montes de Toledo

Casa del Escudero

TOLEDO
in Modern Times

FEET
0   500   1000   1500

0   100   200   300   400   500
METERS

The Text of
THE LIFE OF LAZARILLO DE TORMES, HIS FORTUNES AND ADVERSITIES

Fig. 1 Title page of *La vida de Lázaro de Tormes y de sus fortunas y adversidades* (Medina del Campo: Mateo & Francisco del Canto, 1554). Courtesy of the Biblioteca de Extremadura.

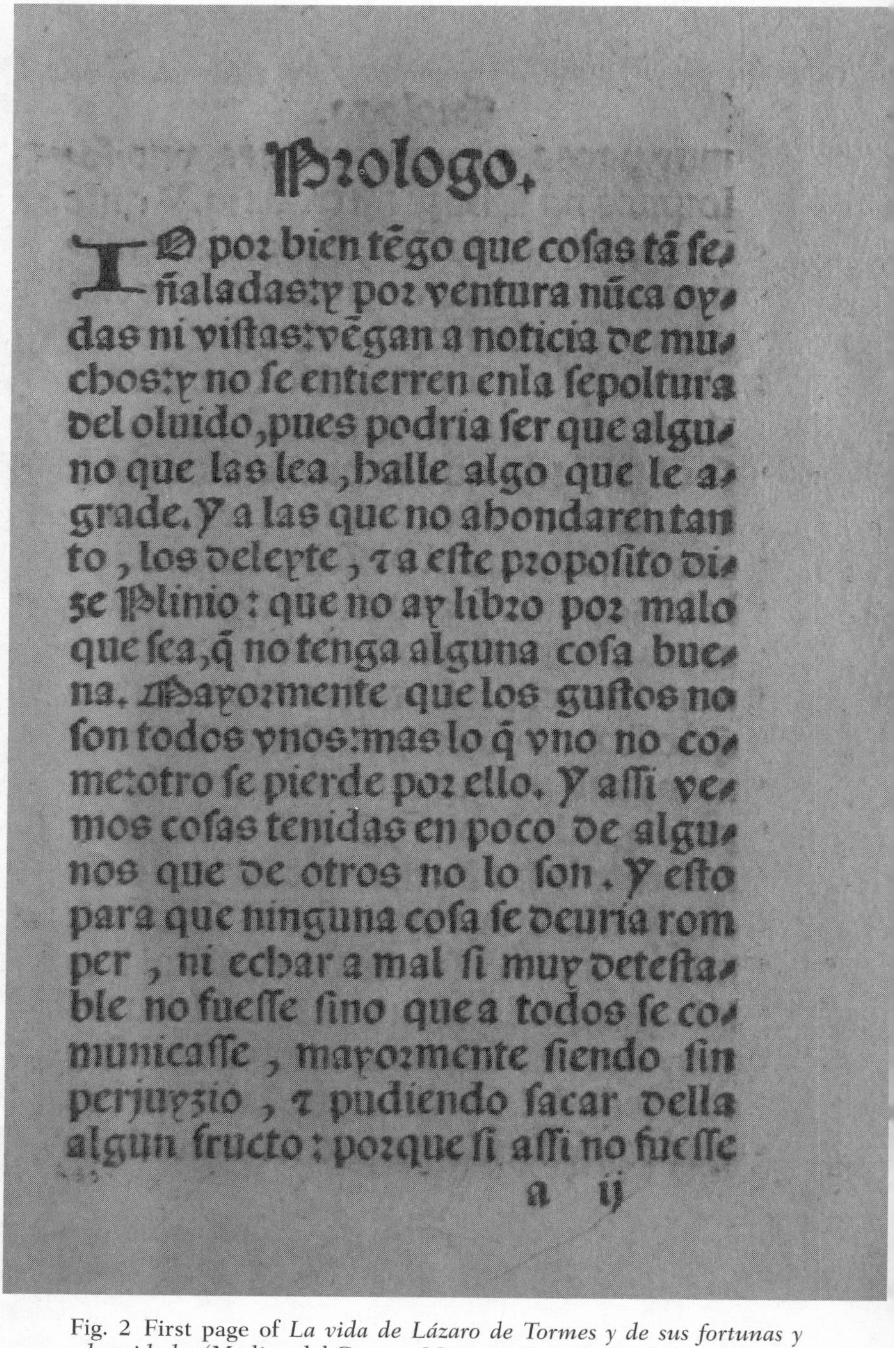

Prologo.

YO por bien tégo que cosas tá se/
ñaladas:y por ventura núca oy/
das ni vistas:végan a noticia de mu/
chos:y no se entierren enla sepoltura
del oluido,pues podria ser que algu/
no que las lea ,halle algo que le a/
grade.Y a las que no abondaren tan
to , los deleyte , τ a este proposito di/
xe Plinio : que no ay libro por malo
que sea,ǭ no tenga alguna cosa bue/
na. Mayormente que los gustos no
son todos vnos:mas lo ǭ vno no co/
metotro se pierde por ello. Y assi ve/
mos cosas tenidas en poco de algu/
nos que de otros no lo son . Y esto
para que ninguna cosa se deuria rom
per , ni echar a mal si muy detesta/
ble no fuesse sino que a todos se co/
municasse , mayormente siendo sin
perjuyzio , τ pudiendo sacar della
algun fructo : porque si assi no fuesse

a ij

Fig. 2 First page of *La vida de Lázaro de Tormes y de sus fortunas y adversidades* (Medina del Campo: Mateo & Francisco del Canto, 1554). Courtesy of the Biblioteca de Extremadura.

Prologue

I believe that things worthy of attention shouldn't be left unheard and unseen, buried in the grave of oblivion. The reader might find them agreeable. Those ready to pay more than passing attention will be rewarded.

In this sense, there is no book, as Pliny says, however bad it might be, without something good in it.[1]

There is no agreement on matters of taste: what one person won't eat another will find delectable. Likewise something might be seen as having little value in one place and appreciated in another. For that reason, nothing should be rejected or destroyed, no matter how unappealing it might be. Truth should be brought to light, without prejudice, seeking to bare some fruit.

If it were otherwise, few authors would write only for one reader, since it is done with much effort. Those who embark on it want to be compensated, not with money but with exposure, their work being seen and read by others, and, if it is of any merit, applauded as well. Cicero states thus: "Honor nurses art."[2]

Does anyone think that the soldier, who sits at the lowest of the social scale, has little regard for his own life? Surely not. It's the desire for praise that makes him get in harm's way.

It's the same with the arts as it is with literature. Such is the case of the student of theology. He talks about the goodness of things and recommends to others paths for the betterment of the soul. Yet ask him if he gets upset when others say: "Your Reverence, your words are wonderful!" Likewise for so-and-so whose jousting was embarrassing yet the jester still celebrates his skills. Would he have liked to hear the truth?

Everything is this way. I confess not to be more honest than my neighbors, as is clear from my clumsy style. No doubt there are parts in my narrative readers will find enjoyable and will recognize in them a person they know, made of good luck, danger, and adversities.

I beg Your Excellency[3] to receive this humble work from someone who would become richer if his talent equaled his desire. So since Your Excellency has written asking for a story, I thought best to begin not in the middle but at the beginning, so as to offer a full picture of myself and also so as those of nobler origins will realize how equally limited they are, since Fortune was as partial to them as to the rest of us, and how much accomplished are those who have

---

1. Pliny, *Epistles*, III, v, 10.
2. Cicero, *Pro Archia*, x, 24.
3. In the Spanish original, *Vuestra Merced*, meaning "Sir, Your Eminence," "Your Majesty," and "Your Lordship."

Fortune against them, for their aptitude and strength will bring them to a safer harbor.

First Chapter. Lázaro Recounts His Life and Who His Parents Were

Your Excellency should know, first of all, that my name is Lázaro of Tormes, son of Tomé González and Antona Pérez, originally from Tejares, a village near Salamanca. I was born on the River Tormes, which is why I have this name. It happened this way. My father, God rest his soul, was in charge of a windmill on the riverbank. He worked for over fifteen years. My mother was pregnant with me, ready to give birth, and one night I came onto this world right there, so I can say I was truly born on the river.

Now when I was eight years old, my father was caught stealing from the sacks belonging to the mill. He was arrested and confessed, denying nothing. He was prosecuted and punished by law. I hope to God he is in His Glory, because the Gospel says they are blessed. There was a campaign against the Moors in those years and my father took part in it, since he was already living away as part of the sentence. He went as a mule driver for a gentleman that went to the campaign. His life ended when he and this gentleman were killed.

My widowed mother, finding herself without a husband and without shelter, opted to approach some wealthy patrons and thus came to live in the city with one of them. She began to cook for certain students and to wash clothes for the stable boys of the Comendador of La Magdalena. So she hung about the stables.

She and a brown-skinned man, one of those who took care of the horses, became intimately connected. He would sometimes come to our house and leave in the morning. On other occasions, he would arrive at our door by day, pretending to buying eggs, and would enter the house. At the beginning of their relationship, I had a rough time with him. I was afraid of him because of his color and his bad demeanor. But when I realized that his arrival meant better food, I started to like him. He always brought bread, meat, and firewood to warm up during winter.

So he kept coming, and their conversations continued. My mother gave birth to a a very pretty little brown-skinned, boy, whom I juggled in my arms and helped to keep warm.

I remember my brown-skinned stepfather playing with the boy one day, and he saw that my mother and I were white and he wasn't. He would run away, afraid of my stepfather. The moment he reached my mother, he would say, "Look mummy, the bogeyman!" Smiling, my stepfather would respond: "*Hijodeputa*! You motherfucker!"

Although still young, I noticed the word my little brother had uttered and said under my breath: "There must be many in this world who run away from others because they don't see themselves!"

It was our bad fortune that the relationship between my mother and Zaide, which was his name, came to the ears of his employer's steward who carried out an investigation. He found that Zaide was stealing about half the oats used for the cattle. He rescued firewood, curry combs, aprons, horse sheets, and blankets. When there was nothing left to steal, he would take the shoes off the horses' feet. All this he would give to my mother to sell for her to raise my little brother. Let us not marvel that a priest or a friar robs his flock to support his vices or those of his peers when love leads a poor slave to act this way.

All that I say is true and then more because they threatened me to make me talk and, since I was just a boy and was terrorized, I testified and even described how I sold a blacksmith some horseshoes when my mother asked me to.

My poor stepfather was whipped and basted with boiling oil. My mother was put on trial, which resulted not only in the usual punishment of ten lashes but her being forbidden to enter the house of the aforementioned Comendador and to have an aggrieved Zaide in her house.

Not to complicate matters even further, my poor mother made an effort and obeyed the court. To avoid danger as well as gossip, she became a servant with the people living at the Solana Inn. There my little brother, suffering a thousand indignities, was raised until he learned how to walk and became an adolescent. He ran errands for the guests, providing wine, candles, and whatever else was needed.

At that time, a blind man came to stay at the inn. Hoping I could be of use to him on the road, he asked my mother if he could take me. She agreed, telling him I was the son of a good man who had been killed for the glory of the faith in the battle of Los Gelves.[4] She said she trusted God that I wouldn't be worse than my father. Since I was an orphan, she begged him to treat me well. He responded that he would and that he embraced me not just as a boy but as a son. So I began serving and guiding my new master.

We spent a few days in Salamanca. My master realized it wasn't a profitable place for him, so he decided to go somewhere else. Before we departed, I went to see my mother. The two of us were crying. She blessed me, saying:

4. I.e., Djerba, an island off the coast of Tunisia, which was the site of important battles in 1510 and 1520.

"Son, I know I won't see you ever again. Try to be good and may God guide you. I have raised you as best I could and given you love. Find your worth."

I went back to my master, who was waiting for me.

We left Salamanca and reached the bridge. There is an animal stone there that almost looks like a bull. The blind man asked me to come close to it. Once there, he told me:

"Lázaro, put your ear close to the bull. You will hear a loud noise inside it."

It was a simple task, and I did it. When he felt I had my head next to the stone, he gave me such a blow that my head crashed against it. The pain from the goring lasted more than three days. He said:

"Dumb one! You must learn. The blind man's boy must know more than the devil himself."

He laughed out loud.

At that moment I felt as if I had suddenly woken up from a stupor. I said under my breath: "He tells the truth. I must be alert because I am alone. I need to figure out how to survive on my own."

We began traveling, and in just a few days he taught me thieves' slang. When he realized I was sharp, he was pleased. He would say: "I can't give you gold or silver; but I'll teach you lessons for life."

He did indeed. After God, he taught me how to live, and because he was blind, he gave me light and prepared me for the path.

I must tell these childish stories to Your Excellency to show you the virtue of men who know how to rise from the lowest levels and how those on top often fall because of vice.

Now, getting back to the blind man and to further tell Your Excellency about my affairs, you must know that in this world there has never been anyone more astute and cunning.

He was an eagle at his trade. He knew a hundred blessings. He recited them in a lower voice, softly, taking a breath, emitting the right sound. The church would resonate with his chant. He put up a humble, devout expression, which he used to his advantage. He made no gesture or faces. He didn't roll his eyes as others do.

Beyond this, he had a thousand ways to steal money from people. He knew prayers for diverse purposes: for women who couldn't get pregnant, for women giving birth, for couples stuck in bad marriages, and for wives eager to recover their husbands' dimming love. He could foretell if a pregnant woman was about to give birth to a boy or a girl. In the case of medicine, he said that Galen[5] knew only half of what he himself did to extract a tooth and cure fainting fits, and

5. Claudius Galenus, or Galen of Pergamon, Greek philosopher and physician in the Roman Empire.

morning sickness. And last of all, if anyone said they were ill, he would say: "Take this, do that, drink herbal tea, get that root."

As a result, the entire world sought him, especially women who believed everything he told them. He earned more in a month than what a hundred blind men earn in an entire year.

But Your Excellency should also know that, even with all the money he collected, I never knew a meaner, stingier man. He almost starved me to death. He gave me less than half of what I needed. This is true because, while he asked for respect and good manners, frequently I almost died of hunger with him. For all his knowledge and experience, I found ways not only to survive but to take advantage of him. To do so I had to be sly so as to get the best of what was going on.

He carried bread and other things in a canvas bag with a metal ring round its neck, which he kept padlocked. He was careful to count everything he put in or took out of it, guardedly so as to avoid having a single crumb stolen from him. I would take the miserable portion he always left for me, which I would finish in two mouthfuls.

After he had locked the bag and relaxed, thinking I was doing something else, I would unpick the bag, bleed it, and sew it up again. That way I didn't get just a nibble but solid chunks of bread and large pieces of bacon as well as sausage. I looked for a convenient time to take action, so as to make him pay for how he treated me.

Whatever I could filch and steal, I put in half *blancas*.[6] When they asked him to recite one of his prayers and gave him *blancas*, as soon as they offered the coin I would grab it, put it in my mouth, and hand him a half *blanca*. No matter how far he stretched his hand, I was quicker in reducing the value of the offering to half. Surely he complained bitterly as soon as he realized what he had in his hand wasn't a whole *blanca*. He said:

"What the hell is this? Since you are with me I only get half *blancas* and before it was a *blanca* and even a *maravedí*? It's your fault."

He also shortened his prayers. He sometimes said only half because he asked me to tug his sleeve as soon as a person who had paid him had gone away. Then he would start advertising again: "Who wants us to recite such and such prayer?"

During our meals, he frequently put a jug of wine next to him. Shrewdly, I would grab it and drink without him noticing before I gave it back. This trick lasted a short time. Soon he would lift it and realize it was lighter. To keep his wine safe, he never let it go again. He kept his hand around the handle at all times. But there was

6. In the 16th century, Spanish currency was made of *ducats* (375 *maravedís*), *escudo* (330 *maravedís*), *real* (34 *maravedís*), *cuarto* (four *maravedís*), and *blanca* (half *maravedís*).

something better than a magnet to attract the jar to me: it was a long rye straw that I introduced into the mouth of the jug, sucking the wine at night. Clever as he was, he sensed what I was doing. From that moment on, he changed his purpose: he placed the jug between his legs and covered its top with his hands. That way he drank the wine in peace.

I had gotten used to the wine and would die for it. Realizing my straw was of little use, I decided to make a little hole at the base of the jug so it could have a jet of wine. I delicately covered it with a wax plug. While we ate our meals, I used to pretend I was cold. To warm myself up, I would place myself between the blind man's legs, near the meager fire we had made. The heat would cause the wax to melt. The fountain would then start to pour wine into my mouth. I placed myself in such way so that no drop was ever lost. When the poor man was ready to drink, he found nothing in the jug. He jumped, cursed, and swore at the jug and the wine. He didn't have a clue what had happened.

"You can't say I was drinking it," I would say, "when you've held it in your hands all the time."

He touched the jug all over until he finally discovered the trick but pretended he hadn't.

The next day, I put the jug in its usual position. I sat under him, ready to drink, unaware of the damage awaiting me or of the blind man's purpose. While enjoying the sweet drops, my face looking up, my eyes shut to better enjoy the flavorful liqueur, the fraught blind man suddenly realized he was within reach of his vengeance. With all his might, lifting with both hands the jug that had given me pleasure and now was about to also bring disgrace, from high above, with all his might, he let it fall right on my face, helping himself. Poor Lázaro, careless and joyful, unsuspecting any of this, literally didn't see it coming out from the sky. The jug and everything in it fell on me.

Such was the little tap that I was knocked out. Pieces of the broken jug got incrusted in my face, injuring it all over. My teeth were broken; I haven't got any to this day.

I didn't like the blind man from that moment on. While he loved me and gave me presents and healed me when I got sick, I was also the recipient of his cruel punishment. He used the wine to wash my cuts. He said, smiling:

"You never know, Lázaro: what makes you sick also heals you and makes you healthy again."

He said other pleasantries I wasn't amused with.

When I had almost recovered from the bashing and the wounds, I pondered if being treated that way was a sign that the old man wanted to get rid of me. So I decided to fight back. I didn't do it before I was sure I was safe and did it right and to my full advantage. Although I truly wanted to put my anger aside and forgive him for hitting me with the jar, I was beside myself for his abuse. He continued to injure me without cause or reason, kicking me on the head and pushing me away. And if anyone asked why he was violent, he would invoke the story of the jug:

"Do you think the boy is innocent? The devil himself isn't as crafty."

Those listening to him crossed themselves, then said:

"Who would ever think that such a young boy could do such bad things?"

They laughed at the story: "Punish him, go ahead. God is on your side."

Whereupon he didn't do anything else.

For that reason, I would always take him through the wrong roads and made him suffer. If there were stones on the road, I walked in that direction. If there was mud, I led him into the deepest part, even though my own feet would be a bit damp. I was ready to lose one eye to make him grieve not having any sight at all. He would shove the top of his cane and beat me on the back of my neck, leaving me with lots of bruises and raw skin. I swore to him I wasn't doing all this out of malice, but because I simply couldn't find better paths. But he didn't believe me, so wise and sharp he was.

To show Your Excellency the extent of this shrewd blind man's ingenuity, I will tell a story among many that happened to me while I was in his company, which I believe makes that astuteness fully clear. When we left Salamanca, he wanted to come to Toledo because it has the richest people, although not known for their generosity. He relied on the trusted proverb: "Better hard of heart than naked." So we took a road leading us through prosperous parts, stopping if we were welcomed, and made a profit. If things were dire, we did a St. John[7] by leaving on the third day.

It happened that upon arriving at a place called Almorox during the grape harvest, a grape picker gave my master a bunch of grapes in lieu of alms. Since the baskets were usually banged around and the grapes are very ripe at that time of year, the bunch would fall apart in one's hand. If it had to put in the sack, it would be ruined along with everything else in it. Therefore, the blind man decided to have a feast, in part to make me happy because that day he had been poking me all the time. We sat down in a fenced-in field, then he said:

"Now I want to be fair with you. Both of us should eat from this bunch of grapes. Take as much as you want. In fact, let's cut it this

---

7. A reference to *"Hacer San Pedro y hacer San Juan"*: 16th-century Spanish refrain about leaving one's patron or moving to another house.

way: you take some and I take some, as long as you promise not to take more than one grape each time. I will do the same until we finish. That way everything will be square."

We agreed and soon started to eat. But when he was in his second pick, the traitor changed his ideas and started to take two grapes at a time thinking I was probably doing the same. When I saw this, I decided not only to imitate him but to speed up and draw ahead: from two at a time I went to three. Soon I was cramming as many grapes in my mouth as I could. Once the bunch was finished, he sat quietly holding the stack. He shook his head and said:

"Lázaro, you fooled me. I swear you've been eating the grapes three at a time."

"No, I didn't," I replied. "What makes you think that?"

The crafty blind man responded:

"Do you know when I knew? When I started eating two and you said nothing."

I didn't reply to that.

In Escalona, where we went next, we passed under some doorway arch and arrived in the house of a shoemaker. There were lots of horns stuck in the wall for the mule drivers to tie their animals to. Some of them hit my master in the head. Rising his hand, he touched one of them, and seeing what it was, said to me:

"Let's go, boy. Let's leave this place. It pretends to feed you while leaving you malnourished."

I had been distracted. When I looked up, I didn't find any food— just coils of rope and saddle straps.

"*Tío*,[8] why do you say that?"

He answered:

"Be quiet, *sobrino*.[9] You will soon find out and know I'm telling the truth."

We went out from under the portico and reached an inn that had a pair of horns on the wall of the door. Some mule drivers were taking care of their animals. He felt for the inn where each day he said a prayer for the innkeeper's wife, sorry for her fate. His hand touched one of the horns and with a big sigh, he said:

"Oh, wicked thing. This thing is dangerous! Do you want to see your name tarnished in your neighbors' mouths? Keep yourself away from evil omens."

When I heard what he was saying, I asked:

"*Tío*, what are you saying?"

"Quiet, *sobrino*. It's a bad dinner I have in my hand, which I'll feed to you if you don't stop."

8. Literally "uncle"; used in Spain to mean "pal."
9. Literally, "nephew." The speaker goes along with the reference to "uncle" to convey kinship.

"I won't eat it," I said, "don't give it to me."

"I tell the truth. You'll live to see it."

We continued until we reached the door of the inn, where I hoped never to arrive, because of what happened there.

It was mostly innkeepers' wives, barmaids, candy sellers, prostitutes, and for other similar women he said prayers, but never for a man.

This made me laugh. Although I was young, I understood perfectly the blind man's discreet understanding of the value of discretion.

But I don't want to digress. I won't tell many notable and humorous anecdotes that happened to me with this first master. I'll tell you what made me leave him and finish the whole thing off.

We were in Escalona, which has a duke of the same name. There the blind man gave me a piece of sausage to grill for him. When I had cooked the sausage and he had eaten it, he took out a *maravedí* from his purse and asked me to fetch him wine at the tavern. Suddenly the devil made a thief of me. Lying next to the fire was a long, thin, rotten turnip left out of the stewpot.

We were there alone, he and I. I let the appetizing smell of the sausage get the best of me, disregarding any of the consequences, throwing all fear aside. While the blind man was taking the money out of his bag, I quietly took the sausage, replacing it with the turnip. Once I had the money, my master took hold of the spit and started to turn it over the fire. The turnip, which had not been meant for the stew, immediately dissolved in it.

I went for the wine and wolfed the sausage with it. When I came back, I found him with the turnip between two slices of bread, not yet having tasted it. As soon as he did, instead of finding the sausage, he was shocked to find a mouthful of turnip. Agitated, he said:

"What's this, Lazarillo?"

"Why are you asking me?" I replied. "Are you blaming me for something? Didn't I just go to fetch the wine?"

"No, no," he said, "I haven't let go of the pan. It isn't possible."

Time and again I swore I had nothing to do with it. It didn't do me any good. You couldn't keep anything from that clever old man. He stood up, seized me by the head, and smelled me from top to bottom. He must have noticed the scent like a good hound. The whole thing was done with agonizing precision. He grasped me, opened my mouth to more than its normal size, and unkindly inserted his long and pointy nose in it. His anger increasing, he reached my throat with the tip of his nose.

In fear, and given the brevity of time I had to digest the black sausage, unsettled as it still was in my stomach, and, with that enormous nose choking me, I felt the need to turn everything back to my master. Even before the nasty blind man could take his trunk out from my mouth, my stomach felt such alteration that it reacted abruptly onto itself so that the nose and the badly chewed sausage simultaneously came out from my mouth.

Oh God! I wished I were dead at that moment—and maybe I already was! Such was the anger of that perverse old man that, if it hadn't been for the nosey people at the whole scene, I'm sure he wouldn't have left me alive. Others helped to free me and I lost most of my hair on my head. His face was all scratched as were my neck and throat. He deserved all this because of the suffering he brought onto me.

The cruel blind man told everyone about the disasters I had caused, recounted every detail one after another. He told them about the episode of the jug and the one about the bunch of grapes and now described what had just happened between us. On the street everyone laughed loudly; it soon felt like a party. I felt abused now by making fun of my disgrace but decided it wouldn't be fair if I didn't laugh as well.

During this time I came to understand that I had been a coward. I felt ashamed. I should have bitten his nose off, of course. I easily could have done since it was halfway down my throat. All I had to do is clench my teeth. That would have done it. I could have replaced the sausage with it. But the nose wouldn't have been able to solve the matter. I wish I had taken things to their limit.

The innkeeper's wife became friendly with me as did others in the place. With the wine I had brought the blind man, they washed up the wounds on my face and healed my throat. The blind man reacted by making fun of everything:

"To be honest, I waste more wine washing this boy in a year than I drink in two. At the very least, Lázaro, you ought to be more grateful for the wine than you are to your father because it has brought you back to life a thousand times."

He then told of the many of times he had knocked my head and scratched my face and cleaned them up with wine.

"I tell you," he said, "if there's any one in this world who should be thankful for wine, it should be you."

People washing me thought it was funny, but I didn't. However, the blind man's prophesy did not prove wrong. Since that time, I often think of him because he must have had the demeanor of a prophet. I am sorry for having been mean to him, although he deserved it, considering what he told me that day, which is as true, as I will let Your Excellency know now.

Thinking about how mean I had been to the blind man, I decided to leave him. I had already been contemplating the idea and had come to the conclusion when this episode happened. A few days later, we left town to go on begging elsewhere. It had rained heavily

the night before and it was still raining at that moment. He was praying near some arcades in the town, where we sought shelter once the
night set in. The blind man said:

"Lázaro, it doesn't look as if it will stop raining soon. As the night
advances, the downpour may even become heavier. Let's find an inn
now."

On our way back, we needed to cross a gulley that was
overflowing.

I told him:

"*Tío*, the water is very wide. I can see a place to cross it without
getting wet. We can jump where it's narrower without getting wet."

He trusted me:

"You're discreet, that's why I love you. Take me to that narrower
side. It's winter now and water tastes bad. It's bad to have your feet
wet."

Seeking a narrower part, I took him out from under the arcades
and brought him straight to the post or stone mast in the main
square, on which the projected roofs of the houses rested. I said:

"*Tío*, this is the narrowest straight."

It was still raining hard. Now the dejected man was getting wet.
In a hurry to escape the rainstorm, with God blinding his understanding (so I could take revenge), he believed me.

"Put me onto the right path and then jump first."

I placed him straight before the post. I made a huge jump, like a
bullfighter waiting for the bull charge, and ended up behind the
post. I said:

"Come on! Jump as far as you can, so you'll land on this side of
the river."

I had hardly finished saying it when, the poor blind charged like a
billy goat, though not before taking a few steps back to gain momen-
tum and jump better. He ended up against the post, head first.
The sound was so loud, it looked as if he had been hit with a pumpkin.
He fell on his back, half dead, his head spilt open.

"How come you smelled the sausage but not the post?" I said.
"Smell! Smell it now!"

I left him in the hands of others coming to his rescue and started
trotting until I reached the gates of the town. I reached Torrijios
before nightfall. I never found out what God did to him, nor did I
try to.

Second Chapter. How Lázaro Settled Down
with a Priest and What Happened
to Him at the Time

Thinking it wasn't secure for me to stay there, the next day I went to a place called Maqueda, where for my sins I come across a priest. I went to him and asked for alms. He asked me if I knew how to help during Mass. I said I did, which was true because, although the blind man had been mistreated me, he had taught me lots of things and this was one of them. The priest accepted me as his servant.

From bad to worse! I say this because in contrast to this man, the blind man was like Alexander the Great,[1] even though he was stinginess incarnated. I won't say much other than it looked as if all the scum of the earth had been compressed into this church figure. I don't know if he was typical or if instead he was part of a special harvest.

He had an old storage chest, which he kept closed with a key that hung from a lace on his cape. He would take in the bread that was brought as an offering to church and put it away in the chest. There was nothing to eat in the house, as there is sometimes in other houses: a slice of bacon hanging up in the smoking room, some cheese placed on a shelf in the pantry, or a small basket with bread remainders left behind on the table. At least looking at these items might console me, albeit I wouldn't touch them without permission.

There was only one string of onions, and that was under lock in a room at the top of the house. I had one of these every four days. I would ask for the key to go grab it, and, if anyone was present, he would reach inside his pocket and with great care he would untie the lace and give it to me, saying:

"Take it and bring it back but don't enjoy yourself too much."

He said this as if all the conserves that are made in Valencia were in the cabinet, but, as I said, there was nothing in the room, except for some darn onions hanging on a nail. He made it clear that if I sinned and took something that didn't belong to me, it would cost me dear. As a result, I was constantly hungry.

Although with me he showed little charity, with himself he was very generous. He normally ate five *blancas* of meat between lunch and dinner. It's true that he shared the broth. As for the meat, I could only hope. I got a piece of bread and wished to God it would satisfy half my craving.

---

1. Alexander of Macedon (356–323 B.C.E), military leader who conquered an empire from Greece to Egypt to northwest India. This reference is to him as generous, splendid, and liberal.

On Saturdays, people eat sheep's head. He would send me to buy one for three *maravedís*. He cooked it and ate the eyes and tongue and neck and brain and the meat on the jawbones. He gave me the bones he had been gnawing on the plate:

"Here, eat them and be merry. The world is yours. Only the Pope has a better life."

"May God grant you what you grant me!" I replied in a quiet voice.

After three weeks, I was so thin I hardly stood on my feet. The grave was near unless God and my wits interceded. I couldn't see how to get out of it. Even if I could, there was no way I could take advantage of his blindness, as I sometimes did with the other one (may God pardon him if his hitting his head against the post killed him). While astute, he didn't have his sight to see what was about to happen to him. But this priest—his sense of sight was better than anyone's.

When we were at the offertory, there was not a single *blanca* he didn't grab before it reached the collecting box. He kept one eye on the worshipers and another on my hands. His eyes would dance in his sockets as if they were made of mercury.

He counted the number of *blancas* that had been collected, and once the collection was made, he would take the box away from me and put it in the altar.

I was never able to take a single *blanca* all the time I lived with the priest, or rather, died with him. I never even brought him a *blanca*'s worth of wine from the tavern. He made the little bit that was placed on the chest last for an entire week.

Hiding his enormous stinginess, he said to me:

"Look, boy, priests must eat and drink well. That's why I don't indulge in excess like the rest of them."

But the bastard lied miserably because whenever we prayed in gatherings or funerals, he ate like a pig from the charity of others and drank more than a quack doctor.

God, forgive me for mentioning the funeral feasts. I was not an enemy of human nature until then. That's because we ate well and were satisfied on these occasions. I hoped and prayed to God so that each day another person died. And when we gave the Sacraments to sick people, especially the Extreme Unction, as the priest orders those present to pray, I was certainly not the last to deliver the prayer and, with all my heart and good will, I begged God not to have mercy on those who most needed it but, instead, to finish them off.

If the health of one of them improve—God forbid!—I cursed the devil. And I blessed anyone who died. In all the time I spent with the priest, almost six months, only twenty people died, and these I believe I killed myself, or, I should say, they died under my watch. For when God saw how close I was to my own painful and

approaching end, I think He preferred to get rid of them and grant me
life. But the days with a scheduled burial weren't enough because on
the ones nobody died I still struggled with daily hunger. So I never
found any rest except in the death, which I wished for myself and
occasionally on others. Needless to say, it didn't come, although I felt
it close sometimes.

I often considered leaving my callous master. I resisted for two
reasons: one is that I didn't trust my legs because of how thin they
were as a result of my starvation, and the other is that I concluded:
"I have had two masters: the first kept me hungry, and, when I left
him, I found this one, who has brought me even closer to the edge of
death. If I leave this one and find one even worse, all there will be is
death itself."

I didn't stir the waters because I was absolutely certain that things
would deteriorate further. One step more and Lázaro wouldn't be
heard in this world.

In my affliction, with which God tests all true Christians, not
knowing what to do, and seeing that things went from bad to worse,
a tinker happened to show up at the door one day while my grudg-
ing master was away. I thought he was an angel in disguise, sent to
me by God's hand. He asked if there was anything to mend. "If you
could mend me, there would be much that you could do to help," I
said quietly so he wouldn't hear me.

Since there was little time to waste, I said to him, enlightened by
the Holy Spirit:

"*Tío*, I have lost the key to the chest and I'm afraid my master will
be angry and beat me. I'll pay you to try if any of the ones you carry
with you would open it."

The innocent tinker began to try one after another of the huge
key holder that hung around him. I helped him with my prayers.
When I least expected it, I saw God's face made of bread in the chest.
I said to the tinker:

"I don't have money to give you for the keys. But take your payment in bread."

He took the best loaf he found and gave me the key. He left very
happily, leaving me even happier more.

I didn't touch anything at that moment so the priest wouldn't find
out and also because I saw myself rich in goods, so hunger suddenly
wasn't a threat anymore. When my miserly master came back, thank
God he didn't notice the loaf the angel had taken with him.

Next day, as soon as he left the house, I opened my bread paradise. I took a loaf in my hands and sunk my teeth and within min-
utes made it disappear. I didn't forget to shut the chest again. Then
I began to cheerfully sweep the house, thinking I had stumbled upon
the remedy to my sorrowful life.

I rejoiced that way and the next. But it wasn't in my fortune that a break from my despair would last long because three days later I caught a recurring fever.

When I least expected it, I saw my tormentor in front of the chest, counting the loaves of bread, moving them around, recounting them again. I pretended I hadn't seen him and started to pray. I pleaded, "Saint John, please blind him for me!"

After counting the days and loaves with his fingers, he said:

"If this chest weren't so secure, I would swear some bread has disappeared. To be safe, starting today I will count it every day. There are nine loaves and a bit left."

"God protect me nine times over!" I said under my breath.

It seemed as if his words had hit me like a hunter's arrow. My stomach sensed the old hunger I had been used to before. He left the house. To console myself, I opened the chest and saw the bread. I worshiped what I saw but I knew I could not receive it.

I counted them because the bastard could have made a mistake, yet I found the amount more accurate than I wanted. The most I could do is to kiss the loaves a thousand times, and as delicately as possible, to scrape some crumbs from the loaf that was already started on. That kept me going that day, not as happy as I had been the previous one.

My hunger increased since my stomach had bread on the prior two or three days and I was dying a terrible death. Such was my agony that I didn't do anything else but open and close the chest to contemplate God's face, as children often say. Seeing me in such state, God himself, who heals those in need, reminded me of a little remedy. Thinking about it, I said: "This big chest is old and broken here and there, although the holes are small. He might think that mice ate the bread. Taking out a whole loaf isn't a good idea. He'll know what happened."

I began to crumble the bread unto some inexpensive tablecloths I found. I took one and left another, so as to make crumbles in three or four. Adding and taking, I ate the crumbs and felt somewhat satisfied. When the priest came back, he opened the chest, saw the tragedy that had befallen him and didn't doubt mice had been the cause of the damage because I had carefully imitated the way they leave a mess behind. He looked at the entire chest from one side to the other and saw certain holes through which he suspected they had entered. He called on me and said:

"Lázaro, look at the disgrace that has befallen our bread tonight!"

I pretended to be puzzled, wondering what had happened.

"What happened?" he said. "Mice don't leave anything alive."

We sat down to eat. Thank God, I was lucky because the bastard gave me more bread that he usually did. With a knife, he scraped off the parts he thought mice had eaten. He gave them to me and said:

"Eat this. Mice are clean."

And so, on that day I ended up eating a bigger portion by the work of my hands (or, I should say, of my nails), which I wasn't expecting.

I had another shock when I saw him take some nails down from the walls and look for planks. He then nailed down all the holes of the old chest.

"Oh, my God," I said under my breath. "How much misery and fortune and disasters befall some of us and how brief the pleasures are in our toilsome life! Here I am, thinking I could improve my situation and overcome my hunger, and I was already happy rejoicing in my good fortune! But I ran out of luck, for now I needed to be more diligent than he was in figuring out my trick (because miserable people like him are never short in diligence). By closing the holes in the chest, he had sealed the door to my consolation and reopened the one to me suffering."

I was still lamenting myself as my entrepreneurial carpenter concluded the job he was doing with nails and pieces of wood. He said:

"Now, you sneaky mice, you'll have to change your strategy because in this house you won't succeed."

After he left the house, I saw what he had done. He didn't leave a single hole open in the old and woeful chest through which even a mosquito could enter. I unlocked it with my now useless key, without hope of being fruitful, and I saw the two or three broken loaves I had worked on, the ones my master thought had been gnawed by mice. I still got a few crumbs off them, touching them gently, like a skilled fencer. Necessity is the best teacher. As always, I spent night and day thinking how I keep myself survive. Hunger showed me the light, since it sharpens one's wit instead of acquiescing it. This was true for me.

I stayed wide awake one night, thinking of ways I could break into the chest and take advantage of its contents. I knew my master was asleep because he would snore, making loud snorts, which he would do only when he was asleep. I woke up quietly. I had decided that day what I would do at night. I had found an old knife and I put it in a special place. I went to the wretched chest. I opened it with the knife where I thought it was weakest and started boring into it. Since it was a chest long in years, it posed no resistance. The wood was soft and rotten. It surrendered itself to me and I was able to make a hole on the side. When I finished, I opened the chest very quietly, groping what was inside until I found the pieces of bread and gave them the same treatment I mentioned before. I was cheerful. I decided to close the chest, return to my bale of straw, and lay down and slept for a while, although not well because I hadn't eaten enough.

It must have been that because at that time and in that situation not even the King of France could have made me sleep.

The following day, my master saw the damage I had done, not only the hole on the chest but the half-eaten bread. He started cursing the mice, saying:

"What to make of this? This house never had mice until now!"

He was telling the truth: if there was a house in the entire kingdom free of mice, since mice don't come where there's no food, it was this one. He again started to look for nails and pulled bits of wood from the house to close the holes. But when night returned, and with it rest, I was back on my feet, with the exact same intentions: what he covered during the day, I uncovered at night.

Such was the chase we were caught in that surely we must have been the source for the proverb: "As one door closes, another one opens." It must have looked as if we had with us Penelope's[2] loom because whatever he wove by day I unwove by night. In a just few days and nights, we had the poor food box in such state that whoever would have wanted to describe it properly would have to say it was looked like a breastplate from another era, given the amount of nails and bits of wood it was decorated with.

When he finally concluded that his tactic was useless, he said:

"This chest is in such bad shape and its wood so old and knocked out, any mouse can get in. At this rate, there will be no place where to store bread. Still, even in such state it is better than a new one, which would cost me three or four *reales*. Since the remedy I've used so far isn't working, I will now try trapping the darn mice inside the chest."

He then borrowed a mousetrap. With slices of cheese he got from neighbors, he made a man-made cat and placed in inside the chest. This was good for me because, since I wasn't going to find much alternative for food, I took advantage of the cheese slices I unhooked from the mousetrap, which the mice swallowed along with the bread.

Seeing that the bread was gnawed and the cheese had been eaten too, and that the mouse that ate them was still to be caught, he cursed and asked the neighbors what could have taken the cheese off the trap and how come no mouse had been caught by the man-made cat. The neighbors agreed that this couldn't be a mouse because it would have been trapped at some point already. A neighbor told him:

"I remember once seeing a snake in your house. That must be the cause of the damage, no doubt. This must be true since it's long, so it can take the bait. Even if the trap catches it, it can easily escape as long as its whole body isn't in it."

2. Odysseus's wife.

Everyone believed in what he said. My master was quite upset. From then on he wouldn't sleep as soundly as before. Any wood worm that made a noise could wake him up, thinking it was the snake gnawing at the chest. He would quickly get on his feet and with a club he kept near his bed table ever since he had been told about the snake, he would belabor the old chest, hoping to scare the snake. The neighbors would wake up with the racket he made and he wouldn't let me sleep either. He would come over to the pile of straw I slept in, and fling it this way and that, in case the snake had come to me and warped itself in the straw or was hidden in my jacket. He had been told that at night these animals come out looking for heat and that they enter babies' cradles and bite them and put them in danger.

Often I would pretend to be asleep most of the time. In the mornings, he would say to me:

"Didn't you feel anything last night? I was after the snake. I think it must have been hidden with you in bed. They are cold and are always looking for heat."

"May God protect me so it doesn't bite me," I would say. "I'm scared to death of it."

He was so sleep-deprived that the snake (or whatever it was) wouldn't dare gnaw the chest at night. But during the day, while he was in church or somewhere else, I would make my raid. When he discovered the damage and continue to look for ways to prevent it, he would walk around all night like a goblin.

I was afraid that at some point he would find the key I kept under the straw. I concluded that the safest way to protect it was to put the key inside my mouth. Since I lived with the blind man, it was as big as a bag in which I was able to insert twelve or fifteen *maravedís*, all in half *blancas*, without them bothering me while I ate. I didn't have another way to keep a *blanca* without the damned blind man putting his hands on it, since he always searched every part of my clothing he could find.

As I say, I would put the key in my mouth every night and would sleep without fear the warlock of my master would come across it. Still, when disaster is on its way, no precaution can stop it. Out of bad luck, or perhaps because of my sins, one night, while sleeping with the key in my mouth—open as it was so I could breathe through the hole in the key, which made me whistle quite loudly as if through a small pipe—my master heard it. He was shocked and became convinced the whistle came from the snake.

He stood up with the club in his hand, and tiptoed so as not to frighten the snake. He approached where I was, certain the snake was in the straw, warming itself up in the heat of my body. He raised the club, hoping to hit it strong enough to kill it once and for all.

With all his might, he delivered such a crack on my head that I was knocked unconscious and split my head open.

He soon realized he had hit me because I gave a great yell at the unexpected blow. Later on, he said that he started calling my name in a loud voice, eager to wake me up.

When he touched me, he realized I was bleeding badly and understood the damage he had caused. He hurried as much as he could to find some light. When he came back, he found me complaining, still with the key in my mouth, never having woken up. Half of the key was out, in the exact same position it had it while whistling.

The snake-killer was frightened, not knowing what the key was for. He looked at it by taking it out of my mouth, and soon understood what it was meant to open, for it wasn't different from the one that hung from him on a lace. He went to test it and proved his suspicion. The cruel hunter must have said to himself: "I have found both the mouse and snake that were eating in my hacienda."

I won't say what happened to me in the next three days. I was in the belly of the whale.[3] Later on, after I had left him, I heard that my master would retell the story of what happened to me to whoever wanted to hear it.

In three days, I came back to my senses and found myself in my straw bed. My head was wrapped in bandages and covered with creams and ointments. Frightened, I said:

"What's this?"

The cruel priest replied:

"I have finally hunted the mice and snakes that were destroying me."

When I looked at myself, I saw how badly bruised I was and realized what had happened to me.

At this time, an old woman who was known as a healer came in, along with the neighbors. She began to remove the bandages I had on my head and to doctor my wound. When they saw I had regained consciousness, they were very happy and said:

"Since he has come back to his own self, God must not make a great deal of it."

They started to retell my adventures and to laugh at them, and I, the sinner, to cry. With all this, they gave me something to eat because I was starving, but their help didn't kick in immediately. So, little by little, I started to feel better, and fifteen days later I was on my feet, without danger (although not without hunger), and almost cured.

The day after I got up, my señor and master took me by the hand and threw me out the door onto the street. He said:

---

3. A reference to the story of the biblical prophet Jonah.

"Lázaro, from now on you're on your own and not my property any more. Look for another master and God be with you. I don't want such diligent servant in my company. You clearly had been a blind man's property."

Making the sign of the cross toward me, as if I had been possessed by the devil, he went back into the house and closed the door.

Third Chapter. How Lázaro Settled Down with a Squire and What Happened to Him

And so I was forced to look for strength in my weakness. Little by little, with the help of generous people, I found myself in this noble city of Toledo, where, by God's mercy, my wound healed in two weeks. While I was ill, I could always relay on alms. Once I recovered, everyone said:

"You're a rascal and a scoundrel. Go on, look for a master to work for."

"Where might I find one?" I asked myself, "What if God, master of the universe, has not created one for me?"

Wandering from door to door, with little to my pocket since charity had gone to heaven, God put me on the way of a squire who was walking the street. He was reasonably dressed, his hair neat, his demeanor that of a distinguished man. He looked at me and I at him. He said:

"Boy, are you looking for a master?"

"Yes, sir," I replied.

"Well, come on," he said. "The Almighty, in his kindness, has allowed me to find you. You must have said a good prayer today."

I followed him, thanking God for what I just had heard. From his manner and dress, it seemed to be the type of man I was looking for.

It was in the morning when I met my third master. He took me around most of the city with him. We passed through the plazas where bread and other provisions were sold. I thought, indeed I wished, that he would buy me some right there, because that was the time when one generally acquired the provisions for the day. But he kept his step and attended to only his own matters.

"Maybe he doesn't like this merchandise," I told myself. "He will want to buy it in some other place."

We wandered this way until it was eleven o'clock. He then went into the Cathedral and I followed him. I watched him attend Mass in a very devout way and do other divine endeavors. He waited until everything was finished and people had gone out. Then we left the church.

We started to go down a street. I was happy even though we hadn't had anything to eat. I considered my new master to be a man who provided well for himself and was sure food would arrive at the right time and the way one wanted and needed it.

The clock struck one, then one thirty. We arrived at a house. My master stood outside and so did I. Hitching his cloak to the left, he drew a key from his sleeve, opened the door, and we entered the house. The entrance was so dark and dismal it frightened anyone entering it. Inside there was a small patio and large, well-kept chambers.

When we were inside, he took off his cloak. After asking me if my hands were clean, we brushed the cloak and folded it. He blew the dust off a bench and fastidiously placed the cloak on it. When he finished, he sat down and asked me all sorts of questions, such as where I was from and how I had come to be in that city.

I gave him a longer account than was needed even though I thought it would be better to set the table ready and place food on it. Still, I lied as best as possible, telling him only the good parts of my story and silencing the bad ones, since it was convenient to do it that way. All in all, this conversation took longer than I wanted. I thought it was a bad omen because it was almost two o'clock and it was easier to come across a corpse than to find food anywhere around.

Next I thought about him locking the door with the key and about there not being anyone either above or below in the house. All I had seen were walls without seeing a single chair, a stool, a bench, a table, not even a chest like my own stand-by. It looked as if I were in an enchanted house. Just as I was thinking all that, he said to me:

"You, boy, have you eaten?"

"No, sir," I replied. "Not since eight o'clock this morning, when I first met Your Excellency."

"Well, I had already eaten my breakfast at that time. When I do that, I never touch anything again until the evening. Keep strong until dinner."

Your Excellency may just imagine that when I heard this, I was about to collapse, not so much of hunger but of realizing the type of adverse fortune that awaited me. I thought of all my past sufferings and started to cry for my bad luck. I remembered the exact moment when I decided to run away from the priest, saying that, although he was a stingy bastard, I might stumble upon someone worse. I wept over my penurious life and my approaching death.

Yet I hid my feelings as best I could. I said:

"Sir, I am a boy who doesn't need to worry too much about eating, thank God. I even pride myself that, among my equals, I have the smallest stomach. All the masters I've had up until now have praised me in this regard."

"That's a virtue," he replied. "For that reason alone I will think more highly of you. Only pigs stuff themselves. Moderation is the measure is a good man."

"Oh, I get it," I told myself. "To hell with the virtue my masters find in hunger!"

I sat next to the door and took out a piece of bread from my sack. I had placed it there from what I had begged. When he saw me do that, he said:

"Wait, boy. What are you eating?"

I walked up to him and showed him the bread. There were three pieces. He took the biggest and best. He said:

"I swear this looks like wonderful bread."

"It's tasty," I said. "So you think it's good, sir?"

"Sure," he said. "Where did you find it? Has it been baked with clean hands?"

"I don't know that," I answered. "But it tastes fine to me."

"I hope so," said my poor master.

Taking it to his mouth, he started to bite it as forcefully as I did.

"Delicious bread, by God," he said.

I ate as fast as I could, since I understood that, with his disposition, if he finished before I did, he would help himself with all that what was left. We concluded almost at the same time. My master began to brush off some small crumbs that had fallen on his clothes. He entered a little room nearby and came out with a jug. It was all chipped and not very new. After he drank, he shared it with me. Restraining, I said:

"Sir, I don't drink."

"It's water," he replied. "You can drink."

I took the jug and drank. Not much because I wasn't too thirsty.

That's all we did until evening, answering his questions in the best way possible. At one point, he showed me the room here the jug had come from. He said:

"Boy, just stand there and look how I make the bed so you can know how to make it from now on."

I stood on one side and he on the other and we made the darn bed. There wasn't much to make because the bed had on it a framework stretched over some benches. The bedclothes covered a miserable mattress. Since it hadn't been washed much, the mattress didn't look like one, although it served its purpose, although it had far less wool that it needed. We smothered it out and beat it a bit to make it softer, which was impossible since one cannot make a rock spongier. It had damn all inside because when we put it on the framework you could see all the slats, making it look like the backbone of a skinny pig. He put a quilt of the same kind over the shameful mattress. I couldn't tell its original color.

Once the bed was made and night was upon us, he said:

"Lázaro, it's late and from here to the plaza it is a long walk. Besides, there are lots of thieves in this city who go after cloaks at night. Let's go along as we are until tomorrow and God shall provide for us. As you can see, I live alone and don't have any provisions now. I have eaten out all these days. But it's better to do it some other way now."

"Sir, Your Excellency should not be worried for me," I said. "I know how to go to bed with an empty stomach. I can do it even more than one night if necessary."

"You'll have a long and healthy life," he responded. "As we said today, there's no better way to reach old age than to eat less."

"If that's the way," I told myself, "I will never die because by rule I have always followed that regime. Unfortunately, it looks as if I'll keep it until the end of my days."

He lay down on the bed using his breeches and doublet as a pillow. He told me to lie down at his feet, which I did. But I couldn't get any sleep. My guts and bones quarreled all night long. I don't think there was a pound of flesh in my body with all the hardships and hunger I had suffered. As it happens, I hadn't eaten anything that day, and hunger and sleep are never friends. All through the night, I cursed myself a thousand times (may God forgive me!) as well as my ruinous fortune. Worse, I hesitated to toss around so many times as not to wake him up that I repeatedly ended up begging God to do away with me.

When morning came, we got up. I began to brush and dab away at his breeches, his doublet, his coat, and his cloak. I was effectively his valet. He dressed very slowly, to his liking. I poured water over his hands. He combed his hair and put his sword into the belt. As he did this, he said to me:

"Ah, boy, if you only knew what a fine weapon this is! I wouldn't sell it for any gold in the world. Of all the ones made by Antonio,[1] none is as fine-edged as this one."

He took it out from its sheath and gently touched it with his fingers. He said:

"Do you see it? I could cut straight through a ball of wood with it."

I said to myself: "And with my teeth, which aren't made of steel, I could cut through a four-pound loaf."

He sheathed his sword again and hung a ring of large rosary beads from his belt. And walked out the door in rhythmic step, his body erect, in a gentlemanly demeanor. He threw one end of his cloak on

---

1. Famous swordsmith in Toledo.

his shoulder and then under his arm, placing his right hand on his hip. He said:

"Lázaro, while I am at Mass look after the house. Make the bed and fetch a jug of water from the river down the road. Lock the door so nothing goes missing. Put the key in the crack so I can get it when I return."

He walked up the street with such swagger and pride that a stranger seeing him would think he was a close relative of the Conde de Arcos,[2] or at least his valet.

"Bless art thou God," I said under my breath, "for handing us the illness as well as the cure. Would anyone meeting my master suspect he missed a good dinner last night, slept in a lousy bed, and didn't have a fine breakfast this morning? Your secrets, oh God, are inscrutable, and so is people's ignorance! Who would be deceived by his demeanor, his attractive cloak and jacket? Who would think that such a fine gentleman stayed all night without a bite, with only a crumb his servant Lázaro kept night and day under his shirt, where it wasn't kept very clean, and that today he washed his hands and face but didn't have a towel, so he used his shirttail? Nobody would even dream about it. Oh God, and how many of these men do you spread throughout the world, suffering pains to protect their honor yet wouldn't suffer for Thee?"

I was at the door, mussing and thinking about these things and other things as my master made his way through the long and narrow street. Once he was out of sight, I turned around into the house and went straight through it, top to bottom, without anything to stop me. I made the miserable bed and as I took the jug to the river to fetch water, I saw my master in a garden, having an animated conversation with two veiled women. Apparently they are of type that isn't absent in that place. In the summer morning, many of these women have the habit of going to refresh themselves, or else have lunch, without taking provisions, in those fresh riversides, confident there will always be someone ready to offer them what they want, as hidalgos in the area are prone to do.

As I say, he was with them, as courtly as Mecías ever was, giving them sweeter compliments than Ovid[3] ever wrote. When they saw he was tender, they weren't ashamed to ask for lunch on the usual terms.

Feeling his pocket cold and his stomach hot, his face lost its color. He stuttered and gesticulated, offering them all sorts of worthless excuses.

2. A reference to Andalusian nobility in the municipality of Arcos de la Frontera in the province of Cádiz.
3. Publius Ovidius Naso (43 B.C.E.–17/18 C.E.), Roman poet and author of the *Metamorphoses*. Mecías (14th century), a Galician poet.

The well-instructed women sensed his hunger and gave up on him.

Meanwhile, I ate a few cabbage stumps for breakfast, diligently, as a new servant is prone to do, without being seen by my master. I returned to the house. I thought of sweeping parts of it in need of cleaning. I waited to see if my master returned in the afternoon with something to eat but my wishes were in vain.

By two o'clock he hadn't return and my hunger was killing me. I locked the door and placed the key where he asked me to and attended to my needs. With a low and sickly voice, my hands resting on my chest, I begged for a slice of bread as if I were gazing at God and my tongue uttered only His name. I knocked at houses that looked the richest. Since I had sucked this trade in with my mother's milk (by which I mean I learned it from a great teacher, the blind man), I was an accomplished disciple. By four o'clock I already had four pounds of bread inside my body and two more hidden in my sleeve and under my shirt, even though this hadn't been a year of plenty and the town wasn't especially known for its charity. I came back to the house. As I passed a tripe shop, I asked one of the women to have mercy on me and she gave me a piece of a cow's foot, as well as a few pieces of boiled tripe.

When I got home, my master was back already. His cloak was almost folded and on the bench. He was walking around the patio. As I came in, he walked toward me. I thought he might be unhappy with my lateness. But God appeased him.

He asked where I was coming from. I answered:

"Sir, I stayed here until nine o'clock. When I saw that Your Excellency wasn't coming, I wandered around the city, asking people for charity. They gave me all this."

I showed him the bread and tripe I was carrying in my coat. He became excited by what he saw. He said:

"Well, I was waiting for you to come for lunch. When I didn't see you, I ate on my own. You are an honest man because it's better to beg in God's name than to steal. Let God have mercy on me if I didn't like what you did. I only ask that people don't find out you live with me. I wish to protect my honor, although I know it's safe because I'm hardly known in this town. Truth is, I shouldn't have come here in the first place!"

"Don't worry about it, Sir," I said. "If anyone asks I'll tell them to go to hell. They won't get a word from me."

"All right, then. Go ahead and eat, you sinner. God willing, soon we'll find ourselves without needing much. Although I should say that nothing has gone well since I moved into this house and I may never leave it again. It must be a curse because anyone who lives here has bad luck and pays for it with unhappiness. This undoubtedly is one of those houses. I promise you not to be here by the end of the month, even if I got it for free."

I sat down at the edge of the bench. Not wanting to seem as a glutton, I didn't tell him about what I had already eaten for supper from the food people had given me. I began to dine by chewing into the tripe and the bread while hesitating to look at my master. He wouldn't leave his eyes from my shirttail, which functioned as a dish at the moment. May God have mercy on me as much as I had on him, because I felt what I felt and I had often gone through the exact same in my own life, and still do. I wondered if it was appropriate to share a morsel with him. Since he had told me he had his lunch, I thought he wouldn't accept my invitation. Finally, I just wanted that wretched man to help himself with what I had gathered, and that he should have breakfast the way he did the day before, because the offering now was better and I wasn't that hungry.

God wanted to fulfill my wish as well as his because, no sooner did I start eating and, my master began to walk around. He then approached me and said:

"I tell you, Lázaro, you're graceful while you eat. I've never seen anything like it. Anyone who sees you eat can't help but feel hungry."

"Your hunger," I told myself, "makes you think I eat with grace."

In any case, I thought I should help him, since he was helping me, and, in doing so, helped himself too. I told him:

"Sir, good work is done with fine tools. This bread is very tasty and this cow's foot so well cooked and seasoned, its taste would water anyone's mouth."

"Cow's foot?"

"Yes, sir."

"It's the most delicious treat in the world. I'd rather have it than pheasant."

"Try it, sir. You'll see how good it is."

I put the cow's foot in his hand as well as three or four portions of the whitest bread. He sat down and started to eat with much impetus, gnawing every little bone better than a greyhound does.

"With oil, cheese, and garlic sauce," he said, "this tastes delicious."

"You're eating it with even better sauce," I said under my breath.

"God, it tastes as if I hadn't eaten anything all day."

"May the good times come and kill you!" I murmured under my breath.

He asked me to bring the water jug. I did. It was as full as when I had brought it from the river. I took that as a signal that my master hadn't eaten anything. We drank and went to bed very happily, as we had the night before.

I don't want to repeat myself. We were like this for eight to ten days, the sinner going out in the morning to find his happiness down the road while poor Lázaro did his duties for him.

I kept thinking about my disastrous life. Having escaped ruinous masters and seeking betterment, I had stumbled upon someone not only who didn't support me but who I had to support instead. Still, I was fond of him, seeing that he couldn't handle himself differently. In fact, I felt pity for him rather than animosity. Frequently I made it back to the lodging with the basics that I myself skipped so he could get along on.

One morning, when he woke up in his nightshirt and went upstairs to relieve himself, I decided to find out if he was as poor as he seemed. Not wanting to attract any suspicion, I unfolded the doublet and breeches that lay folded on the head of the bed. I found a little purse of smooth velvet folded a hundred times. I didn't have a single darn *blanca* in it, nor a sign it had had one in a long time.

"This man is poor," I told myself. "No one gives what he hasn't got. Even more the stingy blind man and the misbegotten priest, who, in the name of God, one kissed His hand and the other had a loose tongue. They each kept me hungry. I was right to leave them and this one I'm right to feel compassion for."

May God be my witness: when I come across any of those gentlemen today proudly displaying their demeanor as they walk, I feel the same pity thinking of how my master suffered. In all his poverty, I enjoyed serving him more than the others, as I've said. I was only unhappy with him a little bit. He wanted me to be less presumptuous. He needed to fantasize less and pay more attention to practical things. In my opinion, this is the well-kept rule among people of his type: with nothing in his pocket, he was all about appearances. May God help him because they are like that until the day they die.

Well, my life was as I'm describing it when my bad fortune, which never quite ceased, brought to an end the shameful living conditions in which I was living. It turns out that year the crops had failed and the city council decided to throw out all poor people who weren't from the town. Those who stayed would be punished with the whip. The law took its course, granting the stay for only four days, after which I saw a procession of poor people parade through the main streets. I became very frightened and didn't go begging anymore.

Whoever has any imagination at all would have witnessed the abstinence and sadness and silence in my household. I was frightened to such degree that I didn't even have a bite for two or three days, nor did I utter a word. I was fed by some women spinning cotton. I knew them, as they were my neighbors. They themselves survived with little, and they gave me a pittance, which barely enabled me to get by.

Still, I didn't feel pity for myself as I did for my poor master. He didn't eat as much as a bite of bread in eight days. At least at home, I can assure you, there wasn't anything to eat. I don't have the slightest idea where or how he went or what he ate. Seeing him come down the street at noon, his head high, his skinny body leaner than a thoroughbred greyhound, made me sad!

With regard to his wretched honor, he took a straw—there weren't many of them in the house—and would go out the door grinding his teeth, with nothing in between them, still complaining about the bad place he lived in. He said:

"No avoiding the unhappiness of this house. As you can see, it's dark, sad, and miserable. As long as we stay here, we'll suffer. I wish the month was over in order to leave it."

One day, while we were in such a distressed and famished condition, by some strike of luck my poor master happened to come across a *real*. He came home with it so proud it seemed as if he had gotten hold of the treasure of Venice. With a happy and graceful gesture, he gave it to me, saying:

"Here, Lázaro. God has begun to alleviate our misery. Go down to the market and buy some bread, wine, and meat. Let's change our luck! And I'll tell you something else so that you're happy: I have rented another place and once the month is over, we shall not be in this one any more. I curse it and the builder who put the first brick in it, because I've suffered badly in it. My God, ever since I came to live in it, I haven't had a drop of wine or a piece of meat, nor have I been able to rest. It's miserable and sad and gloomy! Go right along, hurry up, and let's eat today like counts."

I took the *real* and a jug and was on my way down the street, in the direction of the market, happy and content. Yet it's in my fortune that any pleasure that comes to me must be accompanied by misfortune and this was the case. Walking on the street, thinking of what best to buy that would be fruitful, thanking God infinitely for allowing my master to come across this money, I suddenly stumbled upon a dead man. He was being carried down by lots of priests and people.

I pressed myself against the wall in order to allow them to walk. Once the corpse went by, I saw a woman who was also coming along. She must have been the dead man's widow. She was in mourning. With her were a bunch of other women. She was crying and shrieking:

"Oh my dear husband, where are they taking you? To the sad and accursed house, to the dark and gloomy house, to the house where no one ever eats or drinks!"

While listening, I felt the sky falling. "Oh, darn! They are taking this dead man to my house!"

I turned around and, leaving the procession behind, I broke off my trip to the market. I ran down the street as fast as I could until I reached the house. The moment I entered it, I quickly closed the door, crying for help and looking for my master, hugging him, asking him to come help and defend the entrance door. Upset, thinking something else might be happening, he said to me:

"What's this, boy? Why are you screaming? What have you done? Why did you close the door with such force?"

"Oh, sir," I replied. "Come here. They are bringing you a dead man."

"How so?"

"I came across this procession. A woman was saying: 'Husband and master of mine, where are they taking you? To the obscure and gloomy house, to the sad and accursed house, to the house where no one ever eats or drinks!' Yes, sir. They're bringing him to us."

After my master heard this, while there was no reason for him to be merry, he laughed so loud he wasn't able to talk for a long time. By then I had already shot the bolt, locked the door, and was leaning against the door to defend it. The procession passed by with the dead man and I was still saying I wouldn't open the door to them. After he got tired of laughing and remembered he was hungry, my master said:

"Truth is, Lázaro, you're right in thinking that what the widow was saying pointed in this direction. But since God has ordained otherwise, open the door. Go out and buy us food."

"Just let them turn around the corner of the street, sir," I said.

Finally my master came up to the street door of the house. He opened it and pushed me out. Although I was still terrified, off I went. While we ended up eating well that day, I didn't savor the food. In fact, it took me three days to regain my color. My master roared with laughter every time I made a reference to what had happened.

That's how I spent the time with my poor third master, who was a poor squire. In all those days, I was filled with curiosity why he had come to this part of the country and what he was really doing in it, since from the first day on I knew he wasn't from these parts. It was clear from the fact that he had few friends and was treated differently from the rest.

At last my wish was granted and I found out what I wanted to know. One day, after eating reasonably well and being happy, he told me his whole life and adventures. He said to me that he was from Old Castile. He had left his native land after having come into some tension with a knight rather than taking his hat off to him.

"Sir," I said, "if he was as you say and was higher than you, shouldn't you have taken your hat off first, given that he had done the same to you?"

"It's true. He was from a higher station. And it's also true that he took his hat off to me. But that was as it should be because of all the times I took mine off first. It was the least he could do than be the first."

"It seems to me, sir," I replied, "that it's better not to see what others have, especially since I would be dealing with superiors."

"You're just a boy," he answered. "You aren't attuned to the affairs that relate to honor. Nowadays it's what all men of good morals are concerned with it. You know that I am a squire. I swear to God that if I come across a count on the street and he doesn't take his hat off, and does it the right way, next time he comes I'll know how to avoid entering his house, pretending to have some other business to do, or will cross the street, if there's one, before he reaches me, so as to avoid him. A hidalgo isn't obliged to anybody except God and his king, since he's a man of breeding because this might cost him his reputation. I remember that one day in my own part of the country I put a tradesman in his place. I put my hands on him because every time I saw him, he would tell me: 'God keep Your Excellency.' 'You're a villain,' I said to him. 'Why don't you show your education?' 'God keep Your Excellency,' you say, as if I were just anybody.' After that, and without fail, he would take off his hat to me and address me properly."

"Isn't it good manners," I said, "when greeting another man, to say 'God keep you'?"

"What a foolish notion," he said. "Only men of low standing say such things. Those with standing, like me, need to be addressed with a 'I kiss Your Excellency's hand,' or at least, 'I kiss your hand, sir,' if he who is talking considers himself a gentleman. That's why when the one in my part of the country tried to impose on me without respect, I wouldn't put up with it. I won't put up with these kinds of indignities, now or ever, from any man from the King down who says 'God keep you' to me."

"I'm a sinner," I said under my breath. "That's why God doesn't care about you. Because you don't want anyone to ask him to."

"For the most part," he said, "I'm not so proud as not to have in my native land small dwellings, which, if they were well kept and cultivated, are worth two hundred times a thousand *maravedís*. They are located sixteen leagues from in Valladolid, where I was born, on a street that runs up a street. These dwellings can be turned into big and good ones. And I have a dovecote that, if it weren't falling down, would yield more than two hundred pigeons a year. I have other things I won't mention, which I left because my honor was at stake. I came to this town thinking I would find a good place here, but it didn't happen as I thought it would. I've come across lots of priests and members of the church. But they are limited people who

will never be able to overcome their own circumstance in this life.
And there are gentry of middle stature who solicit my services. But
it's grueling to work to work for them because as a man you must
turn yourself into their servant otherwise they show you the door.
And usually you have to wait between one payment and the next as
often as you're lucky to get your keep. When they want to be sensible and give you something for your efforts, you're paid off in the
dressing-room with a sweaty doublet or a threadbare cloak or coat.
Even if a man is a member of the nobleman's entourage, he still has
to deal with this disgrace. Is there in me not the ability to serve these
characters? By God, if I had to deal with one, I could become a favor-
ite and serve him a thousand times because I would need to lie to
him as well as to the next one and please him in a thousand different
ways. Cherish his arrogance and customs, even though they might
not be the best in the world. I would never tell him something he
wouldn't like, however it might be to his advantage. I would be solic-
itous with his person, in word and in deed. He wouldn't agonize
about doing things meticulously if he isn't going to see them. And I
would fight with his servants so he would think I'm mindful of everything that relates to him. If he scolded one of them, I would slip in
a few barbs so as to incense him and take sides with the servant
who's been blamed. I would say niceties about the work that's been
done but be malicious and a mocker in the household and outside.
I would find ways to meddle in other people's affairs so as to tell him
their stories and do many other such things, which are done these
days in the palace and are esteemed by the señors who live there.
They don't want to see virtuous men in their households. They abhor
them, they look down on them and call them fools and call them
hopeless. They aren't people on whom the masters can relay on. And
there are people taking care of these affairs today, as I say, today,
and I could too. But my fate hasn't allowed me to do so."

My master went on lamenting his adverse fortune, giving me a
profile of him as a righteous person.

While we were at this, a man and an old woman came through
the door. The man asked my master for the house rent and the old
woman wanted payment for the bed. They figured out the numbers
and in two months the total added to more than he made in one
year. I believe it came to twelve or thirteen *reales*. And he answered
very nicely to them: that he would go to the market to change a
doubloon and that they should come back in the afternoon. But he
left and never showed up again.

When they came back in the afternoon, it was too late. I told them
he hadn't returned. Night came and he still wasn't there. I was afraid
of staying alone in the house. So I went over to the neighbors, told
them the whole story, and slept there.

In the morning, the creditors arrived to where I was and asked about the neighbor next door. The women answered:

"Here's his servant and the key to the door."

They asked me about him and I said I didn't know where he was. I said he hadn't come back since he went to change the money and that in my view he had tricked me and tricked them, too.

Once they heard what I said, they went for a constable and a notary. Then they came back with them and took the key. They called me and several witnesses. They opened the door and entered to take the hacienda away from my master until he had paid his debt. They wandered around the entire house, finding it empty, as I've said. Then they talked to me:

"Where in the hacienda are your master's belongings, his coffers and valuables and jewelry?"

"I don't know anything about that," I responded.

"No doubt," they said. "They must have been taken out last night and placed somewhere else. Señor constable, arrest this boy. He knows where things are."

The constable came in. He took me by the collar of my coat and said:

"Boy, you're under arrest unless you say where your master's stolen goods are located."

Never having seen myself in such a situation (I was taken by the collar many times before, but it was always done more lightly, for instance by the blind man, so I could show him the way), I was terrified and began to cry. I promised to respond to anything they wanted.

"All right," they said. "Tell us everything you know and don't be afraid."

The notary sat down on a stone bench to write some inventory, asking me to list what I had in my possession.

"Sirs, according to what my master told me, he has a fine estate with houses on it and a broken-down dovecote," I announced.

"That's good," they said. "Even if they aren't worth a lot, they'll cover part of his debt. In what part of the city does he have them?" the asked.

"In his own land."

"For God's sake, enough with this business," they stated. "And where is his land?"

"He said he was from Old Castile," I said.

The constable and notary had a good laugh. They said:

"Your account is enough to cover your debt, even if it comes to a lot."

The women neighbors who were there said:

"Sirs, he's an innocent boy. He's been with this squire for just a few days. He doesn't know about him more than Your Honors do. We only knows what the sinner took with him from our house. We have fed this boy with what we could, for God's sake. At night he would go back to the house and sleep at his master's side."

When they saw I was innocent, they let me go. The constable and notary asked the man and the woman for their fees. This led to a terrible dispute that made lots of noise. They claimed they weren't forced to pay because there was no property to account for. The others said they had given up another profitable business that mattered to them in order to attend to this one.

After much give and take, in the end the constable's deputy picked up the old woman's old mattress, although he didn't sag under the weight. Then the five of them went off, screaming and shouting.

I don't know how the whole thing ended. I believe the dirty old mattress must have been made to pay for everything. It would have been well-deserved because although it should have been retired long ago it was still doing heavy-duty jobs.

That's how I was let go by my third master. I was finally convinced of my ruinous fate because he made me do everything upside-down. Masters are usually abandoned by their servants. In my case, it was the other way around: my master left me and ran away.

Fourth Chapter. How Lázaro Settled Down with a Friar of the Order of Mercy and What Happened to Him

I had to find a fourth master. This one was a friar of the Order of Mercy. The women next door led me to him. He was family to them. He was an enemy of singing in choirs and eating in monasteries. He loved wandering around, worldly affairs, and spending time visiting people. In fact, I believe he wore out more shoes than all others in the monastery put together. He gave me the first shoes I ever went through in my life. The pair didn't last me more than eight days. I couldn't keep up with him either. For this and for other little reasons I'd rather not mention, I left him.

Fifth Chapter. How Lázaro Settled with a Seller of Indulgences and the Things That Happened to Him

Fate brought me to my fifth master, who sold papal indulgences. He was the most shameless, uninhibited, and abusive dealer I ever saw, expect to see, or think anyone else has seen. He sought different ways and means and devised subtle tricks.

As he entered places where he would peddle indulgences, first he would offer gifts to priests. Nothing of great value or substance: a head of lettuce from Murcia, a couple of oranges when they were in season, a pair of lemons or oranges, a *melocotón*,[1] a pair of peaches, or wonderful green pears. The presents were meant to keep them happy so they would help him in his business, summon the parishioners to buy the indulgences.

When they thanked him, he would find out how learned they were. If they said they understood Latin, he wouldn't speak a word of it, so as not to make a mistake. Instead, he would use elegant and well-turned *romance*,[2] in which his tongue would find eloquence. And if he found out that the clergy were reverends (by which I mean, with more money than education, and ordained improperly), he would carry himself like Saint Thomas,[3] talking to them in Latin for two hours. At least it looked that way, even if it were less.

When he didn't succeed in selling indulgence, he would take a dishonest route. People didn't like this approach, since he would take advantage of them. Since it would take too long to describe everything he did, I will tell about one of his sly and clever dodges, to prove my point.

He had been preaching in the Sagra of Toledo for two or three days, displaying his usual eloquence. Yet no one was buying a single indulgence, nor, as far as I could tell, was anyone interested. He was fed up, and, thinking what to do, he summoned everyone to come again the next day so he could try unloading his goods.

After supper that night, he and the constable began to gamble. Soon after, they had a discussion and a fight began between them. He called the constable a thief and the constable called him a forger. At the accusation, my master seized a small spear he found lying on the porch. The constable put his hand on a sword he had on his belt.

A ruckus ensured. The fighters were quickly surrounded by guests and neighbors, who tried to separate them. They tried to get away so they could kill each other. There was lots of noise. The house was full. Realizing they wouldn't be able to duel with their weapons, the fighters again resorted to insulting one another. The constable told my master he was a forger and that the indulgences he was selling were fake.

When it was clear the combatants wouldn't come to their senses, the villagers decided to take the constable away from the inn. This infuriated my master even more. The guests in the inn and the neighbors begged him to stop being angry. In the end he went to sleep and everyone departed too.

1. Peach.
2. Castilian
3. Thomas Aquinas (1225–1274), Catholic philosopher and theologian.

In the morning, my master went to church and asked them to ring the bell for the Mass. He wanted to give a sermon. All the village came, still talking about what had happened the night before, saying the indulgences were false and that the constable, during the fight, had made this clear publicly. My master was in such bad mood, everyone hated him even more.

The pardoner climbed into the pulpit and, in his sermon, encouraged people not to be left without the benefit the indulgences would provide them.

When he was at the height of his talk, in through the church door came in the constable, pretending to pray. He stood up and, with a loud voice, started to say coherently:

"Good people, please hear me for a minute, and then you can listen to anyone else you want. I came here because of this charlatan who is talking to you. He fooled me, saying that if I helped him in his business, we would share the profits. But now I realize the damage he would do to conscience and to your pocket. I regret my decision and declare to you openly that the indulgences he sells are false. You shouldn't believe him or have a part in all this, since I, *directe ni indirecte*,[4] am no longer involved in the deal, renouncing from now on any partnership. If at some point he is punished for his false statements, you are my witness that I am no longer with him, nor am I helping him. I am trying to show him in his true light and declare his maliciousness."

That was the end of the speech.

Several worthy men that were sitting in the congregation stood up and, so as to avoid further scandal, were ready to throw the constable out of the church. Fearing excommunication, my master made a gesture with his hand, asking them not to become an obstacle in his wish to offer a rebuttal. Once again, there was silence as the constable said everything as I have reported it.

When he was finished, my master asked that, if he had anything else to add, now it was the right time to state it.

The constable said:

"There is much more to say about you and your lying, but it's enough for now."

Then the constable fell on his knees in the pulpit, clasped his hands, and, gazing heavenward, said the following:

"God, from whom nothing is hidden, to whom everything is known, and for whom nothing is impossible! You know in truth how unfairly I am being portrayed now. Yet, as far as I am concerned, I forgive him, so that You, my God, may forgive me as well. You shall not pay attention to him, for he knows not what he does or says. The

4. Judicial formula (Latin).

injury done to You, I beg thou not to forget. For those congregated here, who might have perhaps considered buying indulgences from this man, and believing his false statements, will not buy one after all. And since all this is also in detriment of the rest of the people, I beg You, oh God, not to falter in your response, for I have proof here of a miracle, which is the following: that if what this man says is true, that I am the one bringing evil and falsity, may this pulpit sink into the ground, with me in it, and let us be buried seven feet under, where we will perish. But if what I declare is true, and he, persuaded by the devil, so as to take away from those here present their estimable wealth, is spreading evil, let him be the one that is punished, his villainy known to all."

No sooner had my master finished praying when the unhappy constable fell off his bench and hit the floor with such power that the entire church shuddered with the impact. He began to howl and foam at the mouth and twist his face into weird expressions, flinging his feet and hands around, rolling back and forth on the floor.

The screams and shouts were so loud the congregation couldn't hear anything. A few people were shocked and frightened.

Some of them said: "May God help him!" Others: "It serves him well, perjuring himself like that."

Finally a number of those present, and as far as I could see not without trepidation, approached him and grasped his arms, as he was punching those around him. Others seized his legs and held them tight. He was shaking like no beast I have ever seen in the entire world. They kept him immobilized for a long time. More than fifteen men were on top of him. He was a handful. If they hadn't subdued him, he would have kicked them on the face.

While all this was going on, my master was on his knees in the pulpit, his hands clasped and gazing up to heaven, crying and making noises, as if in communion with a godly essence. No one in the church was able to pull him away from his divine contemplation.

Some good men approached him and, saying something, shook him out of his trance, begging him to help the poor man who was dying. They asked him not to look the at the past or to the bad comments made of him, since he had already received punishment for them. If there was anything he could do to stop the danger and torment the man was suffering, for God's sake he should do it. In their view, the guilt of the guilty had already been proven. Thus his truth and good heart were needed now because God doesn't see the need in prolonging revenge and punishment.

As if waking up from a sweet dream, my master the pardoner looked at them, then looked at the delinquent and everyone around him. He said very slowly:

"Good people, you should never plead for any man whom God has shown his will. But as He commands us not to spread evil and to forgive any offense, we may confidently implore His Majesty to pardon this man who offended him by placing an obstacle in the way of His Holy Faith. Let us all kneel."

Everyone went down on their knees and, facing the altar, began to sing a litany in a low voice with the priests. My master came with the cross and the holy water, and when had chanted over the constable, his hands facing heaven and his eyes almost unrecognizable, he began reciting a prayer as a long expression of devotion. Everyone cried (as it often happens during sermons on the Passion, when the preachers and congregation are at their most devout), begging Our Lord, since He doesn't want sinners to die but for them to go on with their life so as to repent, that a man like the constable, having been led astray by the devil, who counseled him in death and sin, be forgiven and granted life and health, so that he could repent and confess his sins.

Having done this, he asked them to bring the indulgences and put one on the constable's head. And immediately the sinful constable, little by little, started to feel better, coming back to his senses. And when he regained his wits, he kneeled again next to the pardoner's feet and asked for an apology. He confessed that what he had said had been guided by the devil, in order to cause my master injury and take revenge against his fury. Also and more important, he said he did it because the evil wanted to benefit from it all by not having the indulgences bought.

My master forgave him and they became friends again. Soon there was such a rush to buy indulgences that almost no living soul in the place was left without one: husband and wife, sons and daughters, boys and girls.

The news of what had happened circulated in the surrounding area. As soon as we would reach a particular village, there would be no need for a sermon or to call everyone to church because people would come to the inn where we would stay like pears to a basket. So we did between ten to twelve villages around there, where my master sold some thousand indulgences without having to preach a sermon.

When he performed his act, I confess to also having been sinful, since his persuasive touch also led me astray, as it did many others. Yet in seeing my master and the constable laughing, proud at how they managed their joint business, I came to understand how one had benefited from the other and how inventive my master really was.

The following happened in another place, which I'd rather not name to protect its honor. My master preached two or three sermons but God knows his trick didn't take effect. He quickly understood what was happening, telling people they had a year to pay. It didn't do any good. They were to such a degree uninterested, it was clear his efforts would go to waste. So he had them ring the bells for our farewell service. Once his sermon was done, and having said good-bye from the pulpit, as he was coming down, he called me and the clerk (I was carrying his saddlebags). My master asked us to climb the first step, and he took all the pardons which the constable was carrying in his hands, and he placed the saddlebags I had at his feet. Then he returned to the pulpit, smiling, and started to throw his indulgences down to the congregation, ten and twenty at a time, saying:

"My brethren, take these pardons that God sends you and return home with them. Don't be in pain because the redemption of pious Christians who are in captivity in this land held by the Moors is a worthy effort. Our faith must not be denied and those who reject it shall go to hell. Help them at least with your alms and with five Paternosters and five Ave Marias, so they can leave the bondage they are in. Your money will benefit the parents and brothers and debtors you have in Purgatory, as you may see in the holy indulgence."

When people saw him throwing them away, as if they were handed by God, they took as many as possible. They even got copies for children in their cradle and for deceased family members, counting their children and servants, from the oldest to the youngest on their fingers. There was such a rush that my old coat was almost torn to shreds. I assure Your Excellency that in more than an hour there were no more pardons left in the saddlebags. It was necessary to go to the inn for more.

Once all were taken, my master, in the pulpit, asked his own clerk and the town clerk to stand up and count the names of those who would benefit from the holy indulgences and the pardon of the holy indulgences, so that he could know who now had copies and those names be written down.

Everyone listed the ones they had taken, listing, in order, the children, servants, and deceased relatives they had taken them in the name of.

Once an inventory was done, my master asked the mayor, since he needed to go someplace, for the clerk to authorize the list and keep a record of those who were included in it, which, according to the notary, there were around two thousand.

When all this was done, he said good-bye with a face wreathed in smiles and we left the town. But even before we did, my master was asked by the assistant priest and the town councilors if the indulgence was good for children still in the mother's womb.

To which he responded that, according to the studies he had done, it wasn't the case. They could ask the wisest theologians, more knowledgeable than he was, and that was what his opinion was worth.

So we went our way and everyone was delighted with the business we had made. My master said to the constable and the clerk:

"What do you think of those villagers, who when they hear we are Old Christians,[5] they expect to be saved without performing any acts of charity or handing over any of their goods? Well, I swear in the name of Pascasio Gómez the lawyer for whom it is possible to take ten captives from Algiers!"

We went to another village in the area, next to Toledo, on the way to La Mancha, where we came across people even more obstinate about buying indulgences. My master and all the rest of us performed our duties in two fairs. At the end of it it we had not sold even thirty pardons.

When my master realized that perdition was upon us and that we would end up in ruin, he came up with an idea to get rid of the indulgences we had left. On that day, he was in charge of High Mass. Once the sermon was done, he was back in the altar. He took out a cross he was carrying that was as almost a hand's breadth. Without anyone looking, he placed it on a lighted brazier, in the back of the missal, at the top of the altar (it had been put there to warm the hands because it was very cold). Once the service was over and he blessed everyone, he took it with a small handkerchief. The cross was well wrapped up in his right hand, and in the other hand he had an indulgence. He descended the altar holding the two until he reached the last step, where he pretended to kiss the cross. He invited the congregation to come and worship it. The magistrates came first, then the elders of the place, one by one, as it is always done.

The first one was an old magistrate. When he came to the altar, my master told him to delicately kiss the cross. But he burned the magistrate's face and took the cross away immediately. When my master saw that, he said:

"Slowly, sir! This is a miracle!"

Some seven or eight others did the same. And he told everyone:

"Slowly, señors. A miracle!"

When he realized he had enough elders with a burned face to serve as witnesses of the miracle, he refused the cross to be kissed again. He returned to the top of the altar and preached wonders, saying that because of their uncharitable attitude God had permitted this miracle to happen. The cross, he said, needed to be taken to the cathedral for the bishops to see and that it had burned because people were mean.

There was such a rush to take his indulgences that even two clerks and the priests and the sacristans weren't enough to write all the

5. Category used in medieval Spain to distinguished between families with Christian roots and those who descended from *converso* Jews and were called New Christians.

names. I am sure we sold more than three thousand indulgences, as I told Your Excellency.

Later on, as we departed, he took the holy cross with great reverence, as it should be done, saying he needed to get it gilded, as is only right. He was begged by the town council and the clerics to leave the cross there, as a reminder of the miracle performed in that place. He refused. After being pestered, in the end he relented. He was given another older silver cross that probably weighted two or three pounds, according to what they said.

And that's how we left, happily with the exchange and good business we had done. Nobody else witnessed what he did except for me. I climbed to the top of the altar to see if there was anything else in the plates, to store it away, maybe to turn it later into cash. When he saw me, he put his finger on his mouth, signaling me to be quiet. I acquiesced although once I saw the miracle he performed I was eager to let the whole thing out yet the fear of being punished by my astute master persuaded me to say not a word. So I kept it all to myself. He forced me to swear that I wouldn't reveal his miracle. That is what I have done—until now.

I was only a boy. Yet the trick impressed me very much. I asked myself: "How many others swindle innocent people?"

In total, I was with this my fifth master almost four months. Even with him I suffered a lot, though he fed me well, at the expense of the priests and other clergy he found in the places he prayed.

Sixth Chapter. How Lázaro Settled Down with a Chaplain, and What Happened While He Was with Him

After this, I settled down with a master tambourine painter. I helped him mix colors. I suffered a thousand ills with him, too.

By that time I was already a young man. One day I entered a cathedral and a chaplain took me under his wing. He put me in charge of his donkey and four jars of water and a whip. I began to carry water around the city. This was my first step toward having a good life, because I had a stable diet. Of my earnings I gave my master thirty *maravedís* a day. On Saturdays I earned everything for myself. And on weekdays I kept everything I made beyond thirty *maravedís*.

I did so well at this trade that with the profits I made in four years, I had enough to dress myself in better clothes than the secondhand clothes I wore before. I bought an old fustian[1] jacket and a worn coat with braided sleeves. I also got a cloak which had had a fringe once

1. Cotton fabric.

and a sword—one of the first ones Cuellar[2] ever made. Once I was respectably dressed, I told my master to keep the donkey as I didn't want the job any more.

Seventh Chapter. How Lázaro Settled Down with a Constable and What Happened to Him

Once the chaplain bid me farewell, I settled down with a constable, becoming his bailiff. But I barely stayed with him long because I thought the job was dangerous. One night some fugitives threw stones at my master and me and chased us with sticks. I ran away, so they didn't get me. My master waited for them and they beat him badly.

As I was thinking how to settle down, have a more restful life and save enough for my old age, it pleased God to enlighten me and put me on the way to a fruitful path. With the help of friends and gentlemen, all my hardships and struggles until would be compensated by achieving my ambition: a job in the government. No one who works in those positions faces obstacles.

To this day I have such job, in the service God and Your Excellency. My duty is to cry up the wines sold in this town and to announce actions and lost property. I also accompany criminals being punished and publicly announce their misdeeds. To put it in plain words, I am a *pregonero*—a town crier.

One day, while performing my job, a petty thief from Toledo was being hanged with a good-quality hempen rope. I paid attention to this detail as I remembered what the blind man had said in Escalona. I regretted having taken advantage of him, since he had taught me much. Next to God himself, it was thanks to him that I reached my present position.

Things have gone well for me. I do my job easily. All aspects and responsibilities in this line of work make their way to me. To such an extent that any investor selling in wine in the city is aware of Lázaro of Tormes is a go-between. Without me the path shows no profit.

At this time, the Archbishop of San Salvador, a friend and servant of Your Excellency, witnessed my ability and manners in crying out wines. He made an arrangement for me to marry one of his maids. Realizing such arrangement would be beneficial to me, I agreed. And so I married her. To this day I don't regret it. She has a good nature and is dutiful and responsible. I also have full trust in my Archbishop. He gives her a bag of wheat every year. On Easter there's meat. Occasionally there are a couple of loaves of holy bread or a pair of old stockings. He rents us a small house next to his. And nearly every Sunday and holidays we eat in his house.

2. A village in Segovia, famous for its production of swords.

There is never a shortage of rumors. They don't leave us in peace. People say I don't know what goes on when my wife makes his bed or cooks for him. May God help those who lie.

To confess, I myself have been suspicious during this period. Sometime I have to wait long after dinner. Sometimes it gets even worse. I frequently recall what the blind man from Escalona told me, with his hand on the horn. Though to tell the truth, I have the impression the devil brings him back to my mind so as to bring discord between me and my wife. But it didn't help him anyway.

She isn't a woman who pays attention to this kind of mockery. And my lord the Archbishop made me a promise I know he will fulfill. He made it to me one day in front of her:

"Lázaro of Tormes, nobody who pays attention to this type of gossip can be happy. I say this because I wouldn't be surprised if somebody, seeing your wife enter my house. . . . She comes in and leaves with her honor intact, and yours is too. Don't pay attention to what others say. Only look at good deeds and at what brings you benefit."

"Sir," I responded, "I have made up my mind to do good and surround myself with fine people. To be honest, some of my friends have told me all about it. They have proven to me that before our marriage, she gave birth three times. I speak with reverence to Your Honor because she is here."

Whereupon my wife swore such fearful oaths, I was sure the house would come down. Then she began to cry, to curse the priest who married us. Such was her grievance that she wished she had died before the priest had given us his blessing. I took one side of her and my lord the other while we talked her out of that state. We pampered her until she stopped crying. She made me swear I would never raise the issue again, that I would be content on allowing her to come and go, day and night, since she was a virtuous woman. So we three reached an agreement.

To this day, no one has heard us speak again about the situation. Whenever anybody wants to say something about her, I stop them. I say:

"Look, if you're my friend, know that I don't want to hear about it, since friends aren't made to upset you. She is what I most cherish in the world. I don't want anything to happen to her. God has blessed me by putting her at my side, more than I deserve it. I pray to the Holy Ghost that she is as virtuous as any woman within the confines of Toledo. If anyone says otherwise, I shall kill him."

So no one says anything and I have peace at home.

All this took place the same year as our victorious emperor entered this illustrious city of Toledo and held his courts here amid celebrations, as Your Excellency no doubt has heard. In this period I was at the height of my prosperity and the summit of all good fortune.

In due course, I will inform Your Excellency of what happens to me in the future.

CONTEXT

ILAN STAVANS

Censorship and the *Lazarillo*: An Appraisal[†]

My intention in this brief assessment is to simply situate the publication of *Lazarillo de Tormes* in 16th-century Spain, a time in which freedom of expression was severely impeded.

The Holy Office of the Inquisition (the full title was *Tribunal del Santo Oficio de la Inquisición*) was established in Spain in November 1478 by the Spanish monarchs. Other European countries had similar institutions, but this one is known for its particularly vicious effort to quench dissent. (The kingdom of Aragon had a papal inquisition much earlier, in 1232. Its impact visibly diminished over time.) With the opening of a route by Christopher Columbus in 1492, the line of control extended itself across the Atlantic, where the Inquisition had two main branches, one in Peru, the other in New Spain (known today as Mexico).

The impact of the Spanish Inquisition in the shaping of the social, political, and economic fabric—in the collective self—in Hispanic civilization cannot be overemphasized. It later served as a promoter of the Counter-Reformation, halting progress at all levels. For centuries Spain had been the stage of *La Convivencia*, the coexistence of the three Abrahamic religions: Judaism, Christianity, and Islam. In what became a nation-building effort to unify religion and the state that sought as its mission the *"reconquista"* of land from infidels, Christianity consolidated its dominating role. The Jews were expelled through the Alhambra Decree, issued in March 1492, and the *Moriscos* (e.g., former Muslims who had converted or had been coerced into conversion) were thrown out in April 1609.

With Christianity as the only acceptable faith, the Inquisition functioned as a repressive institutional body devoted to protecting Christians and denigrating Jews and Muslims. (Very few Protestant cases are part of its history.) It ordered conversion by non-Christians in 1492 and 1501. Orders of conversion forced people to abandon their ancestral religious practices, and, as a result, as new order was formed, based on family lineage. That lineage distinguished between the Old Christians, which descended from Christian families able to trace back their genealogy at least three generations, and the so-called *Cristianos nuevos*, New Christians, whose conversion had been recent. While the former were validated as *castizos* and authentic believers, the new class of New Christians,

† Written for this Norton Critical Edition.

while seen as arriviste, was financially entrepreneurial and eager to prove its place in society, at home and abroad.

The designation of *converso* referred to individuals who were recent arrivals to the Christian faith and could be used derogatorily. Crypto-Judío, in turn, meant that a person was publicly Christian but privately still Jewish. The Inquisition created a fearsome atmosphere of censorship. Acquaintances, friends, neighbors, and family were encouraged to denounce those whose loyalty to Christianity wasn't absolute. Those caught in disloyal acts were imprisoned, at times tortured, and even burned at the stake in ritualized performances called *autos-de-fe*.

From 1507 to 1517, the Inquisitions of the kingdoms of Castile and Aragón split, each having its respective branch. Otherwise, the institution was rather homogeneous. Overall, its function was hierarchical. At the top was the Grand Inquisitor, under whose oversight the whole structure depended. (Arguably the most famous among the approximately fifty, and perhaps the most vicious, was Tomás de Torquemada, who served from its inception in 1483 to 1498 and before holding this post was the prior of the Dominican Convent of Santa Cruz, in Segovia.) The Grand Inquisitor headed the Council of the Supreme and General Inquisition, made of up six members. There were up to twenty-one different tribunals throughout the Spanish Empire.

In the publishing sphere, inquisitorial censorship was strict. Books needed approval for release from a committee and regularly included in the front matter an acknowledgement of having passed the test. Depending on the period (the Inquisition was in place in Spain, unlike other places in Europe, until July 1834, well after the height of the Enlightenment), the strict regulations were neither clear nor openly stated. Ideas believed to endorse the Reformation in all its facets were considered dangerous. To stigmatize them, to establish its code, it printed an Index of Forbidden Books (*Index Librorum Prohibitorum*) concerning Spanish-language titles. The first index appeared in 1551. It was reissued in 1559, 1583, 1612, 1632, and 1640. Among the extensive authors and titles in the list were Jorge de Montemayor, Lope de Vega, *La Celestina*, and *Lazarillo de Tormes*. (Sometimes a censored book was published outside of Spain, escaping inquisitorial control.)

The effect of such censorship is multifold. Of course, books deemed unacceptable almost invariably didn't reach the public eye. But the atmosphere of terror also tied the tongues of successful authors, who often opted for nonthreatening topics to avoid persecution. In the case of *Lazarillo*, releasing the narrative anonymously—especially one emphatically anticlerical in its content—was a way for that content to reach readers without the author's becoming a

CATHALOGVS

libroru̅, qui prohibe̅tur ma̅dato Illu̅strissimi &
Reuerend. D. D. Ferdinandi de Valdes
Hispalen̅. Archiep̅i, Inquisitoris
Generalis Hispaniæ.

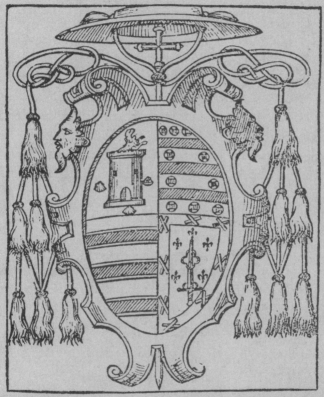

NECNON ET SVPREMI SANCTÆ
ac Generalis Inquisitionis Senatus. Hoc Anno.
M.D.LIX.editus.

❧Quorum iussu & licentia Sebastianus Martinez Excudebat
PINCIÆ.

❧Esta tassado en vu Real.

Fig. 3 Title page of the Spanish Index of Forbidden Books (1559) compiled by Ferdinand de Valdes while he was Inquisitor General of the
Spanish Inquisition. Reprinted in *Tres índices expurgatorios de la Inquisición Espanola en le siglo XVI* (Madrid: Real Academia Española, 1952),
p. 59. Courtesy of the New York Public Library.

¶Imagen del Antichristo, compuesta primera-
mente en Italiano, y despues traduzida en romance por Alonso de peña fuerte.

¶Institucion dela Religion christiana en romance. Impressa en Vuittemberg, año de. 1536. sin
nombre del autor.

¶Instituciones de Thaulero, en romance.

¶Iustino historiador, en romance.

¶Iubileo de plenissima remission de peccados,
concedido antiguamente: y en el fin del dize.
Dado en la corte celestial del Parayso, desde el
origen del mundo, cõ priuilegio eterno, firma
do y sellado cõ la sangre del vnigenito hijo de
Dios I E S V Christo nuestro vnico y verdade-
ro redemptor y señor.

¶Itinerario de la oracion.

L

As lamentaciones de Pedro.

¶Lazarillo de Tormes, primera y segũ
da parte.

¶Lengua de Erasmo, en romançe y en
latin, y en qualquier lengua vulgar.

¶Lectiones de Iob en metro de romance.

¶Leche de la fee.

¶Libro de la verdad de la fee, hecho por el mae-
stro fray Ioan suarez.

¶Libro de suertes, en qualquiera lengua.

¶Libro impresso en romance, en el qual se prohi
be que ninguno de consejo a otro que no se case, ni sea sacerdote, ni entre ē religiõ, ni se arcte

a conse

Fig. 4 Entry in the 1559 Spanish Index of Forbidden Books showing the
censorship of *Lazarillo de Tormes*. Reprinted in *Tres índices expurgatorios de la Inquisición Española en le siglo XVI* (Madrid: Real Academia
Española, 1952), p. 103. Courtesy of the New York Public Library.

target. In his critical edition (Madrid: Real Academia Española, 2011), Francisco Rico offers a valuable summary (pages 115–28) of the possible authors behind the endeavor and the methods, some involving digital humanities, to "unmask" the author, although Rico stresses that such detective work is not only doomed from the outset but probably goes against the author's intentions. In any case, the attempt to make the volume widely available in Spain was curtailed, first in 1559, when it was listed in the Index, then in 1573, when an expurgated edition, without the Fourth and Fifth Chapters, made it out. Translations of the novella into French (1560), English (1576), German (1617), and Italian (1622) were based on a Belgian edition that escaped inquisitorial scrutiny.

In my view, *Lazarillo of Tormes* is an extraordinary example of anti-establishmentarian literature that seeks to simultaneously entertain and denounce. This example is all the more impressive for having circulated during an epoch of authoritarianism that sought to dramatically curtail freedom of expression. That epoch left a deep scar in Hispanic civilization. However, this book stands as a symbol of a rebellion that used humor as a tool to satirize social excesses, particularly of the Catholic priests and the aristocracy. The fact that it has a child as protagonist allowed it to point the finger in favor of the innocent and vulnerable and against the rich and powerful.

TERESA DE ÁVILA

From The Way of Perfection[†]

Chapter II

THAT THE SISTERS ARE TO BE CARELESS CONCERNING CORPORAL NECESSITIES, AND OF THE GOOD THAT IS IN POVERTY

Think not, my sisters, that because ye must not study to please secular persons ye shall want maintenance: hereof I dare secure you. Never seek by human artifices and industries to maintain yourselves, for thus ye will die with famine, and that justly. Fix your eyes on your spouse, for He must maintain you. If He be pleased, those least affected to you shall even against their wills find you diet, as ye have seen by experience; and if thus doing ye died of hunger, oh, happy the nuns of St. Joseph! Forget not this for the love of our Lord; and having quitted all revenue, quit likewise all care about

---

[†] From Teresa de Ávila, *The Way of Perfection*, trans. Abraham Woodhead, ed. A. R. Waller (London: J. M. Dent, 1902), pp. 5–10. Originally published 1565–67.

diet—all is lost else. Those whom our Lord would have take rents, in good time let them mind such cares, since it is very fit, as agreeing with their vocation; but as for us, sisters, it is improper. Taking care about an income from others seems to me to be thinking on what others possess, when, for all your care, another doth not alter his mind, nor ever the more intends to bestow his alms. This care leave to Him who is able to move all—to wit, the Lord of Revenues and of their possessors. By His command we are come hither. True are His words; they cannot fail: heaven and earth shall fail first. Let us not forsake Him, and fear not His forsaking us. If at any time He should leave you, it shall be for your greater benefit—as the saints lost their lives when slain for our Lord, which proved but the augmenting of their glory by their martyrdom. A good exchange this, to dispatch immediately with all the world and enjoy eternal satiety. Mind it, sisters; for this will much concern you when I am dead, and I therefore leave it you in writing; though, whilst I live, I shall remember you of it, as seeing by experience the great benefit thereof. When I have least I am freest from care. And our Lord knows that, to my best understanding, our over-abounding more afflicts me than our want. I know not whether it be because I have seen our Lord presently supply us, otherwise it were cozening the world to make ourselves poor when we are not such in spirit but in appearance only. My conscience would trouble me, as I may so say, and in my opinion this would be, for such as are rich to ask alms—and God grant it be not so. For where these immoderate desires of others giving us are, they may one time or other beg this out of custom, or some may ask what they want not, peradventure of one that needs it more; and, though the donors lose nothing, but gain, yet we may lose thereby. God forbid this, my daughters. Whenever such case happens I had much rather ye should have rent. In no wise busy your mind about this, I beg of you, as an alms for the love of God. And let the meanest of you, when at any time she perceives it to be practised in this house, cry out unto His Majesty, and in humility acquaint the Superioress therewith, telling her that she goes wrong; this is of such consequence that by little and little true poverty may thus come to be lost. I trust in our Lord it will never be so, and that He will not forsake His handmaids; and that this which ye have made me write may, if for nothing else, serve you for an alarm to awaken you. And believe me, my daughters, since for your good our Lord hath made me a little to understand the advantages that are included in holy poverty, and those that try will find it so, though perhaps not so much as I, because I not only was not poor in spirit, notwithstanding that I professed the being such, but in spirit a fool. It is a good that compriseth in it all the goods of the world; it is an ample seignory. I repeat it again and again, it is a kind of lording it over all the goods of the world by him that despiseth them. What care I for kings and lords if I desire none of their estates nor strive to humour them, if I must on the contrary, for their sakes, never so little in anything displease God? Or what care I for their honours if I understand, wherein a poor man's chiefest honour consists—namely, in being really poor? I hold, for my part, that honours and riches almost ever do go together, and that whoever desires honour doth not detest wealth; as likewise, whoever hates money little regards honour.

Understand it rightly; for methinks this point of honour always carries along with it some little interest of estate also, and money— it being a kind of wonder to see one honoured in the world if poor; rather, though he deserve respect, he will be little esteemed. True poverty carries a certain eminency with it, that there are none that suffer by it. I speak of poverty undertaken only for God's sake; it needs not to please any but Him. And it is very certain that, by needing none, one retains many friends. This I have seen sufficiently verified by experience, and because there is so much written concerning this virtue as I am not able to understand, much less to express, that I may not prejudice it by commending it I say no more thereof. I have spoken only what by experience I have seen, and I confess I have been too absorbed in it as not to observe it myself till now, but since it is said, let it go for the love of God. Since, then, our badge is Holy Poverty, and that which at the first founding of our Order was so highly esteemed and so rigidly observed by our holy fathers (for one who knew it told me they kept nothing one day against the next), now that it is not with so much perfection practised in the exterior, let us at least endeavour to retain it in our interior. We have but two hours to live—the reward is exceeding great; and were there nothing in it save the merely accomplishing what our Lord hath counselled us, the very imitating His Majesty in anything were an ample recompense.

These are the arms and motto that must be drawn on our banners, which in everything we should desire to observe—in house, apparel, words, and in our thoughts much more. Whilst this is done, never let them fear the decay of the discipline of this house, through God's assistance, for, as St. Clare said, "The walls of poverty are impregnable. With these," she said, "and those of humility, she desired to enclose her monasteries." And I dare warrant, if it be truly observed, both chastity and everything else is much better fortified thereby than by very stately buildings, which, for the love of God and of His precious blood, take heed of, I beseech you. And if, with a good conscience, I may wish that the same day ye build a costly house it may fall down and kill you all (supposing, I say, a good conscience), I do wish it, and pray to God for it. It looks very ill-favouredly, my daughters, to build stately houses with the poor's stock. This God

forbid. But let ours be every way poor and mean. Let us in something
resemble our King, who had no house save the stable at Bethlehem
where He was born, and the cross where He died—houses, these,
wherein little pleasure could be taken.

I—but those that build great houses surely understand themselves,
and have other pious intentions; but any corner may suffice thirteen
poor women. Notwithstanding, I tell you that (since such strict
clausure requires it, and it also conduceth to prayer and devotion) if
they have a piece of ground with some small hermitages to retire to
their prayers in, well and good; but stately buildings, large houses,
or anything curious, God deliver us from. Ever remember that it
must fall at the Day of Judgment, which, whether it shall be shortly
or no, we know not; and for a house of thirteen poor women with its
fall to make a great noise is not fitting, since the really poor are to
make none, they must be persons without noise, thereby to excite
compassion.

Oh, how would ye rejoice to see one, for an alms bestowed
upon you, delivered from hell! Since all this is possible, for that
ye remain very much obliged to pray continually for such as these
who give you maintenance; since it is our Lord's will also that,
though all comes to us from Him, we should likewise prove grateful
to such persons by whose means He supplies us; and this neglect
ye not.

I know not what I began to speak of, I have so digressed. I conceive it was our Lord's pleasure, for I never intended to write
what I have here said. His Majesty protect us ever with
His hand that none recede herefrom. Amen.

FRAY LUIS DE LEÓN

The Night Serene[†]

When I contemplate o'er me
    The heaven of stars profound,
And mark the earth before me
    In darkness swathed around,—
5   In careless slumber and oblivion bound;

Then love and longing waken
    The anguish of my soul;

[†] From *Hispanic Anthology: Poems Translated from the Spanish by English and North American Poets*, translated, collected, and arranged by Thomas Walsh (New York: G. P. Putnam's
Sons, 1920).

Mine eyes with tears are taken
   Like founts beyond control,
10   My voice sighs forth at last its voice of dole:—

O Temple-Seat of Glory,
   Of Beauteousness and Light,
To thy calm promontory
   My soul was born! What blight
15   Holds it endungeoned here from such a height?

What mortal aberration
   Hath so estranged mankind
That from God's destination
   He turns, abandoned, blind,
20   To follow mocking shade and empty rind?

No thought amid his slumber
   He grants impending fate,
While nights and dawns keep number
   In step apportionate,
25   And life is filched away—his poor estate.

Alas!—arise, weak mortals,
   And measure all your loss!
Begirt for deathless portals,
   Can souls their birthright toss
30   Aside, and live on shadows vain and dross?

Oh, let your eyes beholding
   Yon pure celestial sphere,
Unmask the wiles enfolding
   The life that flatters here—
35   The little day of mingled hope and fear!

What more can base earth render
   Than one poor moment's pause,
Compared with that far Splendor
   Where in its primal cause
40   Lives all that is—that shall be—and that was!

Who on yon constellation
   Eternal can set gaze,—
Its silvery gradation,
   Its majesty of ways,
45   The concord and proportion it displays,—

In argent Wonder turning
  The moon doth nightly rove,
Squired by the Star of Learning
  And melting Star of Love,
50   She trails with gentle retinue above—.

And lo! through outer spaces
  Where Mars is rolled aflame!
Where Jupiter retraces
  The calmed horizon's frame
55   And all the heavens his ray beloved acclaim!

Beyond swings Saturn, father
  Of the fabled age of gold;
And o'er his shoulders gather
  Night's chantries manifold,
60   In their proportioned grade and lustre stoled!—

Who can behold such vision
  And still earth's baubles prize?
Nor sob the last decision
  To rend the bond that ties
65   His soul a captive from such blissful skies?

For there Content hath dwelling;
  And Peace, her realm; and there
Mid joys and glories swelling
  Lifts up the dais fair
70   With Sacred Love enthroned beyond compare.

Immensurable Beauty
  Shows cloudless to that light;
And there a Sun doth duty
  That knows no stain of night;
75   There Spring Eternal blossoms without blight.

O fields of Truth-Abiding!
  Green pasturelands and rills!
And mines of treasures hiding!
  O joyous-breasted hills!
80   Re-echoing vales where every balm distils!

MIGUEL DE PIEDROLA DE BEAMONTE

[The "Soldier-Prophet"]†

* * *

We, the Apostolic Inquisitors who fight heresy, depravity, and apostasy in the city and kingdom of Toledo,[1] together with the ecclesiastical magistrates, have heard the testimony in the criminal case that was and is pending before us, between the party of the first part, Licenciado Sotocameño,[2] Prosecutor for this Holy Office, and the party of the second part, the accused defendant Miguel de Piedrola of Beamonte, born in Marañón in Valle de Campes [Campezo?], near Logroño, who currently resides in Madrid. Because of the information against him, the defendant has been brought before this Inquisition. Asked to give the story of his life, he said:

"From the time I was five or six years old, I was cared for by a priest who taught me to read. Because of some mischief I had made, I was afraid [to remain in Marañon] so I went to Alegría, where I stayed with a potter (*ollero*). The potter's trade didn't appeal to me, so I decided to go to a village near Logroño where the priest, to help me, gave me the vessel (*acetre*) of holy water, which is the way they help poor boys pay for their studies. On Sundays I carried the holy water and a knapsack from house to house, begging for alms.[3] With money I got, I paid for grammar lessons. I studied for about three months, but, seeing that I was stupid and couldn't learn anything, I decided to stop studying. I started singing and took to wandering, working as a servant in various places for assorted masters. Then I went to Sicily and became a soldier. There, during the Gelves [Djerba] campaign, I was captured [by the Turks] and sent to Constantinople.[4]

---

† From "Miguel de Piedrola de Beamonte, called the Prophet," in *Inquisitorial Inquiries: Brief Lives of Secret Jews and Other Heretics*, trans. and ed. Richard L. Kagan and Abigail Dyer (Baltimore: Johns Hopkins UP, 2013), pp. 89, 91–107. © 2004, 2011 The Johns Hopkins University Press. Reprinted with permission of the publisher.

1. Piedrola's Inquisition case file has not been preserved, but his inquisitorial autobiography is recorded in an abbreviated copy of his trial record that was sent to Philip II. Our transcription and translation are based upon this document in Archivo General de Simancas: Estado, leg. 165, fol. 340. An eighteenth-century copy, "Vida y sucesos estranissimos del profeta, ni falso ni santo Miguel Piedrola en tiempo de Phelipe segundo," may be found in the Biblioteca Nacional, Madrid, ms. 10.470, fols. 1–117.

2. Pedro de Sotocameño was appointed *fiscal* (prosecuting attorney) of the Toledan tribunal of the Inquisition in 1565. He served in this office until his death in 1607. The inquisitors who presided over this case were Dr. don Rodrigo de Mendoza, Dr. don Lope de Mendoza, and Lic. Andrés Fernández. The recording secretary was Joseph Pantoja.

3. Piedrola is describing work as an altar boy.

4. Piedrola refers here to the defeat of the Spanish forces gathered at Djerba, in North Africa, by a Turkish fleet in July 1560. The victorious Turks captured and enslaved hundreds of Spanish soldiers. Some of these, Piedrola apparently among them, were transported to Istanbul. Note that Piedrola refers to Istanbul, capital of the Ottoman Turks [from 1453 until the 20th century], by its former Christian name of Constantinople.

I had been previously taken captive three different times. I was in Constantinople for six or seven months when I heard the voice that used to speak to me. The voice told me to escape and bring certain words of warning to Naples, which I brought to the general and he in turn to His Majesty.[5] I believed what the voice had said, since it told me the way to escape and the escape route, and I escaped. I made it to Corfu and was once again captured and taken to Constantinople, where this time I was imprisoned for about seven or eight months. There, the same voice told me to escape and bring with me the same words of warning as last time. Believing what the voice said, as I did, I got safely to Naples. After I'd wandered around Italy and Spain for a while, I rejoined my regiment and was captured a third time. I was in Constantinople working as a boatman for more than a year. As I traveled from Constantinople to Galata and other points along the Black Sea in a ship, the same voice as before came to me and told me to escape and take with me nine other captives and a guide. I escaped with them and took my words of warning to the Viceroy of Sicily and the Commander of the Navy. Serving as a soldier in various places, I ended up badly wounded after one skirmish and was again taken prisoner. The voice told me that I should escape and that on the road I would find someone to guide me. Thus, having served with distinction in the war and having given many important words of warning, I returned to Spain. There, His Majesty showed his thanks to me with a certain annuity from [lands in] the Kingdom of Navarre. I then went to serve him in the rebellion of the Kingdom of Granada.[6]

"When I came back to Madrid, I learned that I was a fourth degree descendent of the valiant nobleman de Piedrola. Because of my lineage and my pretensions to the title, I won a sentence [of nobility] in my favor."[7] [In a shining example of Piedrola's lack of concern for linear narrative, he next tells of his return from Flanders without having mentioned his departure, which appears to have been sometime around 1566.]

"When I came back from Flanders, I gave His Majesty certain advice and letters signed with my name, which dealt with how he

---

5. In the sixteenth century the Spanish Habsburg monarch was also king of Naples and of Sicily and was represented in both by a viceroy.

6. Piedrola refers to an uprising of the moriscos living in the southern city of Granada and its surrounding mountains, known as the "Second Revolt of Alpujarras," 1568–70 (the first revolt took place in 1499). Following the second revolt, Philip II forcibly resettled the granadine moriscos in small groups throughout Castile. These moriscos were later expelled from Spain in 1609–14.

7. Petitions for nobility were relatively common in early modern Spain. In this case, Piedrola was claiming to be the descendant of a certain Luis de Beamonte, a nobleman from the town of Piedrola and the leader of a faction that had successfully defended the kingdom of Navarre against the territorial pretensions of the fifteenth-century Aragonese monarch Juan II.

could best preserve his kingdoms and estates. All these letters were written in a natural discourse, in which I reflected on such matters as a man naturally does. However, other information I knew supernaturally, such as the news that the Frisians and the Malines[8] in Flanders would be the first to rebel [against the king] and that if the situation were not dealt with as I advised, a certain prince would not succeed his father in the monarchy. And really, this is the way it was. The Frisians and the Malines rebelled about six or seven years after that, and the royal person I referred to died within the same period of time I had specified.[9] His Majesty sent a secretary to inform me that I was to leave the Court and never again to take up a pen to write. I told the secretary that I trusted in heavenly justice. I also told him that if he did not do penance for bringing me this news, as I had [noble] lineage and the title of Prophet, and in light of the information and ability these gave me, [I warned him that] his son would marry in a foreign land and he would burn in a fire of pitch, which later came to pass. The secretary asked me why this should be his fault, since he was only obeying orders. I told him that he should ask Elijah why the captains who had burned in the fire were at fault, since they, too, could make the excuse that they were only obeying orders.[1]

"After the secretary made inquiries as to why I hadn't left the Court as I'd been ordered, I received notice that the king had, after consulting with an important adviser, ordered a fort built near [the city of] Tunis.[2] I said that it wasn't a good idea to build [the new fort] before taking down the one that was already there. Instead, the king should route people, munitions, and artillery through La Goletta.[3] If he didn't, within a year all would be lost. This last bit of information came from my supernatural gift for prophecy, while the idea of dismantling the fort, reusing its artillery, and the rest was human discourse and the result of my experience as a soldier with that particular site and fort and as a man of war.

8. These are references to people living in Friesland, a region in the Netherlands, and the Flemish city of Malines, both of which then were part of the Spanish Netherlands. The so-called Dutch revolt against Spanish rule began in 1566 and marked the beginning of a protracted conflict that culminated in the independence of the Dutch Republic—today's Netherlands—in 1648.
9. Piedrola's chronology is confusing. The Revolt of the Netherlands began in 1566. Here he is probably referring to the death of Philip II's eldest son, don Carlos, in 1568.
1. Here Piedrola refers to the Old Testament prophet Elijah, who chastises messengers sent to consult a pagan oracle on the king of Israel's behalf (see 2 Kings 1). The king orders three of his captains, each with fifty soldiers, to summon Elijah. Two of these captains and their regiments are burned to death by heavenly fire, but the third captain recognizes Elijah as a man of God and pleads with him for his life. This captain and his men are spared the fate the others suffered.
2. This fortress Piedrola refers to is probably that of Bizerta, constructed in 1573 as part of the Spanish war effort against the Ottoman Turks.
3. La Goletta was a Spanish fortress near Tunis.

"I told the secretary that I was going to serve in a certain battle. I went to Naples, where, as in other places, I repeated my warning about La Goletta. The same day the news arrived that this fort had been lost.[4] I had been dictating to a friend a letter to His Holiness [the pope], their Majesties the Emperor and the King of France, and the confessor [of Philip II of Spain?], in which I cited the prophet Malachi where he warns the kings and princes about a certain thing and tells them that, among other curses that the prophet would bring upon them, he would curse them with poverty and with constant persecution.[5] My friend asked me how I knew what the prophet Malachi had said if I had never read a book or studied. I told him he could go look it up, but this was what the prophet had said. I got so mad at him over this that I tore up the letters. Later, when I saw my friend again, I told him that I hadn't really been angry, but that I'd felt a spirit inside me that made me do that and the rest of the things I had done since I was a child.[6] My friend and I got back together and rewrote the letters.

"While I was walking [with my friend] around Naples, near the Spanish barracks, at dusk, a very little child, about fourteen months old, came out of a house. He was holding a dried palm leaf, about half a foot long, in his right hand. It sounded to me like he was saying, 'Ah, Ah, Ah.' When the child came near me, I moved aside so as not to step on him, and I let him pass. The child gave me his hand (his left hand came up to the tops of my stockings, or hose) and he stayed that way until I took the palm, which he held out to me in his right hand, showing me that he wanted to give it to me. I refused to take the palm, saying, 'Innocent, this palm is not for me but for others responsible for having brought me out of my country so that I could do my duty.' But my friend told me to take it, because it was a divine mystery. I told my friend that at the entry to Jerusalem it was said that Christ had received the children saying 'ex ore Ynfantium perficisti laudem.'[7]

---

4. La Goletta was captured by the Turks in August 1573.

5. There is no reference in Malachi to the prophet's rebuking kings and princes, though he does take issue with priests. Piedrola here may be referring to Malachi 2, where the prophet brings Hebrew priests this message from God, "If ye will not hearken, and if ye will not lay it to heart, to give glory unto My name, saith the Lord of hosts, then I will send the curse upon you . . . ye have corrupted the covenant of Levi, Saith the Lord of hosts, therefore have I made you contemptible and base before all people" (Mal. 2:2, 9). (All quotations from the Old Testament are from *Tanakh: A New Translation of the Holy Scriptures according to the Traditional Hebrew Text* [New York: Jewish Publication Society, 1985].) The confessor Piedrola refers to here is probably Fray Diego de Chaves, whom he met in 1578.

6. Note that Piedrola makes several references to the "mischief" or misdeeds he has committed since childhood but that these references are always oblique.

7. Matthew 21:16: "Out of the mouth of babes and sucklings thou hast perfected praise." As the inquisitorial scribe noted in the margin of the transcript, the correct quote reads, "ex ore infantium et lactantium perfecisti laudem." When Jesus enters the temple in Jerusalem, the children in the temple cry out, "Hosanna to the Son of David"

"On our way back to the house, I suggested that my friend and I take a closer look at the text of Malachi that we'd discussed before, in which it says 'revertimini ad me, et revertar ad vos Dio.'[8] I decided to buy a Bible from the booksellers, and having bought it, I brought it to my house and placed it on a table on its spine. The book fell open to the aforementioned prophecy of Malachi, and there was an illustration of Malachi with a palm in his hand.[9] I was astonished to see the engraving of the prophet Malachi holding a palm and also to see that the book had turned to that page without anyone's having opened it. Since the child had given me a palm the previous afternoon, when I saw Malachi painted holding a palm, it seemed to me to be a mystery that the child had given me a palm and then that Malachi had one. The Bible had opened to the part God had wanted it to, the part where Malachi warns the princes. I decided, on my own [initiative], to go through the Bible page by page to see if any other prophet had a palm. None did. But in one of God's mysteries, when I went back to the Bible and turned the same pages backward, I found another prophet with a palm. I told myself that I should not believe that it was another prophet, since this engraving was simply a duplicate of the first.

"Some very important people heard about this, and together with them I went to find the child who had given me the palm the day before. We found him in his mother's arms. In response to our questions, she said that the child was fourteen or fifteen months old, and that he could only toddle a little, holding on to things, like all children his age. She didn't know who had given him the palm. The child's name was Marco Antonio. One of the people present swore by the habit of Santiago[1] that Saint Matthew and Saint Mark are mentioned the margin of the text of Malachi and that he thought Saint Anthony had written on the subject. He told me to take his words down as testimony, but I didn't consent, explaining that God's works would be discovered in their own time. With that, I ended the conversation and we all left, each to his own home and me to mine, where I returned to writing the letters I sent the princes.

"After that, I gained courage and pride and began to say what I felt, which is that I was in God's service. A short while later I had

---

(Matt. 21:15). It is this "perfect praise" to which Jesus refers. This and all further quotations from the New Testament are from the King James Version.

8. Piedrola here refers to Malachi 3:7, "Return unto Me, and I will return unto you, saith the Lord of hosts." The correct Latin quote reads, "revertimini ad me et revertar ad vos dicit Dominus exercituum et dixistis in quo."

9. Note that no reference to palm leaves occurs in Malachi's text.

1. The habit of Santiago is the cloak emblazoned with the insignia of the Spanish military order of Saint James, or Santiago.

various meetings with the Lord Don Juan of Austria[2] and the Viceroy of Naples, during which I tried to get them to make peace. In particular, I spoke with Lord Don Juan and told him that I would have to write to his servants that which is written in Ecclesiastes, 'vidi servos in equis,' which means, 'I have seen servants upon horses.'[3] [I told him that] unless he followed the orders I was about to give him, when he left for Flanders things would begin to go badly for him.[4] If he followed my instructions, he would rule over all his enemies in the states of Flanders. But if he didn't do as I said, he would lose and end up bad off. His servants would become lords and he a servant. This is what I wrote in a memo I sent him. . . .

"At this time, various noblemen [passed through Naples] on their way to Turkey, where they planned to do very difficult things. Consulting with the Viceroy of Naples, I told him that for various reasons, which I gave him, the noblemen's task was an impossible one and that they should not go forward with it. The Viceroy responded that they had to try. I then set in writing, with my signature, [my prediction] that the noblemen would come to no good, and that they should not go forward. If they did, it would cause great loss and offense and the noblemen would end up on the gallows or suffer some similar punishment. I said all of this speaking as a prophet and as prophecy, and this is what came to pass, as is well known. One was garroted, one was hanged, and the third went blind and deaf.

"At this same time the Commander of the galley fleet in Naples had been run over by a carriage. Believing that he was about to die, the Commander wanted to pass his property on to his son, but I stopped him, saying that he was not going to die. I went to the Commander's house and told him that he wasn't going to die, since his heart, which at other times could be troubled when he was suffering adversities, was healthy and calm. In short, he wasn't going to die. That very afternoon, the Commander recovered. The next day he was fit and soon he was cured. I attributed [my knowledge

2. Don Juan of Austria, King Philip II's half brother, commanded Spain's Mediterranean fleet in the early 1570s. He had previously commanded troops in the Alpujarras War, which may have been how Piedrola was acquainted with him.
3. "Vidi servos in equis," from Ecclesiastes 10:7, "I have seen servants upon horses and princes walking as servants upon the earth." In early modern Europe, riding horseback was a sign of nobility. Ecclesiastes 10:7 is preceded by this quote, also germane to Piedrola's warning to Don Juan: "There is an evil which I have seen under the sun, like an error which proceedeth from a ruler: Folly is set on great heights and the rich sit in low place" (Eccles. 10:5–6).
4. If this conversation actually occurred, it probably can be dated to 1576–77, as Don Juan was sent to Flanders to 1577 in order to quell the Dutch revolt against Spanish rule. Don Juan had little time to accomplish this goal, because he died the following year.

of] this to supernatural and divine inspiration, which God reserves for His divine mysteries.

"I also counseled the Viceroy of Naples about the governance of his kingdom and his household. Much, or most, of what I told him I said as a human man. But along with that, as later events would show, part of what I said came from my supernatural gift. Seeing that Naples was not well governed, as it should have been, and that in some ways this was my fault, in His Majesty's service I left Naples and returned to Spain. While I was traveling through Rome, His Holiness sent word that I should come and see him at a certain time, which he indicated. I replied that I wished to be excused from the audience, since my first thought was with His Majesty and no other living person. If it pleased His Holiness, however, he could command that I be brought to him forcibly, since I was in his court and jurisdiction. With that, he told me to go on my way. I promised to pay him a longer visit on the way back.

"A few days after I left Rome, I arrived in Florence, where the Duke [of Florence] begged me to go and see him. I told him that if I had business with him, I would go and see him. But if he had business with me, he should send me his questions. If, after that, he still had to see me, he would have to bring me to him by force of law, as the Holy Office has done, since I didn't have the authority to come to him any other way. I said, 'tollierre me et mitite me in mare' (take me up and cast me forth into the sea), as Jonah had said.[5] Even though my life is not equal to that of Jonah, as far as prophecies were concerned, like Jonah, I had said things about the future as a prophet. Thus spoke the Lord through the Prophet Ezekiel, chapter 33, where it says, 'That which is predicted will come to pass, because I have placed here, as I have already done, prophets among you and they will know.'[6] If the duke still wanted to see me, well, I was on his lands and in his city and he could have taken me by force to his palace to see me, which he didn't do. Rather, he let me go without seeing me.

"From Florence I went to Genoa, where, after I had seen its most important buildings, the [Spanish?] Ambassador who happened to be there asked me how I liked the city. I told him, resolutely, that my spirit had moved me for various reasons to say that there would soon be plague and discord in the Republic. He asked me when this would come to pass. I told him that the plague would come in less than five

5. When a storm hits the ship on which Jonah is traveling, the passengers draw lots to see which of them has provoked the wrath of God. Jonah draws the short straw and is asked to name his own punishment: "Then said they unto him, 'What shall we do unto thee, that the sea may be calm unto us?'" Jonah replies, "Take me up and cast me forth into the sea; so shall the sea be calm unto you" (Jon. 1:11, 12).

6. There is no reference in Ezekiel that matches Piedrola's misquote. Ezekiel 3:3 reads, "And He said unto me: 'Son of man, cause thy belly to eat, and fill thy bowels with this roll that I give thee." The reference to Ezekiel 33 as opposed to 3:3 may have been a mistake of the scribe who prepared this transcription, or it may have been Piedrola's error.

months. And so it happened, because it [the plague] arrived after only four months. I said all of this as a prophet, since this is how I understood it in my spirit. In short, as I have said, it happened in this way.

"From there I went to Barcelona, where I saw a certain important person and tried to persuade her to make peace [with certain people]. She did not do this or other things I asked her to do. As it says in the Holy Scripture, [I predicted that] she would forget the death of her husband with the death of her son, though I didn't say when her son's death would happen. This frightened her. I told her, moreover, that for other reasons, she would be punished by seeing no male of her line survive to inherit. Her son would die within a very short time. I said all of this with the utmost assurance, knowing infallibly that this person's son would die, as I have said."

[We, the Inquisitors] asked whether or not he had said this as a prophet or not. He answered that proof of the gift of prophecy required the [involvement of] the Pope [*summo sacerdote*], and that he did not know how the Inquisitors, without a special letter from His Holiness, could have jurisdiction over him and his affairs. [Piedrola continued as follows:]

"As you know, I am a prophet. As such, I have spoken to pontiffs, kings, and magnates and to the guardians of these kingdoms. Many of my prophecies have come true. I state this clearly because I don't want harm to come to you, as has come to all others who have dared to persecute me without my having committed a crime deserving [of punishment]. I won't tell you any more than I've told everyone else."

Continuing with his story, he said:

"When I arrived in Madrid, some advisers told me that His Majesty wanted me to tell him about things I spoke of earlier, that had happened while I was in service in Naples. I replied that I would have to meet either with his royal person or in his presence, with a small group of priests and other ministers of state, so that I could speak more effectively. What I proposed was approved, in accordance with the reasons given by His Majesty. A few days later, His Majesty sent certain important ministers of his to meet with me. When we met, they told me that His Majesty wanted me to tell them whatever it was I had to say. I replied that on matters concerning his office it was the king's duty to hear people so that he could act on what was said. It was better not to go through third parties because kings have the virtue of being able to understand advice better when they receive it [personally] than when they receive it through other means. If His Majesty wanted to hear me, I was ready to speak with him. If not, I had carried out my duty in predicting what it was my duty to predict. If His Majesty didn't want to hear me, I would return to Rome, as I had promised His Holiness.

"The ministers told me that the king's hand would not be forced. They told me I would do well to say what I had to say to those who were here. I replied that kings must hear prophets in person, and that when Nebuchadnezzar asked of Daniel that which was now being asked of me, the prophet responded that the reason such a cruel sentence had been imposed was because he was not in the King's presence and that they should take him to Nebuchadnezzar.[7] I myself didn't want to follow any path except that which the Prophet Daniel had taken. Even though I wasn't as saintly as the Prophet Daniel, as far as predictions were concerned, I had my supernatural gift of prophecy and I was a prophet nonetheless. The Catholic Church does not prohibit this, but if it did, I would serve the hand [of the Church].

"Just before dawn, while I was sleeping, about two days before the ministers and I had this chat, I dreamed that I saw the figure of a kind and well-proportioned priest with gray hair and a beard and a biretta pulled down until just above his eyes. He came over to my bed and stood over me, straddling my legs. Lacing his fingers together but with his palms open, he bent over three times, striking my chest and saying each time, 'Dominus Piedrola, Dominus Aaron' (The house of Piedrola is the House of Aaron).[8] The second time he said this, he raised his voice and hit me harder. The third time he struck me so hard that it seemed that the blow had crushed my chest into my ribs, and his voice was so strong that it rang in my ears as if someone had shot off a cannon next to them. With the last blow and at the sound of his voice, I awoke, awed and frightened of the vision.

"I began to wonder what it could mean. Then I remembered the text of Saint Paul, where it says that none but he who is called by God as Aaron was will be given honor.[9] It seemed to me that the three times I was called represented the same thing as when God called to Samuel three times while he was sleeping.[1] Or, perhaps, if this vision wasn't meant to call me to prophecy, perhaps it was meant to call me to the priesthood. But considering that in the past I had predicted so many things, I was persuaded that it was

---

7. Once again, Piedrola has managed to mangle Scripture. In Daniel 2, King Nebuchadnezzar orders the wise men of Babylon, Daniel included, to be imprisoned and then executed on account of their failure to recount and interpret his dream correctly. He also believes that their prophecies have been false. When Daniel is told the reason for the order, he asks the king's guard to bring him before Nebuchadnezzar. He then provides the king a true interpretation of his dream, upon which "the King Nebuchadnezzar fell upon his face and worshiped Daniel" (Dan. 2:46).
8. See Psalm 115:12: "The Lord remembers us and will bless us: He will bless the house of Israel, he will bless the house of Aaron."
9. Hebrews 5:4: "And no man taketh this honour unto himself, but he that is called of God, as was Aaron."
1. I Sam. 3:3–18.

meant more to call me to prophecy and predictions rather than to the priesthood.

"Two or three days later, after the meeting [with the king's ministers] I mentioned, I heard a voice in my sleep which called to me three times, saying 'Piedrola, Piedrola, Piedrola.' When I opened my eyes and looked around, I was on a high mountain. At its top was a large nest of eagles, brown, white, and black.[2] On their heads they wore imperial and ducal crowns, heavily adorned with different stones. As I was looking up from the base of the mountain, I saw a black raven in the sky, coming [from the west] as if from Portugal. In his beak the raven held a round sphere like the ones astrologers draw, except this sphere was dripping and was the color of recently spilled blood. A few drops of blood from this ball fell to the ground. The raven arrived and landed on the western part of the nest, from whence he had come flying. The eagles in the nest fled toward the east, where I was, turning their beaks and faces toward the raven, who flew out of the nest. The raven flew toward me in pursuit of the eagles and landed on my left arm with the ball, dripping blood, still in his beak.

"When the eagles saw the raven leave the nest, they went back to the other side of it, across from where the raven had been, but they kept their heads and faces turned to the spot where the raven was. It should be noted that the eagles, even though they had fled from the raven, never left their nest unprotected. Instead, they were on the other side of it, across from where the raven was, with their faces and beaks turned [toward him]. The raven on my arm called to me three times, saying 'Piedrola, Piedrola, Piedrola, feed the eagles this, which I have brought.' I, frightened to see that I had approached the eagles' nest and they had fled from me, told the raven, 'Since you are naturally so contrary, you must dare to feed the eagles.' The raven laughed and told me, in Spanish, that since he was supernatural he was not afraid of eagles.

"In reply, I said, 'Well, now, there's no reason you should ask me [to feed the eagles]. I know perfectly well that supernatural things can't be judged as natural things can. Try again.' Then the raven flew up to the nest on the eastern side to where the eagles had gone when the raven flew in from the west. Perched on the nest, the raven opened his wings and flapped them three times, like swans do when they call their children. I saw that the eagles had gone toward the raven and had begun to eat the ball he carried in his beak, which showed that they approached him with fear and awe. Then, frightened by seeing the eagles eat what the raven had

---

2. In Ezekiel 17 a similar dream is narrated, in which eagles represent the king of Babylon who displeased the Lord by breaking his covenant with him.

carried, I awoke and remembered my dream with the certitude that it was a prophetic vision, as I will explain shortly.

"I had doubts as to whether I should tell anyone of my prophetic vision or whether I should keep quiet for fear that talking about the vision could put me in danger. Suffering thus, I decided to look at the Bible which I called [Scripture?] which was the name of the one I had in my hand, the one I had bought in Naples. I took it off the table and opened it. The first thing I came upon was Jeremiah, the part where the Prophet says, 'He who has a dream, tell it now. He who has a word, tell the word.'[3] I wasn't satisfied with this, so I went back and opened the Bible a second time. By chance, I opened it to the part where it says, 'If there is among you any prophet of the Lord, I will appear to him in a vision or a dream and I will speak to him now.'[4] With that, it seemed to me that duty obligated me to tell of this vision.

"I gathered the members of my household together, men and women, and I told them the same things I just mentioned, reminding them of some previous predictions that they knew had come to pass. [The Raven,] I said, . . . was the messenger of death for a generation of the House of Austria.[5] The ball was the grave state of the Christian republic, especially of the priesthood. The rings that encircled the ball were the scheming and violent treachery that hindered any attempt at good government. The blood that fell to Earth was the injustice of those who suffered unjustly with no remedy for their pain save their cries to the heavens. The blood that fell to Earth was also a cry to God against the oppressors, like the cry of the just Abel's blood against his brother, the homicidal Cain. The mountain was Christianity, while the nest was the generation and the house of Austria, the guardians of Christianity. The different colors the eagles had were the generations of the House of Austria. That is to say, the black eagles were the kings and emperors, male and female, who are currently reigning. The brown ones were those who are to succeed to the throne. The white eagles were those from the House who were not to succeed or govern. The different crowns represented the different states. The different stones which adorned the crown were the virtues that all princes have and also the obligation they have to be virtuous so that they may bring glory to their kingdoms.

3. Piedrola may be referring to this passage in Jeremiah 23:28: "Let a prophet who has a dream tell the dream; and let him who has received My word report My word faithfully."
4. Numbers contains this passage in which the Lord addresses Miriam, Aaron, and Moses: "And He said: 'Hear now My words: if there be a prophet among you, I the LORD do make Myself known unto him in a vision, I do speak with him in a dream'" (Num. 12:6).
5. The House of Austria refers to the Habsburg monarchy, which came to power in Spain starting with Charles I (aka Charles V) in 1516 and ended with the death of Charles II in 1700.

I told everyone of this vision and interpretation since that was the will of God and was from God, and so that I would not incur the punishment of the prophet Ezekiel, where Ezekiel says that if a watchman sees the knife coming and doesn't sound the horn and the sword comes and kills, the guard should be arrested for his evil act.[6]

"When a certain person told me that His Majesty wished to know what complaint I had with him, I asked only why His Majesty had not met with me, as I mentioned above. I had not stopped wanting to see him. Even though I had made up my mind because of this to go back to Italy, some people immediately detained me. I sent His Majesty a letter explaining what I needed him to do to right the wrong and redress my complaints. Later, these people brought me a letter from His Majesty. In it, he commanded me to go on a certain day to the [royal] palace, where he would grant me an audience and where we would discuss our business. In response, I asked why His Majesty had written this if he didn't have to. He didn't have to see me, except that, in some way, what happened with the Prophet Micah and the king Ahab might happen to him.[7]

"Even if I were to go to the king and talk to him, he didn't have to make use of what I told him, since he didn't have to do anything. My response frightened the person and he told me I was crazy. I replied that I had always been this way. Those who denounce things in God's name have always been taken as crazy. Look at Job and his friends. So that the truth may be known, I told this person I would go to the palace whenever His Majesty wished, though His Majesty would not see me for some time to come. To date I have not yet spoken with him.

"I had decided to go back to Italy when by order of His Majesty I was detained and ordered to tell a gentleman about the dream of

---

6. Ezekiel 33:1–7: "The word of the Lord came to me: "O mortal, speak to your fellow countrymen and say to them: When I bring the sword against a country, the citizens of that country take one of their number and appoint him their watchman. Suppose he sees the sword advancing against the country, and he blows the horn and warns the people. If anybody hears the sound of the horn but ignores the warning, and the sword comes down and dispatches him, his blood shall be on his own head. Since he heard the sound of the horn but ignored the warning, his bloodguilt shall be upon himself; had he taken the warning, he would have saved his life. But if the watchman sees the sword advancing and does not blow the horn, so that the people are not warned, and the sword comes and destroys one of them, that person was destroyed for his own sins; however, I will demand a reckoning for his blood from the watchman. Now, O mortal, I have appointed you a watchman for the House of Israel; and whenever you hear a message from My mouth, you must transmit My warning to them."

7. Piedrola has incorrectly attributed the prophecies of Jeremiah to Micah, who does not mention King Ahab at all. It is likely that Piedrola was referring to Jeremiah 29:21, "This is what the LORD Almighty, the God of Israel, says about Ahab son of Kolaiah and Zedekiah son of Maaseiah, who are prophesying lies to you in my name: 'I will hand them over to Nebuchadnezzar king of Babylon, and he will put them to death before your very eyes.'"

the raven and other predictions regarding Flanders, which I mentioned earlier, which threatened, among other things, the death of a certain prince. I looked up at a crucifix and said to it, "Well, you know, Lord, that this must be true. I beg you to let it be known." Within four days' time there came letters with the news of the deaths of some important personages. As it seemed to me that the heavenly punishment had begun, I left Madrid, shaking the dust from my boots and garments at the outset, as testimony that I had done my duty by telling of the vision. I was now on my way to do my duty to His Holiness.

"A certain person asked me how I had seen and then denied the aforementioned prophecy of the raven. I told him not to tire himself out and to go with God. The duty of the Prophet is not to be subjected to those sorts of questions, and I was under no obligation to answer them. Even Jeremiah, a Prophet from the time when he was in his mother's womb, had never dared to ask questions of Baruch, the prophet whose secretary and servant Jeremiah had been.[8] As my interlocutor was a certain doctor, he could not touch me. Although he may have worn a great crown, in return for his impudence it would not be covered with a miter. The same thing happened to another doctor who bothered me, while nothing happened to me. Since I was a child it has been my experience that those who persecuted me have come to bad ends. . . ."

In the next passage Piedrola went to Barcelona, where the viceroy, without the king's knowledge, ordered Piedrola to participate in an ecclesiastical debate with various learned clerics. Piedrola, according to his own version of events, made an excellent showing. The clerics were amazed and wondered if Piedrola's knowledge was diabolical. Piedrola then traveled to Rome, where he had an audience with the pope. No visions came to him during his audience, so Piedrola asked the pope for indulgences and left. He then went to Sicily where he met with the viceroy, talked about Spanish misgovernment of the island, and predicted that the viceroy's son would die if he left Sicily to join the Spanish army about to invade Portugal, a reference that suggests that this conversation occurred in 1580 as Philip II's forces invaded Portugal in the spring of that year. In passing, Piedrola repeated the claim that the inquisitors had no right to arrest him or to keep him in prison without special permission from the papacy, since only the pope had jurisdiction over prophets. In making this argument, in which he invoked Joseph and other Old Testament prophets, Piedrola asserted, "I am a prophet, neither holy nor false."]

8. In Jeremiah 36:4, Jeremiah mentions Baruch as an inferior (a scribe commanded to take down Jeremiah's own words). No mention is made of Baruch as Jeremiah's master or teacher.

We [the Inquisitors] asked Piedrola what kind of voice he heard and if he saw a body along with the voice or if he only heard a voice. He answered:

"Sometimes the figure of a man or a woman appears to me in dreams. Other times I only hear a voice and can't see the body it's coming from. In some dreams I see people wearing all manner of dress. Some are priests, others monks, farmers, or courtiers. Some are naked or dressed in various types of women's clothes. When I'm alone, these spirits talk to me and, only when I'm asleep, they talk to me about things that are in the Lord's service. . . .

"I wish, if it please God, that I didn't have the gift [of prophecy] or that the Church and its ministers would order me not to have this ministry so that it would no longer torment me. The figure of Christ himself has spoken to me, but sometimes I don't know who it is who's speaking to me. I do know that it's a good spirit, because of what it says. It always tells me things about the glory of God and His Catholic Church. Anything else that might be against this, I reject as a diabolical illusion."[9]

We [the Inquisitors] asked Piedrola various questions, to which he responded:

"That which I know as a prophet may be corrected by another, greater prophet, as when Jeremiah corrected Baruch. But, on the subject of who is allowed to correct me, I'm not sure if the Pope alone has the authority to distinguish between true and false prophets. I do know, however, that prophets are obligated to appear before their superiors and the judges who call them. If I have said anything wrong, such as the prediction that the Inquisition has no jurisdiction over me because of what I thought the Lateran Council had said (which is that priestly authority is secondary to the gift of prophecy), I have only said it out of zeal and with the best of intentions.[1] If I've committed a crime, any judge can arrest me. The Holy Office is the greatest tribunal in the world. I give myself over to it as the Catholic Church demands I do. If you have found me lacking in anything, then bear my good intentions in mind and pardon me."

In another audience we [the Inquisitors] had with him, which we had at his own request, Piedrola said:

"I've remembered that when I was arrested I may have said some disrespectful words in anger. This weighs on me because I didn't behave humbly, which would have been the right thing to do. It also

---

9. Diabolical illusion was itself an inquisitorial crime (*iluso, ilusente*). Piedrola here may have been trying to avoid adding more charges to the list the Inquisition had already compiled against him.

1. The Fifth Lateran Council (1512–17), at the start of its 11th Session, decreed that the papacy was the ultimate arbiter in matters of prophecy and prophetic discourse.

weighs on me that in this tribunal I have said some disrespectful things. For this, I beg you to pardon me and have mercy on me, an illiterate idiot who has studied the Bible only a little bit. I only did what was necessary with the dreams as with the prophecies written in my letters. If I've said anything the Holy Catholic Church doesn't agree with, pardon me and have mercy on me. I am an idiot. Correct me. If I've said or written anything against the Holy Catholic Church, I'll retract it since I, from the first, have retracted it in my mind. . . . I've never had a pact with the Devil nor been deceived by him. I never meant to seek honors for being a prophet. The truth is that much of what I've said I've said as a human being, based on the vast experience I've had in the business of war. Because these things, and a couple of things I've said in relation to them, turned out to be true, and because I couldn't have known them through human knowledge as I could with some other things, it seemed to me that, somehow, they were prophecies, as I've said and as my papers show.

"I think I've erred most in believing that certain things have happened and in believing that the things I dreamed were prophecies and in giving these dreams more credit than they were due. . . . Many times I've written papers that told of when I heard the voice, but the truth is that the voice didn't tell me anything. I didn't even hear it. Instead, all of what I've said I've said according to human knowledge and then embellished with some sayings from the writings of the Prophets, from the flower of the Bible and the Holy Doctors and other similar authors, and the Catechism written by the Pontiff and other prelates and people, so that I could use their words. . . .

"The truth is that I'm not a prophet, God forgive His Holiness, the Cardinals, the Inquisitors General, His Majesty, and the rest of His Majesty's servants, ministers, and counselors, both clerical and lay, whom I asked twenty years ago to disabuse me of the notion that I am a prophet. Since others told me that I was, you should pardon me since I acted in good faith, modeling my actions on those of the prophet Baruch. . . .[2] Have mercy on me and consider my noble blood, my life, past and present, and my intention, which was to glorify God and ensure the good governance of the state, since the poor were oppressed and the clerics did not always pay attention to that which Saint Paul said, 'curio en anathema en pro fraccuibus meis,'[3] and that which Moses said, 'Give me the Book of

---

2. Baruch, son of Neriah, is mentioned only briefly in Jeremiah (Jer. 36:4–32). Baruch faithfully transcribes the prophecies of Jeremiah. When Jeremiah is unable to go to the temple to deliver the prophecies himself, Baruch goes in his place.

3. It is likely that Piedrola refers here to the following biblical quote, which he has uttered in mangled form. Romans 9:2–4: "optabam enim ipse ego anathema esse a Christo pro fratribus meis qui sunt cognati mei secundum." For I could wish that myself were accursed from Christ for my brethren, my kinsmen according to the flesh (KJV).

Life.'[4] I have erred out of a Christian desire to do good and from not having anyone to disabuse me [of the belief that I am a prophet] until now. I beg God, if He hears me, to make me my own judge as He did with Jonah when they asked Jonah what sentence he wanted to give himself when the fates turned against him. He said, 'Take me and throw me into the sea.' I say to you, take me and put me in an insane asylum for however long you think is necessary."

[Piedrola again called himself an "illiterate idiot" and pleaded for mercy on the grounds that he was noble. He then repeated his request to be put in an insane asylum. The prosecutor Sotocameño formally accused Piedrola of "being a prophet who was neither good nor approved by the Church," who "preached to frighten people" and who "pretended to be a prophet" when in fact he was not. Piedrola defended himself by claiming that he was "soft in the head" and unable to understand the Bible that he had purchased in Naples.]

"I have only sinned in that I was dishonorable and passed myself off as a prophet. . . . From my childhood I've naturally been inclined toward piety and, seeing that there was no other way to become [closer to God], I thought it a good idea to fake these things to frighten and entertain people, though not to harm them. I know that each one of us fulfills his obligation as best he can. Nobody forced me to do this, but since I didn't take up any other sort of craziness, I took up this one. . . . I have lived the most exemplary and virtuous life I could, and I hope you, in your mercy, will take this into account. Because I am crazy, I ask that you please put me in an insane asylum. . . . I lost my wits after I purchased the Bible in Naples, and people in my home-town, where I committed a certain offense, have always thought I was crazy. . . . Pardon me for having offended the Holy Book and for having wanted to count myself among the number of the prophets.

"Most of the fault lies with all those who put it into my head that the visions I had were prophecies. It is not surprising that a crazy man like myself should believe these people. Because of them, others were fooled. I didn't understand the harm I had done until I came before the Holy Tribunal of the Inquisition, where I thank God for having brought me, which made me see that I had chosen a path to evil."

[Prosecutor Sotocameño closed the case for the Inquisition by stating that Piedrola was a "heretic, apostate, disturber of the peace in the republic, usurper of divine and celestial authority, arrogant, seditious, scandalous, a trickster, and a con man who had a pact with the Devil and who declared and signed himself to be a true prophet

---

4. Piedrola may be misquoting from this passage, in which Moses says to God, "But now, please forgive their sin—but if not, then blot me out of the book [of life] you have writ-ten. The Lord replied to Moses, "Whoever has sinned against me I will blot out of my book [of life]" (Ex. 32:32–33).

of God, neither false nor meritorious . . . and who claimed to be subject neither to His Holiness nor to His Majesty in Earthly things. As far as divine things were concerned, they were subject to him, but not he to them." Sotocameño added that he also suspected Piedrola of necromancy and Protestant (or, in Inquisition parlance, "Lutheran") heresies. Piedrola admitted to having "spoken like a mad man, like an unbridled horse" but maintained that his intentions were good and that he deserved inquisitorial mercy because he was "an idiot."

In the end, because of his "good confession, repentance and tears," the inquisitors granted Piedrola mercy, according to their definition. They sentenced him to appear in an *auto de fe*, abjure *de levi* and forbade him to ever again read the Bible or other Holy Scriptures, own paper, write letters, or speak of religious matters. They also sentenced Piedrola to a five-year prison sentence, which in inquisitorial vocabulary was called "perpetual jail."]

∗ ∗ ∗

MIGUEL DE CERVANTES

Don Quijote of La Mancha[†]

Volume 1, Chapter 12

—what a goatherd came and told them

Just then, one of the youngsters who fetched supplies from the village came over, saying:

"Do you know what happened in town, my friends?"

"How could we know?" one of the goatherds answered.

"In that case," the young man went on, "let me tell you. Our famous student-shepherd, Grisóstomo, died this morning, and they're whispering he died of love. It's that damned Marcela, Guillermo the Rich's daughter—the one who goes all over the place dressed like a shepherd."

"You mean Marcela?" one of the goatherds said.

"That's who I said," the youngster replied. "And the funny thing is that, in his will, he says he's to be buried out in the fields, as if he were a Moor, and right at the foot of Corktree Fountain Rock, because that's supposed to be the place where he saw her the first

† From *Don Quijote: A Norton Critical Edition*, trans. Burton Raffel, ed. Diana de Armas Wilson (New York: Norton, 1999), pp. 63–66. Copyright © 1999 by W. W. Norton & Company, Inc. Used by permission of W. W. Norton & Company, Inc.

time—and they claim he used to say that, too. And there's other stuff in his will, things the bishops down there say can't be done, and shouldn't be done, because it's like the heathens. But his great friend, Ambrosio the student, who dressed like a shepherd, the way Grisóstomo did, says it all has to be done just the way it's written down, without leaving out a thing, and it's got the whole village in an uproar. But in the end, or so they say, it'll be done the way Ambrosio and all his shepherd friends want, and tomorrow they'll bury him just where I said, with a great big show. I think it's really going to be something to see, and me, I'm not going to miss it, even though I'm not supposed to go back down tomorrow."

"We'll all go," answered the goatherds, "and we'll draw lots to see who has to stay and take care of everybody's goats."

"You're right, Pedro," said someone, "but you won't have to do all that, because I'll take care of the whole business. And don't think I'm nice, or not interested. It's just that I stepped on a sharp stick, the other day, and I can't walk."

"In any case, we thank you," answered Pedro.

Don Quijote asked Pedro to tell him more about the dead man, and about the shepherd girl, to which Pedro responded that, as far as he knew, the man had been a rich gentleman's son, who'd lived in a nearby village, and that for many years he'd been a student at the University of Salamanca, and then come back home, with a reputation for both wisdom and scholarship.

"And they say he particularly understood all about the stars, and what they're doing up there in the sky, the sun and the moon, because he knew just when there'd be a clips."

"An *eclipse*, my friend, not a *clips*," said Don Quijote, "meaning an obscuring of those two great heavenly bodies."

But Pedro just went on with his story, not concerned with trivialities:

"And also, he could predict when it would be a good year or an arren one."

"You mean *barren*, my friend," said Don Quijote.

"*Barren, arren*," answered Pedro. "You end up in the same place. But I can tell you it was his predictions, because they listened to him, that made his father and his friends very rich. They did whatever he told them to. He'd say: 'This year, plant barley, not wheat.' Or: 'This time, you can plant chickpeas and not barley. Next year we'll have a bumper olive crop, but for three years after that you won't get enough to squeeze out a drop of oil.'"

"That's called astrology," said Don Quijote.

"I don't know what it's called," replied Pedro, "but I do know he understood all this, and even more. Anyway, it wasn't more than a few months after he came from Salamanca when, one day, he surprised everyone by dressing like a shepherd, wearing a sheep-skin coat and carrying a staff, and giving up those long scholar's robes he used to wear, and at the same time Ambrosio, his old friend, who'd been a student with him, started wearing shepherd's robes, too. I forgot to say that the dead man, Grisóstomo, was a great one for writing ballads and songs—so much so, that he wrote carols for Christmas Eve, and plays for Corpus Christi, and the young fellows from our village acted in them, and they all said they were really good. But when the village people all of a sudden saw these two scholars dressing like shepherds, they were really surprised, and couldn't figure out why they'd done such a strange thing. Now, about then Grisóstomo's father died, and he inherited a big estate, not just in land, plus a lot of cattle—I mean, all kinds, cows and horses and mules and sheep and goats—and a lot of cash, all of it his and nobody else's, and really, he deserved it, because he was a nice man and charitable and he was good to honest people, and just to look at him was like getting a blessing. Pretty soon everyone knew the only reason he'd changed his clothes was so he could wander around these wild places, chasing after that shepherd girl, Marcela—the one our youngster talked about, before—because poor Grisóstomo, may he rest in peace, fell in love with her. So now let me tell you, because you ought to know, just who this girl is, because maybe, or maybe not, you'd never in all your life hear anything like this, even if you lived as long as Sarna."

"You mean, *Sarah*," replied Don Quijote, who couldn't stand how the goatherd mangled his words.

"Sarna [*sarna*=scabies] lives long enough," answered Pedro, "but señor, if you go on correcting every word I use, I can talk for a year and never get to the end."

"Excuse me, my friend," said Don Quijote. "I only interrupted you because there's such a big difference between *Sarna* and *Sarah*. But your reply is a very good one, since *Sarna* does live longer than *Sarah*, so go on with your story, and I won't contradict you any more about anything."

"Well, then, my very dear sir," said the goatherd, "let me say that there's a farmer in our village who's even richer than Grisóstomo's father, and his name is Guillermo, and besides his huge fortune God gave him a daughter, whose mother died the most respected woman anywhere around here. It seems to me I can see her right now, her face just like the sun on one side and the moon on the other, and on top of all that she was a hard worker and a friend to the poor, and I think this very minute her soul ought to be happy with God, up there in the other world. The loss of such a good wife killed her husband, Guillermo, leaving his daughter, Marcela—who was very young and very rich—in the custody of her uncle, a priest whose pulpit is in our village. The little girl grew so beautiful that we were all reminded of her mother, who'd been very beautiful, but it still seemed the daughter would outdo her. So it happened that, by the time she reached fourteen or fifteen, no one had ever seen her without blessing God for making her so lovely, and most of them were hopelessly in love with her. Very wisely, her uncle kept her carefully hidden away, but in spite of that her reputation grew, as much for her beauty as for her wealth, and it wasn't just among our own people but with everyone for miles and miles around, and some of the very best people, too, and her uncle kept being asked, and begged, and bothered to let them marry her. But he was a very upright man, a good Christian, and though he would have liked to have her married as soon as he could, because he saw she was of age, he didn't want to do it without her consent—and it wasn't that he had one eye on the profits he earned from her estate, while they waited for the girl to get married. And let me tell you, they said the same thing all over the village, praising their good priest—and I'm sure you know, sir knight, that in little villages like these everything is chewed over and people whisper about everything, so you'll realize, as I do, that a priest has to be powerfully good before his parishioners are forced to say good things about him, especially in villages."

"That's true," said Don Quijote, "but go on. This is an excellent tale, and you, my good Pedro, tell it in fine style, most gracefully."

"May I never run out of God's good grace, that's what matters. As for the rest of it, you'll understand that, although her uncle brought forward everyone who wanted to marry her, and told her all about each of them, asking her to pick and choose as she pleased, all she'd ever reply was that she didn't want to get married just then—and besides, since she was so young, she didn't think she was ready for the responsibilities of marriage. All of which seemed to him reasonable excuses, so her uncle stopped bothering her and waited for her to grow a little older, so she'd know how to choose a companion who'd suit her. He said, and quite rightly, that parents have no right to push their children into a way of life against their will. And then, when you couldn't have expected it, suddenly there was fickle Marcela, turned into a shepherdess. And no matter what her uncle and everyone else in town did to talk her out of it, she made up her mind to go out in the fields with the other shepherdesses and take care of her own flocks. And since now she was right out in public, and everyone could see her beauty, I couldn't even begin to tell you how many rich bachelors, gentlemen and farmers, got dressed up like Grisóstomo and went wooing out in those fields. One of them, as I told you, was our late lamented himself, and they say he'd gone beyond loving her: he absolutely adored her. But don't think just because she chose to be so independent, and live such a free life, with so little protection—or none at all—that she gave any sign, not even any appearance, that her virtue and chastity had suffered. No, she was so careful about her honor that, of all those who wooed and courted her, not one ever boasted, and in truth not one of them could have boasted, that she'd given him even the tiniest, smallest prospect of getting what he wanted. She doesn't avoid either the shepherds' company or their conversation, and she treats them courteously and pleasantly, but if she finds they have any designs on her, even if it's as honest and upright as matrimony, she hurls them away like a cannon. And yet, living this way, she does more damage, here on this earth, than if she carried the plague, because her pleasantness and her beauty draw the hearts of those who deal with her, and then they court her, and they love her, but her scorn and honesty drives them to despair, and they don't know what to say to her, except to call her cruel and ungrateful, and other things like that, which is in truth how she acts. And were you to stay around here, señor, some day you'd find these hills and valleys echoing with the moans of disappointed lovers. Not far from here there's a spot with almost two dozen tall beech trees, and there isn't one of them that hasn't had its smooth bark cut into, to write Marcela's name, and on some there's a crown just above, as if her lover wanted to proclaim that her beauty wears, and deserves, the crown of all womanhood in the world. Here, there's a shepherd sighing; over there, one's moaning; down there, you hear passionate love songs, and up there, hopeless dirges. There'll be someone spending the whole night, sitting at the foot of some tall oak tree or steep crag, never once closing his weeping eyes, lost, carried away by his thoughts: the sun finds him there, in the morning. And there'll be another, unable to ease his sighs, unable to find relief, lying stretched out on the burning sand, in the full heat of the most furious summer afternoon, sending his lament to the merciful heavens. And the beautiful Marcela triumphs over this one, and that one, and these, and those, forever free and confident. But everyone who knows her is just waiting to see where her arrogance ends, and who'll be the lucky man to get the job of trying to tame such a fierce temper, trying to enjoy such fantastic beauty. And since everything I've told you is the unquestionable truth, I'm sure what the youngster told us about Grisóstomo's death is equally true. So I advise you, señor, not to miss his funeral, tomorrow, which will really be something to see, because Grisóstomo has a lot of friends, and from here to where they've been told to bury him isn't more than a mile or two."

"I'll have to, indeed," said Don Quijote, "and let me thank you for the pleasure of hearing such a delightful story."

"Oh!" answered the goatherd. "But I don't know even half of what's happened to Marcela's lovers. Maybe tomorrow, on the way to the funeral, we'll bump into some shepherd who'll tell us everything. And for now, I think you'd better sleep indoors, because the night air might hurt your wound, even though the medicine I put on it is so good that you really don't need to worry about anything bad happening."

Sancho Panza, who could have sent all the goatherd's talk straight to the devil, said he thought his master ought to sleep in Pedro's hut. Which his master did, spending the whole night thinking of his lady Dulcinea, in imitation of Marcela's lovers. Sancho Panza settled down between Rocinante and his donkey, and slept—not like some rejected lover, but like a man who'd been kicked and beaten half to death.

JUAN DE LUNA

From The Second Part of the Life of Lazarillo of Tormes[†]

II. *How Lazaro Embarked at Cartagena*

By nature I didn't last very long with my masters. And it was that way with this one, too, although I wasn't to blame. So there I was, miserable, all alone, and in despair; and with the clothes I was wearing everyone scoffed and made fun of me. Some people said to me, "That's not a bad little hat you have, with its back door. It looks like an old Dutch lady's bonnet."

Others said, "Your rags are certainly stylish. They look like a pigsty: so many other fat little ones are in there with you that you could kill and salt them and send them home to your wife."

One of the soldiers—a packhandler—said to me, "Mr. Lazarillo, I'll swear to God your stockings really show off your legs. And your sandals look like the kind the barefoot friars wear."

A constable replied, 'That's because this gentleman is going to preach to the Moors."

They kept teasing and taunting me so much that I was nearly ready to go back home. But I didn't because I thought it would be a poor war if I couldn't get more than I would lose. What hurt me most was that everyone avoided me like the plague. We embarked at Cartagena: the ship was large and well stocked. They unfurled the sails, and a

† From *The Life of Lazarillo of Tormes, His Fortunes and Misfortunes as Told By Himself, with Sequel by Juan de Luna*, trans. Robert S. Rudder with Carmen Criado de Rodrí- guez Puertolas (New York: Frederick Ungar, 1973), pp. 122–131. Reprinted by permis- sion of Robert S. Rudder.

wind caught them and sent the ship skimming along at a good clip. The land disappeared from sight, and a cross wind lashed the sea and sent waves hurling up to the clouds. As the storm increased, we began losing hope; the captain and crew gave us up for lost. Everyone was weeping and wailing so much I thought we were at a sermon during Holy Week. With all the clamor no one could hear any of the orders that were given. Some people were running to one place, others to another: it was as noisy and chaotic as a blacksmith's shop. Everyone was saying confession to whoever they could. There was even one man who confessed to a prostitute, and she absolved him so well you would have thought she had been doing it for a hundred years.

Churning water makes good fishing, they say. So when I saw how busy everyone was, I said to myself: If I die, let it be with my belly full. I wandered down to the bottom of the ship, and there I found huge quantities of bread, wine, meat pies, and preserves, with no one paying any attention to them. I began to eat everything and to fill my stomach so it would be stocked up to last me till judgment day. A soldier came up and asked me to give him confession. He was astonished to see how cheerful I was and what a good appetite I had, and he asked how I could eat when death was so near. I told him I was doing it so that all the sea water I would drink when I drowned wouldn't make me sick. My simplicity made him shake with laughter from head to foot. I confessed a number of people who didn't utter a word with the agony they were in, and I didn't listen to them because I was too busy eating.

The officers and people of high rank escaped safely in a skiff, along with two priests who were on board. But my clothes were so bad that I couldn't fit inside. When I had my fill of eating, I went over to a cask full of good wine and transferred as much as I could hold into my stomach. I forgot all about the storm, myself, and everything. The ship started to sink and the water came pouring in as though it had found its home. A corporal grabbed my hands and as he was dying he asked me to listen to a sin he wanted to confess. He said he hadn't carried out a penance he had been given, which was to make a pilgrimage to Our Lady of Loreto, even though he had had many opportunities to do it. And now that he wanted to, he couldn't. I told him that with the authority vested in me, I would commute his penance, and that instead of going to Our Lady of Loreto, he could go to Santiago.

"Oh, sir," he said. "I would like to carry out that penance, but the water is starting to come into my mouth, and I can't."

"If that's the way it is," I said, "the penance I give you is to drink all the water in the sea."

But he didn't carry that out either because there were many men there who drank as much as he did. When it came up to my mouth

I said to it: Try some other door, this one is not opening. And even if it had opened, the water couldn't have gotten in, because my body was so full of wine it looked like a stuffed pig. As the ship broke apart a huge swarm of fish came in. It was as though they were being given aid from the bodies on board. They ate the flesh of those miserable people who had been overcome by a drop in the ocean, as if they were grazing in the county pasture. They wanted to try me out, but I drew my trustworthy sword and without stopping to chat with such a low-class mob, I laid into them like a donkey in a new field of rye.

They hissed at me: "We're not trying to hurt you. We only want to see if you taste good."

I worked so hard that in less than half-a-quarter of an hour I killed more than five hundred tuna, and they were the ones that wanted to make a feast out of the flesh of this sinner. The live fish began to feed on the dead ones, and they left Lazaro's company when they saw it wasn't a very profitable place to be. I found myself lord of the sea, with no one to oppose me. I ran around from one place to another, and I saw things that were unbelievable: huge piles of skeletons and bodies. And I found a large number of trunks full of jewels and gold, great heaps of weapons, silks, linens, and spices. I was longing for it all and sighing because it wasn't back at home, safe, so that, as the buffoon says, I could eat my bread dipped in sardines.

I did what I could, but that was nothing. I opened a huge chest and filled it full of coins and precious jewels. I took some ropes from the piles of them there and tied up the chest, and then I knotted other ropes together until I had one I thought was long enough to reach to the surface of the water. If I can get all this treasure out of here, I thought to myself, there won't be a tavernkeeper in the world better off than I'll be. I'll build up my estate, live off my investments, and buy a summer house in Toledo. They'll call my wife "Madam," and me they'll call "Sir." I'll marry my daughter to the richest pastrycook in town. Everyone will come to congratulate me, and I'll tell them that I worked hard for it, and that I didn't take it out of the bowels of the earth but from the heart of the sea. That I didn't get damp with sweat but drenched as a dried herring. I have never been as happy in my life as I was then, and I wasn't even thinking about the fact that if I opened my mouth I would stay down there with my treasure, buried till hell froze over.

III. How Lazaro Escaped from the Sea

I saw how near I was to death, and I was horrified; how near I was to being rich, and I was overjoyed. Death frightened me, and the treasure delighted me. I wanted to run away from the first and enjoy the second. I tore off the rags that my master, the squire, had left me for the services I had done him. Then I tied the rope to my foot and began to swim (I didn't know how to do that very well, but necessity put wings on my feet and oars on my hands). The fish there gathered around to nip at me, and their prodding was like spurs that goaded me on. So with them nipping and me galloping, we came up to the surface of the water, where something happened that was the cause of all my troubles. The fish and I were caught up in some nets that some fishermen had thrown out, and when they felt the fish in the nets they pulled so mightily, and water began to flow into me just as mightily, so that I couldn't hold out, and I started to drown. And I would have drowned if the sailors had not pulled the booty on board with their usual speed. What a God-awful taste! I have never drunk anything that bad in my entire life. It tasted like the archpriest's piss my wife made me drink once, telling me it was good Ocaña wine.

With the fish on board and myself as well, the fishermen began to pull on the line and discovered the spool (as the saying goes). They found me tangled up in the rope and were astonished, and they said, "What sort of fish is this? Its face looks like a man's. Is it the devil or a ghost? Let's pull on that rope and see what he has fastened to his foot."

The fishermen pulled so hard that their ship started to sink. When they saw the trouble they were in, they cut the rope, and at the same time they cut off Lazaro's hopes of ever becoming one of the landed gentry. They turned me upside down so I would empty out the water I had drunk and the wine, too. They saw that I wasn't dead (which was by no means the worst that could have happened to me), so they gave me a little wine, and I came back to life like a lamp with kerosene poured in. They asked me all kinds of questions, but I didn't answer a word until they gave me something to eat. When I got my breath back, the first thing I asked them about was the shackles that were tied to my foot. They told me that they had cut them to get out of the danger they had been in. Troy was lost and so were all of Lazaro's great desires: and right then his troubles, cares, and hardships began. There is nothing in the world worse than to have fancied yourself rich, on top of the world, and then to suddenly find yourself poor and at the bottom of the ladder.

I had built my castles on the water, and it had sunk them all. I told the fishermen what both of us lost when they had cut off my shackles. They were so angry that one of them nearly went mad. The shrewdest one said they should throw me back into the sea and wait for me there until I came up again. They all agreed with him, and even though I objected strongly, their minds were made up: they said that since I knew the way, it would be easy for me (as if I would be going to the pastry shop or the tavern!).

They were so blinded by their greed that they would have thrown me out if my fortune (or misfortune) had not arranged for a ship to come up to us to help carry back the fish. They all kept quiet so that the others wouldn't find out about the treasure they had discovered. But they had to leave off their evil plan for the moment. They brought their boats to shore, and they threw me back with the fish to hide me, intending to hunt for me again when they could. Later, two of them picked me up and carried me to a little hut nearby. One man who didn't know the secret asked them what I was. They said I was a monster that had been caught with the tuna. When they had me inside that miserable pigsty, I begged them to give me some rags to cover my naked body so I could be presentable.

"You can do that," they said, "after you've settled your account with the hostess."

At the time I didn't understand their gibberish. The fame of the monster spread through the countryside, and many people came to the hut to see me. But the fishermen didn't want to show me; they said they were waiting for permission from the bishops and the Inquisition and that, until then, it was entirely out of the question. I was stupified. I didn't know what they were planning, and so I didn't know what to say or do. The same thing happened to me that happens to the cuckold: he is the last to find out. Those devils cooked up a scheme that Satan himself wouldn't have thought of. But that requires a new chapter and a new look.

CRITICISM

HOWARD MANCING

The Deceptiveness of *Lazarillo de Tormes*†

A critical commonplace, appearing in manuals of literature, introductions to student and popular editions, surveys of "picaresque" literature, and in incidental references, maintains that *Lazarillo de Tormes* is fundamentally different from subsequent Spanish prose works called picaresque. The latter are depicted as baroque works imbued with pessimism and *desengaño*, while the former typifies the ironic, perhaps satiric, but essentially optimistic, spirit of the Renaissance. Representative of such an interpretation is José García López, who, in his popular history of Spanish literature, writes of Lazarillo's lack of bitterness and his healthy, ironic criticism of his masters' shortcomings, asserting that the work's satire falls short of the acerbity of later picaresque novels and praising its noble humanity. He concludes: "El 'Lazarillo' no es, en suma, un libro pesimista."[1] Perhaps the most authoritative contemporary critic who reads the book essentially this same way is Marcel Bataillon, for whom *Lazarillo de Tormes* is a "petit livre satirique et plaisant, . . . un tour de force artistique, . . . un livre pour rire, *de burlas*."[2]

The diametrically opposed interpretation is that of Francisco Márquez Villanueva, who specifically rejects such readings, maintaining that *Lazarillo de Tormes* is no less than an unremitting indictment of society's values, "un alegato sin alternativa contra la vida en sociedad, ferozmente sacrástico y pesimista por sistema."[3] This is essentially a recent interpretation and may be properly considered yet to be a minority report. The gulf between Bataillon and Márquez Villanueva is too great to be bridged; their readings of *Lazarillo de Tormes* are mutually exclusive and irreconcilable. One might ask with Wayne C. Booth the pertinent question, "Can two readers be said to have read the same book if one thinks it ends affirmatively and the other sees the ending as pessimistic?"[4]

The aim of this paper is twofold: (1) to study the structure of *Lazarillo de Tormes* and some of its narrative and stylistic devices in order to describe the moral and ethical reactions of the reader to

---

† From Howard Mancing, "The Deceptiveness of *Lazarillo de Tormes*," *PMLA* 90.3 (1975): 426–32. Reprinted by permission of the copyright owner, the Modern Language Association of America.
1. *Historia de la literatura española*, 13th ed. (Barcelona: Editorial Vicens-Vives, 1966), pp. 181–82.
2. Introd. to *La Vie de Lazarillo de Tormès*, trans. A. Morel-Fatio (Paris: Aubier, 1958), pp. 9, 13, 36.
3. "La actitud espiritual del *Lazarillo de Tormes*," in *Espiritualidad y literatura en el siglo XVI* (Madrid: Alfaguara, 1968), pp. 118–19, n. 83.
4. *The Rhetoric of Fiction* (Chicago: Univ. of Chicago Press, 1961), p. 325.

the protagonist, and (2) to suggest that the traditional optimistic interpretation is in some measure a result of a process of deliberate deception on the part of the work's sophisticated and innovative anonymous author. *Lazarillo de Tormes* itself provides easily overlooked keys to its interpretation and, in the Prologue, even suggests why it is so frequently misread.

It is impossible to disregard our moral reactions when undergoing a literary experience. As Booth has shown so brilliantly, it is specifically the nature of fiction to involve the reader emotionally with the characters: "If we look closely at our reactions to most great novels, we discover that we feel a strong concern for the characters as people; we care about their good and bad fortune. In most works of any significance, we are made to admire or detest, to love or hate, or simply to approve or disapprove of at least one central character, and our interest in reading from page to page, like our judgment upon the book after reconsideration, is inseparable from this emotional involvement" (pp. 129–30)[5]

Seldom has an author so prejudiced the reader in favor of his protagonist as in *Lazarillo de Tormes*. Although incidental prejudicial devices will be discussed below, two means by which the reader's sympathy is evoked stand out: the autobiographical form and comparative characterization. By the latter I mean that Lazarillo— young; frail, innocent—appeals to the reader in comparison with his first masters whose reluctance, refusal, or inability to provide the boy with food works strongly against them. The epithets pegged to the blind man ("mal," "cruel," "traidor," "avariento," etc.), the priest ("mezquino," "mísero," "brujo," "cruel," etc.), and the squire ("pobre," "desventurado," "pecador," "triste," etc.) reveal the boy's (and essentially the reader's) hatred for the first two and pity for the last. This constant labeling is a device employed by novelists to stress the negative judgments such characters are expected to evoke in the reader.[6]

Simultaneously, the innovative use of the first-person narrative form works entirely to the protagonist's advantage. The intimacy of autobiography, by its very nature, invites the reader's sympathy for, and even identification with, the author-hero.[7] The tone of this confessional letter, written in obedience to an inquiry into the

---

5. See also Ch. v, "General Rules, iv: Emotions, Beliefs, and the Reader's Objectivity," pp. 119–47.
6. See Sheldon Sacks, *Fiction and the Shape of Belief* (Berkeley: Univ. of California Press, 1964), pp. 179–80.
7. See Stephen Spender, *World within World*, cited by Roy Pascal, *Design and Truth in Autobiography* (Cambridge, Mass.: Harvard Univ. Press, 1960), p. 163. See also Pascal's Ch. xi, "The Autobiographical Novel," pp. 162–78. In fact, a novelist must work hard at being offensive (as does, for instance, Quevedo in *El Buscón*) in order to overcome this natural reader sympathy and make his first-person narrator antipathetic.

"matter," the "caso," of the Prologue, is intimate and colloquial.[8] The author confides in the reader, reveals to him his innermost thoughts, and at the same time amuses and entertains him. Lazarillo's constant display of wit (through euphemism, hyperbole, puns), his frequent moral-philosophic asides, and his ability to laugh at his own misfortunes all contribute to the establishment of an atmosphere of increasing trust and sympathy on the reader's part.

The extraordinary "Prólogo" to *Lazarillo de Tormes* is a dense fusion of disparate elements—the bravado of the opening words ("Yo por bien tengo que cosas tan señaladas, y por ventura nunca vistas")[9] mild erudition (citations from Pliny and Cicero), suspicious humility ("esta nonada que en este grosero estilo escribo," p. 54), and outright pride ("porque se tenga entera noticia de mi persona," p. 54)—which on balance probably produces a negative reaction in most readers.[1] Furthermore, it is ambiguous and obscure: Why is "agradar" (instead of "enseñar" or "aprovechar") coupled with "deleitar"? What, precisely, is the point of the discussion of "arte"? And, most important, who is "vuestra merced" to whom the work is addressed and what is the "caso" which is alluded to?

But if the effect of the Prologue is negative, that effect is slight because the Prologue is brief and it does arouse the reader's interest and curiosity—to learn, if nothing else, how, in spite of adverse odds, one might reach a safe harbor by hard and skillful rowing (p. 54). When the actual narration of the first *tratado* begins, the reader's mind is set at ease.

The apparent ingenuousness and honesty of the narration of Lazarillo's birth and family life are disarming; the daring, irreverent biblical paraphrasing ("fue preso y confesó y no negó, y padeció persecución por justicia," p. 55)[2] and the irony of euphemism ("un hombre moreno," p. 55; "la posada y conversación," p. 56) bring an approving smile to the reader's lips. An intimate link is forged between narrator and reader with the telling of the episode of Lazarillo's little black half-brother's fright upon seeing a "bogy man" in the visage of his father. The boy cries "¡Madre, coco!" and Lazarillo makes a perceptive philosophic observation on man's inability to see himself as others see him: "¡Cuántos debe de haber en el mundo que

---

8. See Claudio Guillén, "La disposición temporal del *Lazarillo de Tormes*," *Hispanic Review*, 25 (1957), 268–70.
9. Ed. Claudio Guillén (New York: Dell, 1966), p. 53. All subsequent citations in the text are from this excellent edition, lamentably out of print.
1. Stephen Gilman, "The Death of Lazarillo de Tormes" (*PMLA*, 81, 1966, 150), finds the Prologue shocking in its arrogance and bombast and concludes that "rather than enticing the reader, its balance defies and even repels him."
2. For Bataillon this is mere "humorismo clerical de tipo perfectamente inofensivo." *El sentido del "Lazarillo de Tormes"* (Paris: Librairie des Editions Espagnoles, 1954), p. 12. Gilman, however, reads it as a "mock commonplace" popular among New Christians (p. 154).

huyen de otros, porque no se veen a sí mismos!" (p. 56).[3] This first aside to the reader is especially important in establishing the tone of the book as well as in gaining the reader's sympathy.[4]

The illusion that Lazarillo's mother has placed him with a "good master" (p. 57) is immediately dispelled in the scene of the stone bull. The blind man's sardonic laughter and warning, "Necio, aprende que el mozo del ciego un punto ha de saber más que el diablo" (p. 58), underscore the symbolic and prophetic value of the boy's awakening from a state of innocence ("la simpleza en que como niño dormido estaba," p. 58). The protagonist's reaction, "Verdad dice éste, que me cumple avivar el ojo y avisar, pues solo soy, y pensar cómo me sepa valer" (p. 58), sets the tone for the remainder of the book: Lazarillo is to be alone in a cruel and hostile world. From this point on only a moral earthquake could disengage the reader's sympathy.

Throughout the period of apprenticeship with the sadistic blind beggar the reader shares Lazarillo's physical misfortunes: the ringing in the boy's head when it is smashed against the stone bull, the unexpected pain when the wine jug is brought down on his face leaving him scarred and missing some teeth (p. 61), and the moral and physical revulsion of the vomiting scene and the subsequent beating (p. 64). In all of these scenes the narrator is careful not to offend the reader with graphic, naturalistic scenes of violence; rather, he takes him further into his confidence by emphasizing the comic, even at the narrator's own expense.

The blind beggar is not, however, the mere personification of cruelty. His humanity is saved by his sense of humor (recall, for instance, the sarcastic and contagious laughter of "¿Qué te parece, Lázaro? Lo que te enfermó te sana y da salud," p. 61), and his ability to impart to Lazarillo frequent valuable lessons in practical living, which evoke the boy's outright admiration ("que después de Dios éste me dio la vida y, siendo ciego, me alumbró y adestró en la carrera de vivir," p. 58). Neither is Lazarillo entirely innocent, as seen in his admission that he returns no small part of his master's cruelty: "holgábame a mí de quebrar un ojo por quebrar dos al que ninguno tenía" (pp. 61–62). The boy's seething hatred[5] and calculated cruelty

3. Undoubtedly, there are readers who do not enjoy the humor of blasphemy, who might be offended by the loose morality of Lazarillo's mother, or who might feel insulted by what they read as an attempt to place in the mouth of a small boy the mature narrator's ex post facto commonplace moralizing. An example of the latter is J. L. Woodward, "Author-Reader Relationship in the *Lazarillo del Tormes*," *Forum for Modern Language Studies*, 1 (1965), 46.

4. See Douglas M. Carey, "Asides and Inferiority in *Lazarillo de Tormes*: A Study in Psychological Realism," *Studies in Philology*, 66 (1969), 124.

5. The feeling, of course, is mutual. Fernando Lázaro Carreter traces the growth of this intense, human, individualized emotion between master and servant: "Construcción y sentido del *Lazarillo de Tormes*," *Abaco*, 1 (1969), 83–87.

are manifest in the potentially mortal vengeance he achieves at the end of the chapter (p. 66).

Though one might expect that the severity of Lazarillo's action would deserve condemnation, it must be remembered that in fiction, even more than in real life, the philosophy of "situational ethics" prevails. That is, the treatment and the context of an act, and *not* the act itself, determine the reader's reaction; the protagonist, especially, must be able to maintain the reader's sympathy "even when he is engaged in morally culpable activities" (Sacks, pp. 72, 182). In this case, I know of no reader of *Lazarillo de Tormes* who definitively condemns Lazarillo for what he does to the blind man.[6] Francisco Ayala, for example, states that he finds having to reproach the boy's conduct at this point somewhat painful.[7] For Márquez Villanueva, Lazarillo seems to act as the instrument of divine wrath and executor of poetic justice (p. 93). Only this sense of the poetic justice of the scene mitigates the reader's potential outrage at the protagonist's morally reprehensible actions.

If the way in which Lazarillo takes leave of his master at the end of the first *tratado* has a somewhat disturbing effect on the reader, the sequence of events that immediately follow wins back the reader's affection for the foundling. In contrast to the wit and wisdom of the blind beggar, the avaricious priest of Maqueda has no redeeming qualities whatsoever. His miserliness and hypocrisy ("Toma, come, triunfa, que para ti es el mundo. Mejor vida tienes que el papa," p. 68; "Cómete esto, que el ratón cosa limpia es," p. 72) cause the boy even greater suffering than before. The "angelic tinker" who provides Lazarillo with the key to the "breadly paradise" (p. 70) does almost seem heaven-sent. During the long battle of wits between master and boy, the reader becomes convinced beyond all doubt that his sympathies are properly placed, savoring with the youth each new crumb of bread and suffering with him the near fatal blow of the snake-hunting priest (p. 76).

In the traditional folktale the number three predominates, and inevitably the first of three characters (here, the blind man) is the most important while the last of the series (the squire) is the most sympathetic.[8] The priest is an important transitional figure, and Lazarillo's sojourn with him has two vital functions in the work. First, it provides the author with the opportunity for some sharp anticlerical satire and perhaps for a symbolic indictment of the role

6. Francisco Rico, however, records an encounter with such a reader. *La novela picaresca y el punto de vista* (Barcelona: Seix Barral, 1970), p. 52, n. 66.
7. *El "Lazarillo": Nuevo examen de algunos aspectos* (Madrid: Taurus, 1971), p. 39.
8. Alan Dundes, *The Study of Folklore* (Englewood Cliffs: Prentice-Hall, 1965), pp. 133–36. See also Lázaro Carreter, pp. 70–72.

of the church in society.[9] Second, and more important in the overall structure of the work, it provides the background against which the reader's sympathy for the protagonist is intensified.

Both the reader and Lazarillo have high hopes after the encounter with the squire at the outset of the third *tratado*. The pair's peregrinations through the streets of Toledo, attendance at mass, and arrival at the house all promise a turn for the better.[1] But as soon as Lazarillo enters the "casa . . . oscura y lóbrega" (p. 79) with its almost complete lack of furnishings, and learns that the squire is not going to feed him, all turns to despair ("Finalmente, allí lloré mi trabajosa vida pasada y mi cercana muerte venidera," p. 80). To go from bad to worse is difficult enough, but to have one's hopes raised before sinking to greater depths is far more disheartening. The squire's inadvertent dashing of Lazarillo's hopes at the beginning of the chapter foreshadows his conscious abandonment of the boy in the final scene.

The tone and structure of this chapter are quite different from those of the preceding two. Time slows to a near standstill as Lazarillo counts the days and hours (see Guillén, "Disposición," p. 275). No longer is boy pitted against master; rather, the two work in concert to survive at the lowest level. Lazarillo feels more pity than scorn for the squire in spite of the latter's hypocrisy, pomposity, and stress on honor ("la negra que llaman honra," p. 83). The reader, too, though not without reservations,[2] looks with kinder eyes on the first master who does not mistreat the boy physically, who is at least capable of thinking and talking of values other than those of the basest materialism, and who is able to talk about himself, to reveal his most intimate thoughts,[3] to expose the essence of his soul as only Lazarillo had done previously. The most intense and moving pages of the work are those in which the squire and the street urchin feign ignorance of each other's reality and strain to communicate obliquely.

In this chapter Lazarillo lives, almost literally, in the presence of physical death—underscored by the traditional folkloric set piece of "the house without food or drink."[4] Yet, in spite of his near starvation, this is the boy's finest hour. Witness his sentiments:

9. See Anson C. Piper, "The Breadly Paradise of *Lazarillo de Tormes*," *Hispania*, 44 (1961), 269–71.
1. This point is made by Lázaro Carreter: "el lector acompaña a Lázaro desde la confianza a las sospechas y a la evidencia de su pobreza, con pasos muy bien graduados" (p. 103). See also Rico, *Punto de vista*, p. 41.
2. See Lázaro Carreter, p. 73.
3. The squire is hardly a lovable figure—though he is an intensely human one—in his lengthy confession-within-a-confession characterized by a "bitter and querulous tone, . . . burning resentment and perversity" (Joseph H. Silverman, rev. of *La Vie de Lazarillo de Tormès*, ed. Bataillon, *Romance Philology*, 15, 1961, 93, n. 16).
4. For a discussion of how the death imagery of the first 3 chapters increases steadily until it reaches its zenith in Lazarillo's sojourn in the squire's house-tomb, see Gilman, pp. 161–66, For observations on the folk origins of the episode of the dead man, see Lázaro Carreter, pp. 101–02.

Contemplaba yo muchas veces mi desastre, que escapando de los amos ruines que había tenido y buscando mejoría, viniese a topar con quien no sólo no me mantuviese, mas a quien yo había de mantener. Con todo, le quería bien con ver que no tenía ni podía más, y antes le había lástima que enemistad. Y muchas veces, por llevar a la posada con que él lo pasase, yo lo pasaba mal. (p. 87)

What higher moral sentiment is there, especially within the framework of Christianity, than to love ("querer bien") and to make sacrifices for ("pasarlo mal") one's fellowman? Lazarillo has become, in the words of F. Courtney Tarr, "humanized and ennobled by his pity, his loyalty, and his sacrifice."[5] When the squire abandons him, both the boy and the reader feel betrayed. Lazarillo's bitter "acabé de conocer mi ruin dicha" (p. 95) is the note on which the chapter ends.

Abuse and deception are difficult to accept under any circumstances; betrayal by a friend can be "shattering."[6] Though the squire is Lazarillo's most sympathetic master, he is also the cruelest, for he allows Lazarillo to glimpse things the boy has never before even imagined (sensitivity, intimacy, respect), only to turn out to be little different from the others with whom Lazarillo has had contact.

At this point, the anonymous author of *Lazarillo de Tormes* has reached a "critical point" in the work's structure:[7] he can no longer continue his story in the same vein. The protagonist has experienced a series of masters who have been increasingly unwilling or unable to sustain him, and he has suffered in increasing proportion from hunger until eating any less would mean starvation. Meanwhile, Lazarillo has grown in moral stature to as high a point as is humanly possible; to continue this trajectory would be to approach martyrdom and sainthood. In effect, a story has been told and a moral implied. But in order to underscore the point with devastating effectiveness, the framework of the story is expanded; in a few more pages (less than a fifth of the book) the remainder of the protagonist's life is outlined.

Tratado Four surprises the reader with its brevity (it is less than 100 words long) and tantalizing ambiguity (what might be implied by the "por otras cosillas que no digo," p. 96). The entertaining and satiric adventure with the indulgence seller that comprises *Tratado* Five apparently reassures the reader that there has been a return to normalcy. In fact, however, Lazarillo is reduced to the status of a mere observer (an extension of the role he played as he listened

5. "Literary and Artistic Unity in the *Lazarillo de Tormes*," *PMLA*, 42 (1927), 410.
6. See A. D. Deyermond, "Lazarus and Lazarillo," *Studies in Short Fiction*, 2 (1965), 353.
7. See Raymond S. Willis, "Lazarillo and the Pardoner: The Artistic Necessity of the Fifth *Tractado*," *Hispanic Review*, 27 (1959), 271.

to the squire's story shortly before), hardly different from the townspeople who are duped by a master confidence man or from the reader who is also ignorant of the outcome. The result of this episode is one final, and important, lesson in the arts of deception.[8] The sixth *tratado* repeats the formal brevity of the fourth, but it contains some clues that anticipate the outcome of the work. Lazarillo observes that his four-year job as a water seller was his first step upward ("el primer escalón que yo subí para venir a alcanzar buena vida," p. 103), clearly indicating that his life is now fundamentally different from what it had been. He manages to save enough money to dress "honradamente" in old clothes and buy a venerable old sword—in short, to become an "hombre de bien" (p. 103)—ominous evocations of the life-style of the squire from the third *tratado*.[9]

The brevity of *Tratados* Four through Six shocks and puzzles the reader, as do the acceleration in the pace of events and the fact that access is no longer permitted to the protagonist's innermost feelings and thoughts.[1] What happens is that the author uses this interlude to prepare the reader for the final, adult status of the protagonist. Whereas Lazarillo has up until this time occupied stage center, he now steps behind a curtain, hiding himself from the reader while maintaining an illusion of passing time and continuing action, only to emerge in the final chapter as a radically different man.[2] The result of these three brief chapters is to disengage Lazarillo both from his previous existence and from the reader's sympathy (see Willis, p. 275), as well as to foreshadow carefully the protagonist's status at the end of the book.

In no way whatsoever does this section of the book represent an artistic shortcoming; indeed, it is almost as difficult to imagine *Lazarillo de Tormes* being as effective without this link between the first three *tratados* and the last as it would be to conceive of the work's ending with the disappearance of the squire.[3]

8. Lazarillo learns "la [lección] del callar y quedarse al margen cuando conviene, la del silencio en provecho propio," thus preparing him for his role in *Tratado* Seven. Rico, "Introducción," *La novela picaresca española*, I (Barcelona: Planeta, 1967), xlviii. See also p. lxxvi; and, again, *Punto de vista*, pp. 34–35.

9. See C. B. Morris, "Lázaro and the Squire: 'Hombres de bien,'" *Bulletin of Hispanic Studies*, 41 (1964), 238–41.

1. See, respectively, Andrée Collard, "The Unity of *Lazarillo de Tormes*," *Modern Language Notes*, 83 (1968), 263; Guillén, "Disposición," p. 275; and Carey (pp. 120–21), who observes that Lazarillo's asides to the reader, frequent in the first 3 *tratados*, virtually cease in this part of the book.

2. As Willis states, "Almost without our perceiving it, Lázaro has grown under our eyes near the start of Chapter VII from the barely adult to the fully mature man whom we can unreservedly accept as the actual narrator" (p. 277).

3. Tarr, p. 404, and Willis, p. 268, n. 3, offer summaries of the traditional view that these 3 chapters are faulty. It is perhaps surprising to find in some recent studies by perceptive critics, for instance Lázaro Carreter, pp. 56–57, 108–09, and Ayala, pp. 66–68, 72–74, the clichés that the author committed an esthetic blunder, ran out of inspiration, or was unable to complete more than a mere outline of what he had intended to write.

The final chapter begins innocently enough with a passing reference to the protagonist's service with a constable, and is genuinely optimistic concerning his employment as an advertiser or *pregonero* of wines ("quiso Dios alumbrarme y ponerme en camino y manera provechosa," p. 104).[4] But then comes the surprising revelation of the "caso" alluded to in the Prologue: Lázaro (the mature man who has written the book, in contrast to Lazarillo, the boy of the early chapters)[5] is now the town crier of Toledo and lives in the comfort of a petit bourgeois. His wife doubles as the mistress of the Archpriest of San Salvador, Lázaro's business patron, whose favor he curries and rationalizes by feigning not to see how his conjugal honor and his morality are compromised. Taking a cue from the squire's cynical description of how to please a prestigious master (pp. 92–93), Lázaro does more than avert his eyes from his wife's infidelity. By profiting from it and, at least inferentially, encouraging it, he becomes much more than a mere consenting cuckold. To exploit another person sexually for the sake of material affluence is the definition of a pimp. This, rather than a potentially comic deceived husband, is what Lázaro has become.

Claudio Guillén first called attention to "el caso" ("Disposición," p. 269). Its unifying thematic importance in the Prologue and last chapter has been stressed repeatedly and effectively by Francisco Rico, who refers to "el caso" as both the pretext and heart of the novel,[6] and by Fernando Lázaro Carreter, who considers the *ménage à trois* at the end as the single focus which illuminates and, simultaneously, subordinates all other aspects of the book (p. 60). The "caso" then is the "moral earthquake," referred to earlier, needed to shock the reader into a rejection of the character. One simply cannot suffer complacent cuckoldry in a prosperous adult as one can lying, cheating, and vengeance in a starving waif. Although literature frequently offers adulterous heroes and heroines in the most sympathetic of lights, the presentation of Lázaro's moral rise and fall is designed to evoke a negative reaction. The archpriest is offensive in his blatant hypocrisy ("Ella entra muy a tu honra y suya, y esto te lo prometo. Por tanto, no mires a lo que pueden decir, sino a lo que te toca, digo a tu provecho," p. 105). Lázaro is made equally odious by his own cynical sarcasm: "yo determiné de arrimarme a los buenos" (an ironic recollection of his mother: "Mi viuda madre . . . determinó arrimarse a los buenos por ser uno de ellos," p. 55); "es tan buena mujer como vive dentro de las puertas de Toledo"; "en

---

4. This is the first time in the book real optimism is expressed. See Lázaro Carreter, p. 116.
5. With his usual perceptiveness and concision, Guillén says that "Lázaro, más que Lazarillo, es el centra de gravidad de la obra" ("Disposición," p. 271). See also Didier T. Jaén, "La ambigüedad moral del *Lazarillo de Tormes*," *PMLA*, 83 (1968), 130, n. 3.
6. "Problemas del *Lazarillo*," *Boletín de la Real Academia Española*, 46 (1966), 287. See also "Introducción," pp. xlii–liv, and *Punto de vista*, pp. 21–25.

este tiempo estaba en mi prosperidad, y en la cumbre de toda buena fortuna" (pp. 105–06).

With lightninglike suddenness the reader's response to the character has been inverted; admiration for Lazarillo has been replaced by revulsion toward Lázaro. As Lazarillo was betrayed by the squire's desertion in *Tratado* Three, so the reader is defrauded by the emergence of Lázaro in *Tratado* Seven. Anticipating Cervantes, the artist has asserted his independence and his superiority over the mere reader.

Raymond S. Willis has demonstrated that the "inversion" of values "is of the very essence of the book" (p. 273). He has also suggested the contours for a graph of the protagonist's life, tracing his material circumstances and his "picaresque 'enlightenment.'" I would prefer to draw essentially the same graph, but in terms of the alternately ascending and descending physical and spiritual trajectories of the life of Lázaro de Tormes.

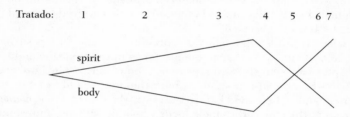

As Lazarillo slowly descends toward starvation he simultaneously ascends in the eyes and heart of the reader to the point where he deserves unreserved admiration. Having reached the limits to which these trajectories can be taken, in the third chapter, the process is swiftly and brutally reversed, so that at the end of the book Lázaro enjoys security and material comfort but is morally bankrupt.

A key to this interpretation is a crucial observation contained in a short moral digression by the protagonist-author early in his career: "Huelgo de contar a vuestra merced estas niñerías, para mostrar cuánta virtud sea saber los hombres subir siendo bajos, *y dejarse bajar siendo altos, cuánto vicio*" (p. 58; italics mine). This statement is traditionally interpreted as an affirmation of the character's worldly success; the italicized clause is either ignored entirely or presumed by inference to apply to the wellborn who suffer hardships.[7] In this sense the statement does little more than repeat the final

---

7. To cite but one example, see Norma Louise Hutman, who states that since "it is the adult Lázaro relating his life, we can take as a declaration of theme his own statement: 'saber los hombres subir siendo bajos.' The entire action thereafter . . . is a logical working out of this sentence." "Universality and Unity in the *Lazarillo de Tormes*," *PMLA*, 76 (1961), 472.

lines of the Prologue: "porque consideren los que heredaron nobles estados cuán poco se les debe, pues fortuna fue con ellos parcial, y cuánto más hicieron los que, siéndoles contraria, con fuerza y maña remando salieron a buen puerto" (p. 54). It seems to me, however, that the *subir-bajar* dichotomy (whether or not consciously intended as such by the author) provides a succinct and complete framework within which Lázaro's entire life unfolds: his material rise—in itself not a negative value—is devalued and overshadowed by the decline of his morality. It is easier for a camel to pass through the eye of a needle than for a rich man to gain entrance to heaven; wealth—even comparative—is obtained only at the expense of the soul.

Lázaro proclaims in his Prologue that he is not "más santo que mis vecinos" (p. 54), which amounts, as R. O. Jones observes, to "another way of saying 'You are no better than I.'"[8] Márquez Villanueva calls this the most important confidential statement made to the reader, and rhetorically asks whether Lázaro is not like all men (p. 92). This, together with the sympathy and identification the reader establishes with Lazarillo, suggests that there is a universal and perhaps symbolic value to the character, that, in the final analysis, the story of Lázaro de Tormes is a parable of us all.

By extension, then, this is the moral lesson demonstrated by the life of Lázaro de Tormes: that man, although possessing the capacity for the noblest of deeds and sentiments, must choose to come to terms with the society in which he lives. The values Lázaro comes to accept are presented as the societal norm, not just for Lázaro in the sixteenth century, but for modern man.[9] Márquez Villanueva observes that Lázaro's acceptance of evil is an outrageous act of free will, which comes about when he does not even have the excuse of hunger, that it is not a matter of a weakness, but of a serious moral sin (p. 95). The book is one of the bitterest and most profoundly pessimistic statements ever made on man's inevitable compromise.

That there is a moral lesson in the book and that it is not necessarily obvious is also suggested in the Prologue. In the second sentence Lázaro states that "podría ser que alguno que las [the "cosas" of his life] lea, halle algo que le agrade, y a los que no ahondaren tanto, los deleite" (p. 53), a statement that has evoked considerable comment. For Stephen Gilman, the replacement of the traditional *aprovechar* with *agradar* "dumps all readers into a single basket. Those who penetrate the surface and those who merely skim will find a synonymous reward" (p. 149). But the author also states that he hopes the reader might "sacar della algún fruto" (p. 53), so that

8. Introd. to *La vida de Lazarillo de Tormes* (Manchester: Manchester Univ. Press, 1963), p. xxix.
9. See Jean Paul Borel, "La literatura y nosotros. Otra manera de leer el *Lazarillo de Tormes*" *Revista de Occidente*, 46 (1967), 94–95.

Rico makes, I believe, a clearer distinction when he interprets "algo que le agrade" as something in the work that the reader perceives as consistent with his own literary or doctrinal ideas; hence the careful reader is promised something of value, some 'fruit' which he must seek out. This fruit, Rico suggests, is most probably some moral or social truth. The reader who is incapable of such penetration remains content with the skin of the fruit, the jokes and tricks ("Introducción," p. lxiv).[1]

This, then, suggests why *Lazarillo de Tormes* is so frequently misread. It is too easy to remain at the surface and not *ahondar*. Many readers stop (or wish they had stopped, or pretend they had stopped) reading after the third *tratado*. *Lazarillo de Tormes* is a wolf in sheep's clothing. Many readers are so beguiled by the charming, witty, ironic little boy—Lazarillo—whose story they have just read that they fail to see, or prefer to divert their eyes from, the base and repulsive creature—Lázaro (in whose image they may see something of their own reflection)—he has become.

"¡Madre, coco!" is the reader's reaction to Lázaro. To which Lázaro cynically responds, "¡Cuántos debe de haber en el mundo que huyen de otros, porque no se veen a sí mismos!"

EDWARD H. FRIEDMAN

From the Inside Out: The Poetics of *Lazarillo de Tormes*†

The most celebrated of poetics, that of Aristotle, established a protocol for tragic drama based in great part on Sophocles's *Oedipus Rex*, a source of inspiration and exemplarity. For one in search of a model for the novel—a form that has lent itself to a multitude of theoretical commentaries yet remains, understandably, rather resistant to a definition that would satisfy all critics—it would seem reasonable to start, if not at the (always problematic) beginning, early on. Here, I would like to look at *Lazarillo de Tormes* (1554) as a narrative vehicle and, more specifically, as a paradigm of the novel. My approach is predicated on the assumption that the anonymous author, who most recently has been identified by Mercedes Agulló Cobo as Diego Hurtado de Mendoza,[1] had a marvelous sense

---

1. See also Silverman, who cites the passage and says, "It seems to me that the author is saying: 'For the superficial, for those who do not scrutinize my work, there is entertainment, but for those who read it attentively the rewards are much greater'" (pp. 92–93)

† From *Philological Quarterly* 89.1 (Winter 2010): 13–30. Reprinted with permission of the publisher.

1. Mercedes Agulló y Cobo, *A vueltas con el autor del Lazarillo* (Madrid: Calambur, 2010). There remains, of course, considerable debate on the authorship of *Lazarillo de Tormes*.

of narrative, substantial artistic sensibility, and a degree of sophistication that many scholars have chosen to underestimate, because of the early publication date and the relative brevity of the document. I would like to analyze the text from the inside out, by describing how Lázaro's narrative initiates and displays its conventions, and how the author anticipates the future course of the novel. *Lazarillo de Tormes* opens with a prologue that is essential to its structural design and to its particular rhetoric, and the story proper consists of seven chapters, or *tractados* (*tratados*), which begin with allusions to the protagonist's birth and lineage and end with references to his marriage and his mature years. This early modern Spanish narrative has been associated with a break from literary idealism and with a movement toward realism, as well as with the origins of the picaresque tradition. It is, at once, a work that continually indicates its precedents and deviates from them. To the extent possible, in determining a poetics of *Lazarillo de Tormes*, I would like to proceed from the descriptive to the prescriptive.

As a work of art, *La vida de Lazarillo de Tormes y de sus fortunas y adversidades* [The life of Lazarillo de Tormes, and his fortunes and misfortunes] links "life" and creativity (and good fortune and adversity) in a brief but brilliant prologue, which serves as a type of theory in practice, and which sets the frame, the tone, and the parameters of the text that follows.[2] Lázaro de Tormes introduces a motif of doubling that marks the entire manuscript and its conceptual base. The author—or the figure of the author—has in his hands what will become a published book. He addresses the product and the potential audience of readers with a combined sense of pride and humility. This is a modest offering, but, as Pliny the Younger points out, there is no book so bad as to offer nothing of value to the reader. The allusion to modesty is ironic, given that the conventional recourse to "false modesty" implies that the author is feigning humility, whereas Lázaro has every reason to act humbly and to perceive himself in humble terms. He "confesses" to being no more holy than his neighbors. In the first half of the prologue, Lázaro presents himself and his book to readers, and, citing Cicero, he notes that honor sustains the arts. The quotation amplifies the elevation-by-association theme and anticipates the crucial role that honor will play in the development of the narrative. Everyone goes in search of praise, and most people are willing to take risks, Lázaro asserts, with specific examples, and he asks to be heard, to be read. We all want to be praised, whether we deserve the endorsement or not, he maintains. If one has gone to the trouble to write a book, that book merits attention, unless it is totally offensive. Lázaro obviously is

2. I refer to the edition of *Lazarillo de Tormes* by Francisco Rico (Madrid: Cátedra, 1987), 3–11. Citations appear parenthetically and all translations are my own.

conscious of the readership and of the need to cater to the public.
At the same time, the "authorial" contact with the reader by the nar-
rator/protagonist blurs the distinction between the historical author
and his alter ego, and thus between the real text and its fictional
pretext. Correspondingly, Lázaro directs his words to two groups of
readers, one external and the other internal, but the prologue,
through its narrative persona, does not differentiate between them.
With no change in voice and no acknowledged transition, the pro-
spective author speaks of a book; the narrator, of the explanation
of a case. By placing the two planes under the rubric of the prologue, the author/"author" highlights the convergence of art and
life and the indispensable element of self-fashioning, in its multiple
applications.

In the second part of the prologue, Lázaro uses the humility topos
to gain sympathy. His unprepossessing origins have had an impact
on all areas of his life, and success, for him, has to be seen in a comparative light. Fate has condemned him to start at the bottom, and
his rise must be qualified and assessed comparatively. He engages
the reader—within the fiction, his narratee, the enigmatic figure of
"Vuestra Merced" [Your Grace]—to judge him, but with low expectations. The rhetorical presuppositions depend precisely on the
interrelated features of lowliness and humiliation. The reader can
appreciate Lázaro's moderate ascent in the social order and can
enjoy, with a sense of distance and of difference, the account of the
trials and tribulations of the protagonist. The fact that fortune has
not smiled on Lázaro forms the core of his argument and a justifi-
cation for his appeal to the literary reader. What remains in the prologue moves from the reader of a book to Vuestra Merced, who
apparently has requested an explanation, in some detail, of "the
case" (*el caso*), to which Lázaro will respond by starting at the beginning (10). This suggests a category of writing unlike the *in medias
res* opening (and the high art) of epic poetry. In reiterative style, the
writer beseeches Vuestra Merced, as he has entreated the reader at
large, to bear in mind the special achievement of those who have
countered the odds and attained success through determination,
extra effort, and skill (*fuerza y maña*) (11). The word *maña*, most
effectively, connotes both competence and cunning. The prologue
ends with a maritime allusion to those who, unfavored by fortune,
have weathered tempestuous seas to arrive at a safe harbor.

The brevity of the prologue to *Lazarillo de Tormes* should not con-
ceal its significance, not only as a key to analyzing the narrative but
as an artistically garbed, as it were, theoretical statement. The author
joins presence with absence, and the book as a consumer object
merges with the explanation as pretext. The obvious mediation
underscores the illusion of unmediated discourse. The middle

ground in this instance is Lázaro's commentary on the composition of his narrative. At the extremes are the author's intervention at the beginning of the prologue and the narrator's remarks that follow. There emerges a paradigm that, intriguingly, resembles the tripartite model of poststructuralism, which places emphasis on the mediating space between the signifier and the signified.[3] *Lazarillo de Tormes* becomes a masterpiece in the creation of mediating spaces. The implied author stands between the historical author and the narrator, exemplified in the confluence of voices and positions in the prologue, and producing an implied reader and a narratee, who operate along with a "real" external reader. The narrator/protagonist moves—sometimes clearly, at other times confusingly—between the child, the young man, and the adult Lázaro. Between truth and fiction lie rhetoric and rhetorical strategies, a current version of which is "spin," the locus wherein transformations of content and of perspective take place. The genre of autobiography necessarily puts a spin on history (and is one of many sources of the demystification of historical objectivity), and the picaresque, as fictional autobiography or pseudo-autobiography, further removes the story from the elusive realm of absolute truth. Somewhat paradoxically, the reader is called upon to mediate both history (*la verdadera historia*, in the words of one of the narrators of *Don Quixote*), and fiction (or fiction-making) in *Lazarillo de Tormes*. The mysterious identity of the author, the summoning of a double audience, the play of book and "explanation," the ambiguities of time and perspective, and the references to the act of composition simultaneously, and cleverly, appreciate, interrogate, and ultimately displace—decenter—history. What lies in the wake perhaps can best be designated as perspectivism.

The prologue to *Lazarillo de Tormes* encompasses numerous aspects of the processes of writing and reading, representation and interpretation. Notably, the author recognizes, before Miguel de Cervantes, the inseparability of life and art. Fiction can strive for, and certainly achieve, a high level of realism, of verisimilitude, and it can camouflage, but not obscure, the conventions that mark differences. A book can hold a mirror to life, and it can become part of one's reality, but it cannot *be* what it represents. The depiction of Lázaro and of Spanish society in *Lazarillo de Tormes* is realistic, but each is a graft—a supplement—and a metonym of something else. On one hand, realism prevails. On the other, the strings that control the figurative puppets show through. That is why, in my opinion, the novel, from its conception, has offered variations on

---

3. For a presentation of the general principles of poststructuralism, see, e.g., Jonathan Culler, *On Deconstruction: Theory and Criticism after Structuralism* (Cornell U. Press, 1982).

the theme of the interconnection of realism and metafiction.[4] The story and the storytelling, like the dancer and the dance, are never mutually exclusive, yet they are discrete entities, with functions of their own. The narrator is a fundamental part of the story, and the story is always in need of a structure and a structuring agent, and, of course, a receiver of messages. The dialectics of story and discourse is validated by the collaboration of the reader. The more self-conscious the act of narration, the more cognizant the reader of the inscription of the writing process, but that inscription can never be elided or excluded from consideration. Novels such as *Don Quixote* and *Tristram Shandy* flaunt their artistic recourses, their "literariness," in the lexicon of Russian Formalism,[5] but novels in the mainstream of realism and naturalism perforce give evidence of their formal attributes, their constructedness. The distinction lies in the proportion to which realism and metafiction coexist. *Lazarillo de Tormes*, as, arguably, the first novel, lies comfortably within the two extremes, highlighting narrative realism as an alternative to idealism while foregrounding the narrative persona, present through his invention of the story and of himself as the protagonist of that story. With perspectivism comes a dual irony: of proximity and of distance.

Tragic drama, epic poetry, and idealistic narrative (such as sentimental, pastoral, and chivalric romance in Spain) tend to accentuate nobility, grandeur, and what might be called a loftiness of spirit. In certain ways, realism conspicuously removes loftiness from the scheme, and the author of *Lazarillo de Tormes* resorts to the extreme position by placing his protagonist in the lower depths of poverty and lineage. The grander precedents seem to favor universal values, although they are hardly bereft of national themes and standards. In contrast, *Lazarillo de Tormes* is a veritable social document of the Zeitgeist of mid-sixteenth-century Spain: its obsessions with genealogy, blood purity, and prohibitions and hierarchies of all stripes. In crafting his narrative, the author shows his debt to the literary and cultural past as he flouts convention. What is new, or novel, about *Lazarillo de Tormes* is its lowering of ideals, its deconstruction of previous centers, its shifting of perspective, and its critique of broad segments of society. The course of the narrative— and, one reasonably might suppose, the course of the composition— will consist of a confrontation with previous forms of fiction, visions of representation, and conceptions of didacticism and audience

---

4. The joint presence of realism and metafiction in the novel is a central argument of my study *Cervantes in the Middle: Realism and Reality in the Spanish Novel from "Lazarillo de Tormes" to "Niebla"* (Newark, DE: Juan de la Cuesta, 2006).
5. See, e.g., Victor Shklovsky, "Art as Technique," *Russian Formalist Criticism: Four Essays*, ed. Lee Lemon and Marion J. Rice (Lincoln: U. of Nebraska Press, 1965), 3–24.

response. The comprehensive enterprise grows from a sought-after tension between the literary legacy and the desire for innovation, and the result is an awe-inspiring brand of performance art. That idea applies perfectly to *Don Quixote*, published some fifty years later, but the author of *Lazarillo de Tormes* beats Cervantes to the punch, so to speak, by self-consciously positing the state of affairs of the narrator as well as of the lead character, by creating a system of gaps and ambiguities that will bring the reader into the frame, and by "ingeniously" mixing realism with metafiction (or the reverse). The author and the reader stand above the narrator/protagonist, but not necessarily above the social propositions and insights into human nature implicit in the text.

The double-pronged prologue to *Lazarillo de Tormes* sets a process in motion and supplies a meta-commentary on that process: on books and their readers, on advancing in a resistant society, on social obligations and restraints, and on events in the life of an individual who is unique and symbolic, manipulative and manipulated. The topic of judgment and defense pervades the distinct planes of the succinct yet richly enigmatic prologue. The narratee Vuestra Merced is one of the judges. The collectivity of readers is another, but so—astutely on the part of the author—is Lázaro himself, an able rhetorician who knows, as does his inventor, how to maneuver language, data, and point of view. The interplay of subject and object, as delineated in the prologue, is among the most striking facets of the narrative. Satire and irony work in tandem, aided by constantly modified vantage points and negotiating spaces. The parallel universes of the prologue—the author and the book, the character and the case, the reader and the narratee, the errant soul and society jointly under scrutiny, and verisimilitude and signs of literariness, of multileveled authorial intrusion—are maintained throughout the narrative. Crucial to the content and to the analysis of *Lazarillo de Tormes* are an identification and analysis of the duplicity of the text, from its openness, its changing associative fields, its rhetorical strategies, and its ironies. Buoyed by citations from authors of classical antiquity, the prologue starts with a reference to the writing and reception of the book and to the honor that can be gained from a literary triumph. The convention of modesty permits the author to apologize for the defects of the book and to insert himself into the equation. As he left-handedly, and thus incisively, sings the praises of his product, he brings up the issue of social determinism in connection with the evaluation of success. The defense of the book segues into what will become a self-defense, a rationale for the choices that Lázaro has made and those that he will contend have been made for him by fortune and circumstance. Lázaro gives the narrative a *pretext* and a narratee, and he leaves the reader in suspense. He promises to start at the beginning, and that is exactly what he does.

The first of seven chapters (*tratados*) deals with Lázaro's birth and early childhood. Here, he is tagged by the diminutive *Lazarillo*, through which he is differentiated from the mature Lázaro who narrates the explanation of the case. In having Lázaro discuss his heritage, the author demonstrates that he grasps, intuitively, the importance of heredity and environment on character formation. Lazarillo is born in a no-man's-land on the river Tormes, to less than illustrious parents. The second he exits his mother's womb, he is consigned to inferior status. His father is a miller who becomes a criminal. Although he dies serving his king and country as a soldier, the progenitor is anything but a hero, despite the narrator's attempt to memorialize him in a positive manner. Through Lázaro's treatment of his background, there emerges a dominant pattern: a use of euphemism that is, or becomes, transparent. Lazarillo's father has been imprisoned for a serious offense; he can fight bravely in combat, but he cannot erase the crimes for which he suffered punishment. Lázaro convincingly could have glorified his father by omitting the details that led to the military service, but he elects—and the author elects—to tell the full story. As Lázaro's account will turn out to be, this is a tale of success, if at all, only in qualified terms. Lazarillo's widowed mother, with little to safeguard her and her son, moves to Salamanca, where she hopes to earn a living, and to associate with good people and thereby live a respectable life, following the dictum "Arrímate a los buenos, y serás uno de ellos" [join with the good people and you will become one of them] (15). When Lázaro the narrator quotes the proverb, he knows that this did not happen. His mother works as a servant at an inn, aligns herself with a black man named Zaide, and gives birth to another son. Zaide is a thief who is apprehended for his crimes, thanks in part to Lazarillo's comments when he is grilled by officers of justice. A major source of irony in the narrative is the failure of Lázaro and of Lazarillo to remain silent when their words incriminate them and others. The abstract construct first denominated "the implied author" by Wayne Booth may have its origins in *Lazarillo de Tormes*; if not, this narrative phenomenon most assuredly has a glorious moment in mid-sixteenth-century Spain.

When Lázaro as narrator enters the territory of euphemism and when his words are rendered ironic, there seems to be a ventriloquism-effect taking place. Lázaro adopts a defensive posture, but he is not completely skillful at defending himself. He finds himself trapped in a paradox of writing (and speaking). When he commits himself to responding to Vuestra Merced's request, he must articulate events that might be better left unrevealed. Looking exclusively at the internal components of the narrative—its direct discourse—one might observe Lázaro (and Lazarillo) as unaware of the ironies of his life and of his storytelling. He seems to forget that his mother's aim of collaborating with upright citizens and of transforming her fate fails miserably, and he even repeats the phrase in the seventh *tratado* when he speaks of his own experiences in Toledo. In Salamanca, the prominent new figures are Zaide and Lazarillo's half-brother, both of whom represent alterity, the polar opposite of the desirable Old Christian standard. When the *hermanico* [little brother] sees his black father, he cries out, "¡Madre, coco!" [Mommy, the boogeyman!] (17). Lázaro comments that even though he himself was only a child, he noticed how common it is for people to flee from others because they do not see themselves. He is setting himself up—or the author is setting him up—for an ironic reversal: his own figurative blindness and his own positioning as the symbolic Other. Lazarillo's first action in the text, his "confession" of Zaide's crimes to the officers of the law, forms part of the cycle of irony that culminates in the final chapter. The motif of breaking silence is one of a number of examples of the ironic base of the text. Lázaro appears to be endeavoring to narrate his story from the most favorable angle, but he comes far from realizing this goal. The author, on the contrary, and through an almost palpable implied author, is quite powerful in having his narrator/protagonist convey the irony of story and discourse. Just as there are two objects at the foundation of the prologue—the book and the response—there are two narrative subjects, each divisible into additional "selves."

As narrative realism will continue to do, *Lazarillo de Tormes* situates its story in a defined time and place. The events and their consequences depend on when and where the characters live and interact. Lázaro is ensconced in what the structuralists were to call the *system* of early modern Spain, which supplies the historical, sociocultural, and ideological contexts for the narrative.[6] Lázaro's birth has geographical, social, and literary weight; he is an outcast without a permanent home and destined to remain in the margins of society. Adding insult to injury, his father and stepfather are criminals, and Zaide occupies a rung on the social ladder even lower than that of Lazarillo's family. Lázaro's mother hopes to expand her horizons in Salamanca, but she goes from bad to worse. The campaign for upward mobility lies at the heart of the narrative, but the theme of descent rather than ascent marks at least the first four chapters, and the change in status in the final chapters is so punctuated with irony that the reader may struggle to measure Lázaro's advancement. This is a sixteenth-century Spanish story, replete with

---

6. Jonathan Culler provides a handbook for structuralism in *Structuralist Poetics: Structuralism, Linguistics and the Study of Literature* (Cornell U. Press, 1975).

members of the clergy and an obsession with honor. It is a story with an intricate narrative plan, and, like *Don Quixote*, a story about the exploits of the title character and about the discourse itself. The author of *Lazarillo de Tormes* brings together linearity, circularity, repetition of images, "the force of blood," growth and psychological development, the interdependence of episodes, and cause-and-effect relationships, framed by fate, social determinism, satire, humor, and irony. In some five pages of text—the prologue and the first pages of the opening chapter—the structural design, the various (and sometimes competing) trajectories, and the essence of *Lazarillo de Tormes* have been laid out.

As Lázaro narrates his story, the implied author recasts his words. As Lázaro submits his evidence, the implied author frequently amends self-defense into self-incrimination. As the text upholds social protocol, the object of satire moves beyond Lázaro to other characters and to society in general. Using a model proposed by Jacques Derrida, James Parr notes in *Don Quixote* a game of inventing and breaking frames, each doomed to be replaced ad infinitum, and the same can be seen in *Lazarillo de Tormes*.[7] The autobiographical model and the first-person narration would seem to grant special control to the narrator, but the mechanisms of fictional (or pseudo-) autobiography and the voice-over of the implied author disrupt the illusion of control. The subject becomes object. Nonetheless, the very centrality of the narrative position, through a double-edged irony, transfers Lázaro from subject-turned-object to a different kind of subject, caught in a fascinating dialectic that will remain a factor in the history of the novel. The conventions of narrative are on display, whether subtly or ostentatiously. Every story is also a meta-commentary on the process of writing and, by extension, on the separation between reality and representation, that is, between what is represented and how it is represented. The *how* includes a requisite discourse analysis, in one form or another. From the first sentence of the prologue, the author of *Lazarillo de Tormes* concedes a space in the text to the reader, who is united immediately with the narratee and with the act of deciphering messages, of arbitrating verbal signs. The movement within the narrative seems geared to rejecting idealism for realism, yet this is realism in the domain of fiction. The realist novel is, then, a bit of an oxymoron, given that it alternately invites the reader to suspend disbelief and to discern the tricks of the trade. Complementing the dichotomy reader/narratee are the dichotomies author/narrator and text/metatext, among others. The prologue and the text proper incor-

---

7. James A. Parr, "Plato, Cervantes, Derrida: Framing Speaking and Writing in *Don Quixote*," *On Cervantes: Essays for L. A. Murillo*, ed. James A. Parr (Newark, DE: Juan de la Cuesta, 1991), 163–87.

porate and integrate the critical, but healthy, opposition of tradition and innovation.

Intertextuality in *Lazarillo de Tormes* links literature with social
codes and norms, through a technique that anticipates Cervantes.
In the prologue, Lázaro embraces classical antiquity through the
quotations from Cicero and Pliny, and quickly announces that he will
start at the beginning rather than *in medias res*. He revises the modesty topos into an ironic paean to the crudeness of his book and to
his humble beginnings. He wants to lower the criteria for judgment
of his document and of his case. The first judgment refers to art,
the second to life, and, collectively, they correspond to the breadth
of referents of the narrative. *Lazarillo de Tormes* is not so much
about parallel lives as about parallel modes of discourse. At every
stage, one can discover intersections with prior texts and institutions. Idealism is deflated and deconstructed. The author takes the
exaggerated pride in bloodlines of chivalric romance to ground zero
(the river Tormes). The spiritual evolution of St. Augustine's *Confessions* and of similar exemplary works moves in reverse order. The
confessions of Lázaro and Lazarillo are secular, even when the language has biblical overtones. This early modern Lazarus may not
rise from the dead, but he reimagines and, on occasion, reinvents
himself. As Lázaro narrates, the past and the present—and the child
and the adult—come together in shared, but, for the most part, dis-
tinguishable, points of view. The author seems to want to complicate the very act of narration and to convert it into an art. The
mature narrator frames the story, as storyteller and, at the conclusion, as the grown-up Lazarillo. Needless to say, he knows all along
in what direction life has led him, but he gives the reader the opportunity to experience the events that he recounts, more often than
not, from his perspective at the moment, with appended observations. This is a far more complex discursive structure than it may
seem on the surface. Lázaro is not narrating randomly. He is trying
to make an argument that will reveal the "adversities" with which
he has had to deal and how he has been able to overcome them. Life
has treated him badly, but he has overcome many obstacles. In order
to win the approval of Vuestra Merced, he chooses details that will
elicit sympathy and perhaps respect. Within the remembrances of
things past, he puts the reader in his place, in a radically new juxta-
position of temporal axes. The discursive schemes of reliving the past
and explaining the present function smoothly; one does not inter-
fere with the other, and both are vital to the full force of the narrative. The narrative persona proceeds in a linear direction, but he
inflects the discourse with a knowledge of the future and with his
peculiar rhetoric. The structure—or, more fittingly, the volume—is
amplified many times over by the interference of the implied author.

Selection and irony have an impact on the forward movement of the narrative.

The protagonist's service to a series of masters comprises the primary portion of the narrative. The length of the description of each contact varies significantly, and this has to do with the role of selection. Lázaro starts with his birth and childhood as he builds up to the "case." He shares useful information, information that he believes will be useful to his defense. The reader can decode the data by focusing on arguments of the self-defense and by focusing on the ironic counterargument proposed (*implicitly*) by the author. Lázaro himself divulges his plan in the prologue: he began with nothing and now enjoys a modicum of success, which, considering the circumstances, should be viewed as an unequivocal against-the-odds victory. The implied author also discloses, or puts into practice, his stratagem. This abstract figure will ventriloquize Lázaro and thereby intrude upon the first-person perspective, and, through ironic mediation, he will make Lázaro's discourse anything but self-promoting. Stated in other words, the implied author will turn the singular and single-minded project into a dialectical competition. The battle enacted in the pages of the narrative is nominally between a specific individual and his society, but the message concerns, more broadly, the place of individual in society, and early modern Spanish society becomes an enforcer of rules and the enemy of anyone who would disregard its tenets and its insistence on decorum.

Beset by more problems that she can endure, Lazarillo's mother entrusts him to a blind man who earns his income by praying for others. The trauma of desertion is intensified by the lessons in life—lessons in reality—that this first master gives his charge. It is evident that the author wants the reader to recognize that the innocent child is figuratively the blind one of the pair, who is abruptly awakened from his simplicity and finally capable of using his visual advantage to escape from months of suffering. Lázaro's narration of his time with the blind man allows the reader to experience the surprise of his initiation into the ways of the world and the disillusionment that accompanies his rites of passage: the violent push into the stone bull, the beatings, his master's nose in his mouth, which smells of sausage, and so forth. Lázaro tells *and* shows. He views his life in retrospect but juggles time and perspective. The blind man overpowers Lazarillo; he himself has learned the hard way, and he wants to teach Lazarillo to fend for himself, and the methods that he employs are not gentle. The author gives the reader the chance to see things from Lazarillo's perspective and to relish the artistry of the text. Blindness becomes a motif. Lazarillo takes revenge on the blind man and plots his escape by inverting the roles; he sees what his master cannot see. This sets up the encounters with his second master, a

priest, and his third master, a squire. The stingy priest comes close
to starving Lazarillo, who must deal with avarice and with a master
who can see. The honor-obsessed squire means well, but he forces
Lazarillo to seek food for both of them at a time in which begging
is illegal. As Lazarillo moves onward, conditions get worse, and the
hunger motif, along with references to the senses, is magnified. By
the same token, elements in the first chapter, such as wine, will
recur and strengthen the irony in the final chapter. Most notably
perhaps, the motifs of speech/silence and vision/blindness—pivotal
to the overriding emphases of the narrative—are introduced in the
opening *tratado*. What may disguise themselves as aleatory thoughts
become part of a calculated system of themes, verbal ploys, satire
(including religious satire), and irony. The world view projected in
Lazarillo de Tormes is infused with pessimism; conflict, evil, and
hypocrisy seem to characterize the human condition.

In chapter 2, the service to the priest of Maqueda compels Lazarillo to increase his survival skills. The chapter hyperbolizes the
preceding chapter in several spheres: religious hypocrisy, greed,
ingenuity, and misery. The imagery is more noticeably biblical (the
coffer becomes a "paraíso panal," or breadly paradise, for example
[56]), the cruelty more pronounced, and the depiction of humanity
harsher. Lazarillo's ruses include the fabrication of a mouse and a
snake that supposedly have access to the food in the priest's coffer.
The young boy becomes animal-like in his behavior, as he resorts to
whatever means at his disposal to survive in the home of a man of
the cloth who is not poor but miserly and unfeeling. Having gone
from the frying pan into the fire, Lazarillo is too weak and too afraid
to flee the second master. Lázaro interweaves his thoughts from
childhood into the narration, and he stresses how every ray of hope
evolves into further distress. No consolation is on the horizon, but
Lazarillo is becoming wiser, a better judge of his fellow men, more
cunning, and more willing to fight to stay alive. When the priest
detects the source of his missing food, he dispatches Lazarillo, whose
fears about his next master prove to be well founded.

The third chapter—Lazarillo's service to the squire—is the most
extended, so its symbolism likewise will be deeper and more profound. The motif of hunger reaches its most pathetic moment in this
chapter, and the theme of survival combines with the theme of
honor. The juncture and the transition help to determine the con-
tinuation of the narrative and of Lazarillo's education and choices.
The squire is a good person, if a bad master. He is the embodiment
of *desengaño*, disillusionment and the recognition of deceptive
appearances. He looks well-to-do, but he has nothing. He presents
himself with unlimited confidence, but he cannot back up his words.
Because he is a nobleman, the squire cannot submit to manual labor,

but he has no means of support and no release from the blind alley in which he finds himself. He is a virtual slave to a code of honor that guides and restricts him. His pride shows through in his interaction with Lazarillo, who must do much of his bidding. In a radical reversal, the servant keeps his master alive, and the master eventually flees from his creditors, leaving Lazarillo abandoned and defenseless. The (con)fusion of time, perspective, and reflection is especially elaborate here. Through abundant asides, Lazarillo/Lázaro portrays the squire with a blend of admiration, sympathy, and contempt. In this chapter, the narrator takes strides to distance himself from the squire as, in asides, he derides his master's obsession with honor, as ill-conceived as it is impractical. There is little regard here for the concept of *honor*, virtue and strength of character, which is unquestionably subordinate to *honra*, public perception, the external over the internal. The implied author is setting Lázaro up for a reintroduction of the theme of honor in the final part of the narration. Religious ritual comes into the frame when Lazarillo confuses the squire's water with wine and in an interlude in which the boy is afraid that parishioners are delivering a corpse to the squire's house. The range and depth of Lázaro's commentaries in the third chapter not only present the squire with great precision and critical acuity, but they place the narrator/protagonist in the role of arbiter. As he judges the squire, so will he be judged as honor reappears in the narrative when Lázaro completes his defense. The inclusion of an impoverished and arrogant nobleman among the masters expands the comparative fields, including the precocious consideration of social determinism, and clarifies Lázaro's yearning for social acceptability and a rise in rank. Lázaro as narrator is conscious of the irony of his service to the squire while overlooking the larger and more pervasive irony of this period in his life.

The fourth *tratado* carries a paradoxical weight by dint of its brevity. Lazarillo's master is a Mercedarian friar who prefers gadding about ("in secular business and visits") to remaining in the monastery, and he takes his servant with him (110–11). Lazarillo quickly tires of traipsing about, and for that reason "and other little items that I won't mention" (*otras cosillas que no digo*), he leaves the friar (111). The chapter concentrates on another clerical figure, it would seem, gone astray. Lázaro's last statement falls into the category of silence that is not silence, or articulated silence, which is, in sum, neither silence nor lacking in irony. The fact that Lázaro would rather not remember what happened with the friar or would not wish to share this information with Vuestra Merced is, paradoxically, telling. Announcing silence constitutes breaking silence, and this chapter underscores that motif and the continued presence of an ironic voice-over. The reader is left to conjecture what actually happened, who was involved in the meanderings, and whether Lazarillo was mistreated or abused in any way. What one can conjecture is that the deleted material was unlikely to have been positive. With this ending, Lazarillo disappears from the visual side of the narrative, and becomes a witness and storyteller in the fifth chapter, which shows how a pardoner and his accomplice, a constable, use religious rituals and beliefs to rook people of their money. This chapter deconstructs the belief that seeing is believing, since acting and deceiving trump reality, or substitute their own version of reality. The dupes are, in a double sense, believers, ready to accept the doctrines and the authority of the Church, as represented by the pardoner. Lázaro points to the techniques of defrauding people, of converting lies into verifiable truths and appearances into reality. He himself sees, and believes, what is going on, and only when the perpetrators discuss the swindle does he comprehend what has taken place. Like the others, he is deluded by the practice of rectitude by swindlers in righteous garb. Literally and figuratively, Lázaro grows here, through a lesson that is as strong, if more abstract, than his being pushed against the stone bull in the first chapter. Humanity is corrupt. No one is immune to betrayal, and no institution, holy or secular, is spared from contamination. Disillusionment waits at every corner. When he reappears in the sixth *tratado*, the protagonist is no longer Lazarillo, but a young man on the verge of adulthood. He has moved from childhood and from the threat of starvation.

Similar to the fourth chapter, but less dramatically so, the sixth chapter is compact in its composition. Lázaro has two masters: a tambourine painter and a chaplain. He writes that with the first master he suffered "a thousand ills" (*mil males*), related to the *otras cosillas* of the fourth *tratado* (125). The chaplain gives him a job as a water seller, and Lázaro spends four years at this task. He saves enough money to buy some respectable secondhand clothes, and, feeling confident and proud, considers himself above that task and moves onward. The decision is a turning point—and a climactic moment—in the narrative. Lázaro has a certain stability and consistency in his life: he has a secure employment and building confidence. The most arresting detail of the resolution is that, for Lázaro, clothes make the man. The outfit that he buys is indisputably like that of the squire of the third *tratado*. Lázaro is earning an honest living through manual labor. Through metonymy, the used clothes signal a new self-image and a new social category. Because the clothes bring to mind the squire, the metonymy includes the fixation on honor. By copying the squire's wardrobe and rejecting manual labor, Lázaro seems to invite the reader to note his concern with higher things in life, such as propriety, social standing, and, most ardently, honor. Assimilating and developing what has preceded it, the sixth chapter locates Lázaro in a different stratum of society and prepares him (and the reader) for the events (and for the ironies) to come. The purchase may figure among the most important commercial ventures in Spanish literature, for it takes Lázaro to the culminating stage of his novel and groundbreaking biography.

The seventh *tratado* opens with a short description of Lázaro's employment as assistant to a constable, a job whose dangers outweigh its advantages. Through God's help, good luck, and the favors of friends, Lázaro finally attains the professional advancement that he has coveted: an "official position" (*oficio real*) as a town crier in Toledo (128). He is put in charge of broadcasting the offenses of criminals. Through his work, Lázaro deals with Vuestra Merced. He also comes to the attention of the Archpriest of San Salvador, who arranges a marriage between Lázaro and a woman in his service. The lady has a less than flawless history, and there is talk of a relationship with the archpriest himself. Tongues begin wagging, and Lázaro finds himself in a bind. The potential, or real, scandal may be the "case" of the prologue. Lázaro's patron advises him to ignore the gossip and act in his own best interest. Lázaro admonishes those around him to keep their opinions in check, swearing to them that his wife is as decent as any woman in Toledo. They seem to have complied, and the narrator notes that this has brought him peace at home. In closing, Lázaro refers to a historical event of 1525 or 1538–39—the entry of the emperor Charles V (Carlos I) into Toledo, where he convened parliament—and observes that "at this time, I was living in prosperity and at the height of all good fortune" ("en este tiempo estaba en mi prosperidad y en la cumbre de toda buena fortuna") (135).

The repetition of images is evident in the final chapter. Wine and grapes are instrumental in Lazarillo's apprenticeship with the blind man. Lázaro is a town crier; he constantly breaks silences, and his work involves criminals. Like his mother, he vows to join with the good people, but exemplars may be in short supply, and, like his mother, his wife cannot detach herself either from misfortune or from a difficult past. The archpriest is yet another figure of the Church who may have transgressed. Little is perfectly clear at the end, but welcome silences continue to be replaced by speech, even by shouts, and ironies compound. Heeding the counsel of the archpriest, Lázaro warns his acquaintances to remain mum on his wife's business and threatens to harm them if they do otherwise, but his discourse on the matter does not enhance the portrait of the lady or remove doubts about her fidelity. Encouraged by his mentor, Lázaro intimidates his neighbors, demanding that they follow his model of figurative blindness and deafness, a model that he cannot sustain because of the pressure to respond to Vuestra Merced's request and because of the book into which that response is inscribed. The reader has a glimpse into Lázaro's adult life and into what he tries to present as a victory for the underdog. In spite of unavoidable setbacks, Lázaro has bettered his position; one cannot deny his accomplishments nor gloss over the distance that separates his early childhood from the creature comforts that he enjoys in Toledo. The reader must give some consideration to the use of the imperfect tense in the concluding sentence, which refers to *then* rather than *now*, and suggests that things may have gotten worse. Perhaps more salient, however, is the matter of Lázaro's state of mind as he reflects on the past. In many ways, the facts speak for themselves. As a child, he had nothing—no name, no parental guidance, no positive role models—and he faced the prospect of starvation. He was mistreated, beaten, and possibly abused. He moved from those abject conditions to integration into society, with a good job, a home, a wife, and supporters. Materially speaking, there is no comparison between his childhood and his adulthood. Lázaro should be satisfied with the way that things have turned out, but is he? The answer, for me, lies in the overriding irony of the text, but I would submit, as well, that the collective data will, and has, led to radically varied analyses (or processing) of the narrative. I believe that the textual markers indicate that when Lázaro gains entry into—according to his perception—the social mainstream, he accepts the requisites of the honor code and must live surrounded by the menacing shadow of dishonor. In the end, many of his commentaries and asides reverberate ironically against him, above all his critique of the squire's obsession with honor. Honor negatively inflects the story of Lázaro's rise, while preserving society's hold on the individual.[8]

Lazarillo de Tormes does not give the reader a ready-made or static protagonist. Lázaro de Tormes grows physically and emotionally in the course of his narration, which complements this development with shifts in point of view and contrasts among narrative stances. An incipient form of multiperspectivism predates and probably influences *Don Quixote*. Along with European writers such as Cervantes and Miguel de Unamuno, among countless others, but earlier, the author of *Lazarillo de Tormes* is a virtuoso in the art of doubling and adept at juggling fragments of text and of thought. With admirable economy, the narrative displays causes as well as effects, circularity as well as linearity, and the author envisages social determinism and encodes this version of fate into the plot. On one plane, the movement is from birth to maturity; on others,

---

8. I argue for Lázaro's acceptance of the honor code in "Coming to Terms with Lázaro's Prosperity: Framing Success in *Lazarillo de Tormes*," *Crítica Hispánica* 19 (1997): 41–56. For a counterargument, see Frank P. Casa, "In Defense of Lázaro de Tormes," *Crítica Hispánica* 19 (1977): 87–98.

time and space are interspersed and rendered indistinguishable. The service to an array of masters directs the linear plot, and, in the end, Lázaro remains dependent on one or more figurative masters. The text is inextricably bound to its social contexts, and realism and verisimilitude are elements within this frame, one frame of many. Specificity does not rob the narrative of its universality, or of its capacity to change with the times. From another angle, the text draws attention to, rather than shields, its literariness, as Lázaro refers to the composition process per se. Self-referentiality, or metafiction, interacts dialectically with the recourses of realism. The work-in-progress crosses with the studied response to the request from Vuestra Merced and with the studied, if often mystifying, counter-narrative of the implied author. The gaps and indeterminacies of the narrative call for intervention from the consumer of the text,[9] and the narrator-narratee engagement is replicated on the level of (implied) author-reader. The result, expressed metaphorically and a little eccentrically, is a sort of thick concoction of parallelism and early postmodernism. The narrative is fully conscious of an intertext—literary, spiritual, and nonfictional—that exalts the ideal and the exemplary, but it moves in the opposite direction and with opposing aim, not unlike those of deconstruction centuries later. Early narrative realism, folkloric traditions, and social satire enter the structure as well, and the particular alchemy of *Lazarillo de Tormes* conducts the reader on a path that will lead not only to the picaresque subgenre, but, with its spirited play of imitation and deviation, to *Don Quixote* and beyond.

The story of *Lazarillo de Tormes* is inspired and imaginative. It takes the topos of literature as a mirror to life and holds the mirror at different slants from previous narrative, with respect to point of view, subject-object relations, personal development and psychology, linear and circular structures. It "paints" the reader into a sharp and powerful Renaissance portrait that comes to be, in its own way, as intense—and as crowded with ideas—as the baroque portraits of Cervantes, Francisco de Quevedo, and Diego Velázquez. For me, the five major lessons of *Lazarillo de Tormes* can be reduced to (1) the expansion of voice, idiolect, point of view, and creative force; (2) the conception of realism with an essential dose of metafiction; (3) the representation of psychological change with linguistic and structural counterparts; (4) the engagement of the reader; and (5) a rhetoric of irony,[1] the ingenuity and profundity of which have

9. I would recommend as a starting point in this area Wolfgang Iser, *The Act of Reading: A Theory of Aesthetic Response* (Johns Hopkins U. Press, 1980), and, by the same author, *The Implied Reader: Patterns of Communication in Prose Fiction from Bunyan to Beckett* (Johns Hopkins U. Press, 1978).
1. See Wayne C. Booth, *The Rhetoric of Fiction* (U. of Chicago Press, 1961), and *A Rhetoric of Irony* (U. of Chicago Press, 1975).

remained extraordinary as life has become increasingly ironic. Irony may be the umbrella or the all-encompassing feature of the narrative, which never ceases to surprise the reader, no matter the number of rereadings. The author exalts language, the institution of literature, and the mental capacity of the reader. He is a true critic, arguing for and against the basic arguments that he introduces, and demanding that the reader exercise judgment. He goes low, but aims high, and this paradox that serves as the first premise of the narrative reconfigures itself as the text progresses. He teaches that the new is always indebted to the old, and Cervantes is one of his best students (as is Jorge Luis Borges, to cite but one additional disciple).

The question of whether a survey of the mechanisms of *Lazarillo de Tormes* could lend itself to a poetics of the novel will depend on the interpreter. Having attempted to proceed from the inside out, I would summarize the inner workings of the narrative as satisfying criteria that seem fundamental to the genre, as follows: (1) a recognizable setting, with attention to details of time and place, but with universal themes; (2) a highly developed discursive structure, with variations of perspective and outlook; (3) a strong linear plot, with a system of symbols and images and with an accompanying cyclical pattern; (4) signs of growth and psychological progression; (5) the joint presence of realistic and metafictional elements; (6) an elaborate use of irony; and (7) a strong involvement of the reader in the interpretive process. Not only does *Lazarillo de Tormes* exemplify the novel as it has advanced, but the revelations and modi operandi of this small work of 1554 can guide readers, writers, critics, and theorists to the novels of the twenty-first century, with vigor, flexibility, and wit.

T. ANTHONY PERRY

Biblical Symbolism in the *Lazarillo de Tormes*[†]

One of the most suggestive assaults on the resistant perplexities of the *Lazarillo de Tormes* has been a number of recent observations on its symbolic or mythical structure. F. Maldonado de Guevara was perhaps the first to see this anonymous masterpiece as representing an antihero of a special kind: "Un antihéroe cuya misión, en una atmósfera espesa y continua de irreverencia, consistió en la burla y la desintegración del primero y mayor de los mitos,

† From T. Anthony Perry, "Biblical Symbolism in the *Lazarillo de Tormes*," *Studies in Philology* 67.2 (1970): 139–46. Copyright © 1970 by the University of North Carolina Press. Used by permission of the publisher. www.uncpress.unc.edu

el mito del *puer asternus*."[1] Although its author did not know the archetypes in a conceptual and scientific way, the critic continues, he grasped them intuitively in the forms available to a Renaissance humanist, in the infancies of Hercules, Mercury, Apollo, Perseus, and chivalric heroes such as Amadís (p. 256). The resulting artistic protest is succinctly characterized as "una parodia del mito del héroeniño abandonado y una meditación existencialista de la dere-licción, de la deyección del Existente en el Mundo" (p. 255). While plausibly explaining details such as Lazarillo's birth in the river or his humble origins, these Jungian categories nevertheless lead to the distortion of several aspects of the novel. For example, in order to illustrate the sexual immaturity proper to the eternal *Niño*, the critic is led to assume that Lázaro does not love his wife (p. 261), an observation that relies too heavily on later developments of the genre and which is contradicted, at least verbally, by the pro-tagonist's own statement ("es la cosa del mundo que yo más qui-ero, y la amo más que a mí," p. 145). More debatable still is the critic's identification of the serpent of *tratado* two with the ser-pents (note the plural) killed by the infant Hercules. To maintain this it is necessary to imagine the serpent(s) as constituting "ries-gos que acechan la vida del Niño" (p. 259). However, Lazarillo is menaced not by serpents but by the priest, and it is the latter's identification of the boy with the serpent that needs explaining. In short, Maldonado de Guevara's general approach is suggestive but, as we shall see, often remote from the novel's intended symbolic universe.

Stephen Gilman also rejects as far-fetched the parallel of Hercu-les slaying the serpents, but he in turn succumbs to the lure of Greek myth in characterizing Lazarillo's blind master as an ageless and "Tiresias-like" prophet.[2] More fanciful still is the suggestion that *tratados* one and seven are parodies of the Oedipus story (Gilman, p. 162, n. 54). Surely the intuitions of a symbolic structure in the *Lazarillo* are validated not through undemonstrable Jungian arche-types or distant Greek myth but rather when related to more likely symbolic traditions. Gilman's chief merit in this respect is to have shown the importance of the novel's interdependent patterns of death and rebirth and, following the lead of a brief essay by Anson

---

1. F. Meldonado de Guevara, "El niño y el viejo: desmitologización en el *Lazarillo* y en el *Quijote*," *Anales Cervantinos*, VIII (1959–60), 254. For the text of the *Lazarillo* I use what is to my mind the most sensible and best critical edition to date, that of José Caso González, Anejo XVII del B. R. A. E., (Madrid, 1967). For biblical passages I use the Spanish translation of Bover-Canters, 6th edition (Madrid, 1961). Finally, I would like to express my gratitude to Mrs. Sandra Briggs, graduate student in Spanish at the Uni-versity of Connecticut, for her gracious assistance with this article.
2. Stephen Gilman, "The Death of Lazarillo de Tormes," *PMLA*, LXXXI (1966), 162. Although the blind man's spirit of prophesy is exaggerated in the first interpolation of the Alcalá edition, his real identity is quite different, as we shall see.

Piper, to have related these to their biblical origins.[3] It is now clear, for example, to what degree of detail the second *tratado* is a symbolic (and ironic) representation of the sacrament of Communion.[4] It seems to me that Gilman's and Piper's excellent demonstrations can and must be developed further, especially if such problems as the poorly understood first *tratado* are to be resolved. A study of religious symbolism, I shall argue, reveals that Lazarillo's "salvation" frequently evokes the New Testament's account of man's redemption, while his fall is coherently patterned after the myth of Genesis.

Bataillon's allusion to the "quelques plaisantes applications des évangiles" in the *Lazarillo* characterizes the usual view that the Bible's function in the novel is essentially humorous and limited to obvious parallels.[5] Yet we shall see how an explicit parallel is often also a hint to a total biblical context which lurks just below the surface and assumes all sorts of forms. For example, the hero's name and his early career as a hungry vagrant evoke the beggar of Luke 16. 19–25, but Gilman's analysis of the central theme of resurrection points to a more profound identification with the Lazarus brought to life by Christ (John 11, 1–44). Those who speculate on the latter part of the hero's name, Lazarillo *de Tormes*, may observe that this biblical figure is also identified by a toponym: Lárazo *de Betania*. Now Bethany is mentioned earlier in the same gospel as being the place where John baptized Christ (1.28). In other words, Betania, the scene of the resurrection of Lázaro in the flesh, is also associated with Man's sacramental rebirth. Now if one accepts the humorous transmutation of Lázaro de Betania into Lazarillo (note the diminutive) de Tormes, might not the hero's announcement that "con verdad me puedo decir nacido en el río" appear as an impious allusion to baptism by total immersion (Christ in the Jordan)? Lest the reader still fail to recognize the ambiance of the gospel of John, the author immediately (and ironically) assimilates Lazarillo's father to the prophet of Christ: "Confesó y no negó" (p. 63). The informed reader supplies the missing words, making them thus all the more emphatic: "y confesó: Yo no soy el Mesías" (John 1. 20). Within the novel's context of "desacramentalization," this humorous evocation of Scripture also ominously announces that Lazarillo's father "is not Christ" and

3. Gilman, "The Death of *L. da T.*," 161–6. Anson Piper, "The 'Breadly Paradise' of Lazarillo de Tormies," *Hispania*, XLIV (1961), 269–71.
4. Gilman, 163–4; Piper, 269–70. I accept the view that the sense of biblical symbolism in the *Lazarillo* is ironic, that the impossibility of spiritual salvation is a dominant theme ("ya la caridad se subió al cielo," p. 102), and that symbols of spiritual rebirth are consistently transferred to secular realities. The most obvious example of this is the purely materialistic sense of renewal ascribed to the wine of *tratado* one and to the bread and "arcaz" of the second *tratado*. Gilman suggests the term "desacramentalization" for this, postulating that the author's hostility "is primarily directed against the 'myths' of the Lazarillo's own century, myths of providence and religious ceremony as well as those of heroism and honor" ("The Death of *L. de T.*," 162, n. 54).
5. Marcel Bataillon, in his introduction to *La vie de Lazarille de Tormes* (Paris, 1958), p. 53.

by implication that his son Lazarillo is not, spiritually speaking, Christ's son.

The mock baptism accompanying Lazarillo's birth sets the tone for his harder initiation into the world's realities at the hands of the *ciego*. If no satisfactory mythical interpretation has yet been offered of the first *tratado*, this is largely due to the fact that the role of its chief protagonist, the blind man, has been neglected or misunderstood. Lazarillo's birth is indeed a fall into unsanctified existence, and the author developed this idea by the images he knew best. The first three *tratados* present many elements of the Genesis myth: Man, the Creator, the Tempter, and the spiritual fall of man. Within this context of damnation, the leading role is played by the Devil, and this is the real identity of the blind man.

Lazarillo continually attributes the satanic qualities of shrewdness and deceit to his master: "Desde que Dios crió el mundo, ninguno formó más astuto ni sagaz" (p. 68). The explicit reference to God's creation of the world invites the comparison with Genesis 3.1: "La serpiente era el más astuto de todos los animales salvajes que Yawveh Dios había producido."[6] The reader is reminded of the devil's successful temptation of mankind through Eve when Lazarillo says of his master: "Andábase todo el mundo tras él, especialmente mujeres, que cuanto les decía, creían" (p. 69). Also, the blind man is thrice called "el traidor," a traditional epithet of the devil.[7]

Like Adam, Lazarillo's fall from a paradise of innocence and delight is described as a new kind of consciousness. Parallel to the opening of Adam's eyes in Genesis 3.7, Lazarillo tells how, following upon his first encounter with the blind man, "desperté de la simpleza en que, como niño, dormido estaba" (p. 67). His state of primitive innocence (*simpleza*) and enjoyment is harshly disrupted by a sudden and terrible punishment that seems to come from heaven. He sits drinking wine, "descuidado y gozoso" and in perfect repose, "estando recibiendo aquellos dulces tragos, mi cara puesta hacia el cielo, un poco cerrados los ojos por mejor gustar el sabroso licuor," when suddenly "verdaderamente me pareció que el cielo, con todo lo que en él hay, me había caído encima" (pp. 72–3).

The relatively high number of references to the devil in the first *tratado* suggests that the presence of the blind man is naturally associated with the demonic. Lazarillo is first deceived by his master through "el diablo del toro" (p. 67); the blind man "daba al diablo el

---

6. The *Diccionario de Autoridades* (Madrid, 1732) lists the following as one of the meanings of *Diablo*: "Se llama asimismo al sugeto que tiene gran sagacidad, sutileza y maña, aun en las cosas buenas."

7. In the famous medieval drama *Le Mystère d'Adam*, for example, Adam summarizes Satan's treachery in a single verse: "Tu es traitres, e sanz foi" (ed. Paul Aebischer, Genève: Droz, 1964, v. 204). Lazarillo refers to "el traidor tan astuto" (p. 71); "el grandíssimo entendimiento del traidor" (p. 74; also p. 75).

jarro y el vino" (p. 72); it is the *demonio* who teaches Lazarillo how to steal (p. 76); the boy refers to his master's "falta endiablada" (p. 70) and to his own retributive "burlas endiabladas" (p. 69). But beyond mere preoccupation with a theme, the last example cited points to the outcome of this association with the blind man: Lazarillo has become en-deviled. The devilish master's dominant quality of "*discreta* consideración" (p. 75) or cleverness is thus transferred to his disciple in the acknowledgement: "*Discreto* eres, por esto te quiero bien" (p. 80). The blind man's role of corrupter affords him considerable pride, and his jests in this vein are thinly disguised hints as to his real identity. He summarizes the lesson of the bull of Salamanca in the following manner: "Necio, aprende: que el moço del ciego un punto ha de saber más que el diablo" (p. 67). The disciple is so diligent, however, as to come to overshadow the "demonio" himself: "Y sí alguno le decía [al ciego] por qué me trataba tan mal, luego contaba el cuento del jarro, diciendo: ¿Pensaréis que este mi moço es algún inocente? Pues oíd si el demonio ensayara otra tal hazaña" (p. 73).[8]

The blind man, then, is not Tiresias but the Tempter who teaches the ways of the world: "Después de Dios, éste [el ciego] me dió la vida y, siendo ciego, me alumbró en la carrera de vivir" (p. 67).[9]

Lazarillo's grotesque metamorphosis into the serpent in *tratado* two can now be understood as merely the logical symbolic outcome of the devil's tutelage.[1] It is also from this perspective that the *clérigo's* parting words take on their intended meaning: "Yo no quiero en mi compañía tan diligente servidor. No es possible sino que *hayas sido moço de ciego*. Y santiguándose de mí, *como si yo estuviera endemoniado*, se torna a meter en casa y cierra su puerta" (p. 99, italics added).

The Creator in Genesis, who placed man into a garden of abundance and delight, is replaced in this novel by the stingy *clérigo* of the second *tratado*. While he pretends to treat his servant well, the cleric in fact is more avaricious than the blind man. When offering

8. The irony of this avowal is that the devil's lessons in *burlas* are about to precipitate his own destruction. In his *Screwtape Letters* C. S. Lewis recalls the adage that Satan cannot stand to be mocked, and violent extinction is the only possible outcome for a devil who has been *burlado* or outwitted at his own game. It is thus not quite correct to say that Lazarillo abandons the blind man, rather that he surpasses and destroys a master whom he nevertheless reveres throughout the novel.

9. It is surprising that no one has yet pointed out this ironic allusion to John 14.61 "Dícele Jesús: Yo soy el camino, y la verdad, y la vida," exactly parallelod by *carrera, alumbró*, and *vida* or *vivir*. The intent of the passage is similar to that of the preceding line, in its use of Scripture to evoke the "life-giving" powers of the blind man: "Yo oro ni plata no te lo puedo dar; mas avisos para vivir, muchos te mostraré" (p. 67, recalling Acts 3.6: "Plata y oro no tengo; mas lo que tango, esto te doy; en el nombre de Jesu-Christo Nazareno, ponte a andar"). Then uses of the Bible to state worldly realities serve to emphasize, in an ironic mode that is by now familiar, that the *vivir* of the blind man is really death, and that this personage who assumes the appearance of Christ is in fact an anti-Christ or devil.

1. Piper suggests the Genesis origin of the serpent ("The 'Breadly Paradise'," 271), but it is Gilman who clearly spells out the identity of Lazarillo and the serpent ("The Death of *L. de T.*," 164).

the boy some bones, he says, "Toma, come, triunfa, que para ti es el mundo" (p. 85), echoing the words of the Last Supper (Piper, p. 270), but perhaps also the Creator's display to Adam and Eve of the world's abundance, "que os servirá de alimento" (Genesis 1, 29). And just as Adam was cast out of Paradise, Lazarillo is excluded from the "arcaz" or Holy Sacrament and, after it is discovered that he is the serpent, dismissed altogether from the house (the Church). The numerous references to death throughout the second *tratado* merely dramatize the fact that, once man's fall into the realities of the world has been consumated at the hands of the Devil, man is rejected and dies.

In the next *tratado* Lazarillo enters a kind of limbo where he experiences neither great joy, as he did eating and drinking in the previous two *tratados*, nor pain from beatings.[2] His master the *escudero* is a spectral being who lives for days without food, totally preoccupied with abstract problems of honor. His house seems like a *casa encantada* (p. 104), without "passos de viva persona" or any belongings whatsoever and yet mysteriously locked (p. 103). Showing no more "aliento de comer que un muerto" (p. 103), the squire finally leads the boy to bed, a "cama negra" or coffin. It is small wonder that, when Lazarillo hears a woman lamenting the death of her husband, he thinks that the corpse is being carried to the squire's house; "¡A la casa triste y desdichada, a la casa lóbrega y obscura, a la casa donde nunca comen ni beben!" (p. 118). The low point is reached ("do acabé de conocer mi ruin dicha," p, 127) when the ghostly squire simply vanishes, and Lazarillo is left a *mozo* without a master, a man without an identity. The spiritual death that is about to unroll in the final four *tratados* is thus already symbolically foreshadowed in the first three: satanic fall, expulsion, and annihilation.

The pendulum of Lazarillo's fortunes begins its upward swing, so the detail of the pair of shoes—his first awareness of clothing—to speak, in *tratado* four, as the boy begins to be reborn to the world, anticipates his first major step forward ("el primer escalón que yo subí para venir a alcançar buena vida," p. 139), his purchase of a suit of clothes. The importance of these details suggests a final parallel with Genesis. It is only after the fall that Adam becomes conscious of his nakedness (loss of innocence). In the *Lazarillo* clothing is one of the instruments of man's social hypocrisy. This clothing permits Lazarillo to enter the society of hypocrites and to live well.

These symbolic patterns permit new hypotheses concerning the novel's structure. Arguments long familiar to critics have viewed the

---

2. The following analysis of the third *tratado* closely follows Gilman, "The Death of *L. de T.*," 165–6.

first three *tratados* as a tryptich unified by Lazarillo's sufferings.[3] Since this tryptich is now seen to portray a symbolic death, it can be related to biblical accounts of death and descent into the lower world in which the number three is significant: Christ's descent into hell, and especially Jonah's sojourn in the belly of the whale, a myth evoked by the lad when describing his period of unconsciousness after being exorcised by the cleric: "De lo que sucedió en aquellos tres días siguientes ninguna fe daré (porque los tuve en el vientre de la ballena)" (p. 98). And like the biblical Lazarus who returned to life on the fourth day, Lazarillo is resurrected (ironically, of course) in the fourth *tratado*. Though largely undeveloped, *tratados* 4–6 thematically balance the first three by describing the hero's rebirth. Finally, in the seventh and final *tratado* the hero "arrives" and, like the Creator on the seventh day, mockingly takes his own *descanso*.

If, as has been often observed, *Lazarillo de Tormes* is not a psychological novel, this may be due not to disinterest—the luminous episode of the Squire alone disproves the supposition—but to its symbolic nature. The main reason for the characters' lack of individuation is that, at least upon occasion, they become figures, in the medieval sense, of biblical heroes. A *clérigo* can sound like the Creator or embody the guardian of Paradise, a *calderero* is almost mistaken for an angel, and a blind man is a strong figuration of Satan. At such moments the novel becomes a theatre where supernatural forces contend and where the great biblical myths are reenacted. Within this novelistic universe the main theme is neither hunger nor anti-clericalism[4] but, as its title suggests, the symbolic death and rebirth of man.

LOUIS C. PÉREZ

On Laughter in the *Lazarillo de Tormes*[†]

Not all previous commentators have agreed that the ending of the *Lazarillo de Tormes* indicates that the protagonist has come to terms with his environment. Perhaps a study of laughter as it appears in the *Lazarillo* will disclose a subjective attitude on the part of the author towards his work. Striking it is that in this book which reputedly evokes much merriment from the reader, the

3. F. Courtney Tarr, for example, views the first three *tratados* as a progressive and climactic treatment of the hunger theme in his "Literary and Artistic Unity in the *Lazarillo de Tormes*," *PMLA*, XLII (1927), 408, 410.
4. Tarr, 404–21, cited and followed by Piper, 269, in his allusion to "the two main themes of the entire work: hunger and anticlericalism."
† From Louis C. Pérez, "On Laughter in the 'Lazarillo de Tormes,'" *Hispania* 43.4 (1960): 529–33. Reprinted by permission of the publisher.

words for laughter, whether in adjectival, substantival or verbal form appear only eighteen times. Apparently the book is not intended as a superficial rib-tickler. This is to say that that which is risible in the *Lazarillo* is treated in a very subtle manner, that the author's main purpose is apparently a deeper one as he suggests in the prologue: ". . . pues podria ser que alguno, que las [cosas] lea, halle algo que le agrade y á los que no ahondaren tanto los deleyte" (70–71).[1]

The first time we encounter laughter, Lázaro is a young boy:

> Y acuerdome que, estando el negro de mi padrastro trebejando con el moçuelo, como el niño via á mi madre é á mi blancos y á él no, huya dél con miedo para mi madre y, señalando con el dedo, dezia:
> "¡Madre, coco!"
> Respondió él *riendo*: "Hideputa!" (83–84)

Thus it is that Lázaro is introduced to sarcastic laughter, laughter that is perhaps tainted with a sense of guilt accompanied by the disreputable term *hideputa*.[2] More important, however, is the fact that it serves as a release mechanism for the guilt the man feels when confronted with the reality of his acts.

Laughter next appears when the protagonist sets out in the service of the blind man. Here too it is tainted with sarcasm. The old man wishes to introduce Lázaro into a society whose mores are apparently based on deceit, trickery and constant fear of harm. He submits his boy to the test:

> "Lázaro, llega el oydo á este toro é oyrás gran ruydo dentro dél".
> Yo simplemente llegué, creyendo ser ansi. Y, como sintió que tenia la cabeça par de la píedra, afirmó rezio la mano y diome una gran calabaçada en el diablo del toro, que mas de tres dias me duró el dolor de la cornada y dixome."
> "Necio, aprende: que el moço del ciego un punto ha de saber mas que el diablo."
> Y *rió* mucho la burla. (89–90)

In this wicked setting the boy passes into a state of awareness—he comes to life: "Paresciome que en aquel instants desperté de la

---

1. All page references are to the following edition: *La vida de Lazarilla de Tormes*, ed. Julio Cejador y Franca, Madrid: Clásicos Castellanos, 1914. The page reference will appear in parentheses at the end of the quoted passage. Italics in quoted passages are ours. We omit the additions of the Alcalá text. First, because we believe the rapid or telegraphic style of synthesis to be the true style of the author and not the later additions and reflections. Second, the additions of the Alcalá text change nothing of what we say in this paper.
2. The use of *hideputa* here is not to be taken lightly. It seems to us that the author wished to imply an awareness of guilt on the part of the stepfather. Bear in mind that it is Lázaro, who is very much aware of the immoral situation, who is doing the observing.

simpleza en que como niño dormido etstaua" (90). What a cruel awakening to life, and the clarion with its shattering sound is laughter, a harsh laughter in the midst of a physically painful experience. Here too, as regards the blind man, it acts as an emotional release for the bitterness the handicapped sometimes feel toward fate. The old man is clearly cleansing himself of pent-up energy and frustration, availing himself of a teaching situation. None the less, from our *atalaya* of four hundred years distance, it remains to us a depressing event as it does also for Lázaro. So much so that it may well serve to explain why our hero never laughs outwardly and why his laughter, besides appearing only once, is suppressed—*risa de adentro*. We refer to the episode in which the old man comes into the possession of some grapes and suggests to Lázaro that they share them and eat by turns. The old man begins. He takes one and Lázaro takes one. The old man takes two, Lázaro takes two and three "y como podia las comia" (107). After they have finished the bunch, the old man speaks: "Lázaro, engañado me has." Lázaro feigns innocence:

> "No comi, dixe yo; mas ¿porqué sospechays esso?"
> Respondió el sagazissimo ciego:
> "¿Sabes en qué veo que las comiste tres á tres? En que comia yo dos á dos y callauas".
> *Reyme* entre mi y, aunque mochacho, noté mucho la discreta consideración del ciego. (107; 110)

Even here in this internal laughter that accompanies victory without the consequences of the physical punishment which the boy usually experiences, the laughter is one touching on emotional release. The boy was expecting some retaliation from the old man. He denies the accusation and waits for the old man's reaction to it. The boy is mildly relieved when he is not maltreated, and laughs, but only inwardly. His laughter does not erupt. It becomes corrosive for Lázaro. The lad never laughs out loud and he is aware of this.

The only other time that Lázaro comes close to laughing is when he deceives the blind man in the sausage episode. The old man discovers that his young guide has substituted a turnip for the sausage. He seizes Lázaro when he returns from his trip to the wine shop and probes with his nose so far down into the poor boy's throat that he causes him to vomit and produce the evidence of the crime. The blind beggar proceeds to take his customary vengeance. The boy is saved by the passing crowd, whereupon the old man explains his evil actions. There is great laughter, and though the boy is in tears, he realizes the humor of the situation:

Contaua el mal ciego á todos, quantos alli se allegauan,
mis desastres y dauales cuenta una y otra vez, assi de la del
jarro como de la del razimo y agora de lo presente. Era la *risa*
de todos tan grande, que toda la gente, que por la calle pas-
saus, entraua á ver la fiesta; mas con tanta gracia y donayre
recontaba el ciego mis hazañas, que, aunque yo estaua tan
maltratado y llorando, me parescia que hazia sinjusticia en no
se las *reyr.* (115)

Yet it is clear in the above passage that he does not laugh. We imagine that in this incident, at the most, a smile crossed his lips. It is
during Lázaro's stay with the old man, during his "education" or for-
mative period that laughter appears most often.[3] It is almost as if
the boy were being surfeited with laughter via different episodes so
as to have his fill of it.

Only once more subsequent to his stay with the blind man, do we
find Lázaro in tears in the midst of laughter. The urchin is in the service of the parsimonious priest. The priest awakens one night to the
hissing of the "snake" which has been stealing his bread from a
locked chest and administers him a crushing blow with a wooden
club. Lázaro is bedridden for two weeks. The priest relates the incident, the people laugh, and Lázaro weeps: "Ay tornaron de nueuo á
contar mis cuytas y á *reyrlas* y yo peccador á llorarlas" (163). This is
without doubt his most punishing physical experience—the culmi-
nation of mingled tears and laughter in the novel. From here on
laughter is never associated with physical punishment.

When next the hero appears as the butt of laughter, a certain
calmness pervades the air. It is Lázaro's most happy episode.[4] His
naïveté causes the proud *hidalgo*, his new master, to burst into

---

3. Besides the instances already cited, laughter appears as follows:
　　"Y si alguno le dezia porqué me trataua tan mal, luego contaua el cuento del jarro,
diziendo:
　　'Pensareys que este mí moço es algun innocente? Pues oyd si el demonio ensayara
otra tal hazaña.'
　　"Santiguandose los que lo oyan, dezian:
　　'¡Mirá quién pensara de un muchacho tan pequeño tal ruyndad!'
　　"Y *reyan* mucho el artificio y dezianle: . . . (103).
　　"Y luego contaua quántas vezes me auia descalabrado y harpado la cara y con vino
luego sanaua.
　　'Yo te digo, dixo, que, si hombre en el mundo ha de ser bienauenturado con vino, que
serás tu.'
　　"Y *reyan* mucho los que me lauauan con esto; aunque yo renegaua" (117–118). Notice
in this last quote how the protagonist reacts in the midst of laughter. Later on in the
novel, laughter will not daunt him.
　　The word *sonriéndose* appears only once in the book—in this chapter: . . . "Lauome
con vino las roturas, que con los pedaços del jarro me auia hecho, *y sonrríéndose*
dezia: . . ." (102)
4. César Barja in *Libros y autores clásicos*, 6th ed. (New York: G. E. Stechert & Co., 1941),
p. 229, comments:

laughter: "*rió* tanto, que muy gran rato estuuo sin poder hablar. . . . Y desque fué ya mas harto de *reyr* que de comer el bueno de mi amo, dixome: . . ." (207). Lázaro has become immune to laughter at his own expense. He does not regard the squire's laughter as an affront. Nor does he comment on the laughter at the end of this chapter when he is, in a sense, the object of ridicule. The *hidalgo* has left his creditors in the lurch. The boy is explaining that his master has some assets which may be used to settle debts he has incurred. He is asked:

> ". . . ¿Y á que parte de la ciudad tiene esso?" . . .
> "En su tierra," les respondi.
> "Por Dios, que está bueno el negocio, dixeron ellos. ¿Y adonde es su tierra?"
> "De Castilla la Vieja me dixo él que era," les dixe yo.
> *Rieronse* mucho el alguazil y el escriuano, diziendo:
> "Bastante relacion es ésta para cobrar vuestra deuda, aunque mejor fuesse." (222)

It is in this chapter that the word *risueño* appears.[5] It is one of the characteristics that Lázaro seems to associate with the squire. Paradoxically enough, with this humane and gentle *hidalgo*, endowed with a certain gay personality, Lázaro learns of *la risa arruladora*. The *hidalgo* is speaking and giving his servant some practical advice of the "what I would do if I found the right person" type:

> *Reylle* ya mucho sus donayres y costumbres aunque no fuessen las mejores de el mundo. Nunca dezirle cosa que le pesasse; aunque mucho le cumpliesse, . . . (215)

This happy encounter with the *hidalgo* comes to an end, and when next we meet laughter, the protagonist is, as it were, on the outside, looking in. The townspeople have just been hoaxed by the cunning

---

". . . *Lazarillo de Tormes* tiene gracia bastante para hacernos tolerable y entretenido lo que de otra manera seria insoportable, o por repugnante o por doloroso. Lo cual no quiere decir que *Lazarillo* sea una obra alegre. No podía serlo." There is no doubt that insofar as the novel as a whole is concerned, Barja is correct. Nevertheless in this chapter Lazarillo is quite happy with this gentle squire, though he has to forage for both. The rogue gets humane treatment from the nobleman, and as F. Courtney Tarr indicates in "Literary and Artistic Unity in the *Lazarillo de Tormes*," *PMLA*, XLII (1927), 410: "Master and servant, instead of engaging in a struggle of wits, as formerly, come to be real companions in misfortune. There exists between them that respectful intimacy so characteristic of *amo* and *criado* in Spanish literature."

5. Con el qual él vino á casa tan ufano, como si ruuiera el thesoro de Venecia y con gesto muy alegre y *risueño* me lo dió, diziendo: . . . (203).
   Y ciertamente, quando mi amo esto oyó, aunque no tenia por qué estar muy *risueño*, . . . (207).
   Mas, aunque comimos bien aquel dia, maldito el gusto yo tomaua en ello. Ni en aquellos tres dias torné en mi color. Y mi amo muy *risueño*, todas las vezes que se le acordaua aquella mi consideracion (208).

and inventive vendor of papal bulls and the constable who have "arranged" a miracle so that the people would purchase bulls. After this drummed-up performance, which had even Lázaro fooled, the vendor and his partner meet outside the town and have a good laugh:

> Quando él hizo el ensayo, confiesso mi pecado que tambien fuy dello espantado y crey que ansi era, como otros muchos; mas con ver despues la *risa* y burla, que mi amo y el alguazil lleuauan y hazian del negocio, conosci cómo auia sido industriado por el industrioso é inuentiuo de mi amo. (242)

Lázaro from this episode passes on to become a water vendor. He earns enough money to buy himself gentleman's clothes, though second-hand, "join the good guys,"[6] and surrender to inactivity, so to speak, by becoming a town crier. The story ends in a climate of criticism and apparent snickering. Laughter appears only in muffled tones. It is frequently suggested but nowhere expressed.

We have been exposed to laughter with sarcasm, laughter with burlesque acts and physical punishment, and laughter with ridicule. When merriment appears it is most often accompanied by a physical or moral blow and Lázaro is frequently in the midst of tears as laughter surrounds him. Never does he himself laugh. As we have already pointed out, only once is he on the verge of laughter.

Every main character involved directly in Lázaro's life experiences a certain emotional release through laughter. The stepfather; the blind man whose tension mounts from one episode to another—his very handicap making him prone to this; the priest whose tension builds up in the snake episode; and especially the *hidalgo* in whom tension and emotion start mounting in the first pages of the chapter. The episode of the vendor of bulls also seems to us to be one in which laughter is used to release tension. The moment of highest tension is reached when the constable goes into his trance act. The release of tension however, via the escape valve, laughter, is postponed until the two frauds meet outside the town and reminisce about the incident. Here Lázaro could have been laughing, yet he does not. In the last chapter, in which the author had the opportunity to close with a great laugh if his intentions were to produce a funny book, he passes it up and leaves us with the feeling that Lázaro continues to suppress his true emotions and continues to live *sin entregarse a la risa.*

---

6. We use this colloquial phrase in order to convey the same cynicism that the author no doubt intended. The Spanish phrase to which we refer is: "Señor, le dixe, yo determiné de arrimarme á los buenos" (263).

These episodes through which the *pícaro* passes cause irreparable damage to him. So much so that they destroy him. He becomes an empty carcass. He stops fighting, moving and inventing. He surrenders to *abulia*. And lest some be misled, this does not typify *la descansada vida* of which Fray Luis speaks. The *pícaro's* life in the end is still full of turmoil, but, like the laughter, the turmoil has subsided beneath the surface. When the author has Lazarillo accept his environment, has him surrender to the cancerous current of life as typified by the clergy of sixteenth-century Spain, to us he predicts the trajectory that Spain is to follow for the next three hundred years. Here in *Lazarillo*, the creeping cancer has already started, the cancer that has nearly destroyed Spain.

The impression we get is that the writing of the book has not served as an escape valve for the author, as it has for all of his characters with one exception, Lázaro himself. Lázaro, who to us seems to be living a life parallel to Spain's, is left in a state of arrested emotion. Unable to laugh and thereby experience emotional release from his tensions, he succumbs to *abulia*. It appears now that Lázaro's lack of laughter is a reflection of the author's own sad meditation on the fate of Spain. The fact is that the protagonist cannot detach himself emotionally from his role because the author, his creator, is too intensely aware of Spain's ills.[7] This is the story of laughter in the *Lazarillo*. In a way it is the very negation of laughter.[8]

---

7. As Bergson points out, in order to laugh at something or someone, you have to detach yourself, if only momentarily:

"Je voudrais signaler maintenant, comme un symptôme non moins digne de remarque, l'insensibilité qui accompagne d'ordinaíre le rire. Il semble que le comique ne puisse produire son ébranlement qu'à la condition de tomber sur une surface d'âme bien calme, bien unie. L'indifférence est son milieu naturel. Le rire n'a pas de plus grand ennemi que l'émotion. Je ne veux pas dire que nous ne puissions rire d'une personne qui nous inspire de la pitié, par exemple, ou même de l'affection; seulement alors, pour quelques instants, il faudra oublier cette affection, faire taire cette pitié." Henri Bergson, *Le rire*, 13th ed. (Paris: Librairie Félix Alcan, 1914). pp. 4–5.

8. "La novela picaresca es en su forma extrema una literatura corrosiva, compuesta con puras negaciones, empujada por su pesimismo preconcibido, que hace inventario escrupuloso de los males por la tierra esparcidos, sin órgano para percibir armonías ni optimidades. Es un arte, y aquí hallo su mayor defecto, que no tiene independencia estética; necesíta de la realidad fuera de ella, de la cual es ella crítica, de la que vice como carcoma de la madera." José Ortega y Gasset, *Obras completas*, 4th ed. (Madrid: Revista de Occidente, 1957), II, 124.

DAVID GITLITZ

Inquisition Confessions
and *Lazarillo de Tormes*[†]

The sixteenth-century Spanish literary landscape is peopled with
various forms of autobiography: discoverers', soldiers' or conquistadors' memoirs,[1] administrative reports,[2] travelers' reports,[3] confessional narrations,[4] and—in a realm less pretentious of "objective
truth"—picaresque novels. Though all of these exhibit some literary aspects, all of these various narrations were first and foremost
reports; that is, as González-Echevarría emphasizes throughout his
article, their rhetorical conventions were framed by the ubiquitous
sixteenth-century genre of the official *relación* (The Law . . .).
Within this context they responded to an institutional request—
either implied or explicit—for an accounting of the circumstances
of the writer's experiences. The expectation is clearly put in the Prologue to the fictionalized autobiography *Lazarillo de Tormes:* "Vuestra merced escribe se le escriba y relate el caso muy por extenso"
(89). The writer's responsibility when faced with such a request is
equally clear: the writer becomes a reporter, crafting a response "por
que se tenga entera noticia de mi persona" (89). In this reportorial
relationship the reporter's position is one of subordination to the
addressee (Levisi, *Golden Age Autobiography* 113). This inequality
of power, and the resulting dependency of the writer on the reader,
leaves the narrator in a precarious state.

Nowhere is this more true than in the autobiographical confessions to the tribunals of the Inquisition which become such an

[†] From David Gitlitz, "Inquisition Confessions and *Lazarillo de Tormes*," *Hispanic Review*
68.1 (2000): 53–74. Reprinted by permission of the publisher, University of Pennsylvania
Press.

1. Margarita Levisi notes the "memorial de servicios" model for three 16th-century military memoirs, those of Jerónimo de Pasamonte, Alonso de Contreras and Miguel de Castro (Autoblografias . . . , 236; see also "Golden Age Autobiography" 99). Even though
most of these were "documentos privados dirigidos a la propia familia o cuanto más a
un grupo restringido de lectores, que por diversas razones deben ser informados de los
acontecimientos ocurridos a sus autores" (14), and were not published until this century, they share the general characteristics we are describing.

I want to thank Sidonie Smith, Walter Barker, and Linda Davidson for critiquing
early drafts of this paper, and the participants in The Howard Gilman International
Colloquium on The Spanish-Jewish Cultural Interaction, where a later version was first
presented, for their comments.

2. See González-Echevarría, *"Humanismo, retórica y las crónicas de la conquista",* and
"The Law of the Letter" for discussions of the *relación* and of the influence of the reper-
torial style of sixteenth-century *letrados* on a variety of authors (Pané, Columbus, Bernal Días, Cortés), literary genres, and particularly *Lazarillo de Tormes.*

3. "Levisi distinguishes between these books, which tend to narrate "hechos observados,"
and soldiers' tales that portray "hechos vividos" (241).

4. Saint Teresa de Avlla's *Su vida* is notable. See also Sor María de San Jerónimo.

important part of the Spanish psychic landscape from the 1480s on, which is to say, in the decades just preceding the boom in autobiographical literature. In fact, over the next two hundred years these confessions may be the most ubiquitous form of the autobiographic genre, comprising tens of thousands of *curricula vitae* narrated to the investigators of the Spanish Inquisition. Although these reports are not generally considered literary documents, they bear many striking similarities to the other forms of report/autobiography with which they are contemporary. Indeed, the exigencies of coping with life in a church-police state, in which at any moment any individual might be ordered to lay out in the form of a *caso* the most intimate details of his life, may well have been one stimulus for the development of the autobiographical genre in sixteenth-century Spain. My point is that the likelihood of being called to account—at least for intellectuals and conversos—tended to fragment one's concept of self by requiring one to be constantly aware of how one appeared to others, and to be prepared at any moment to recount the edited version of one's life to an adversarial higher power. In this atmosphere, the ingrained rhetorical techniques of disclosure and evasion, strategies of self-promotion and vindication, and habits of incessant self-monitoring with their associated hyper-consciousness of one's identity as a reportorial voice, so harrowed the psychic soil of Spain that the autobiographical genres easily took root.

Inquisition dossiers from the 1480s to the 1680s abound with confessions, that is, with transcriptions of focused narrated autobiographies. When the Holy Office began to gather data in a new district, it customarily proclaimed a period of grace during which Catholics[5] were required to come forth and confess—that is, testify—to any heretical acts of deed or of speech of which they might have notice. These included acts which they themselves might have committed, or acts which they had witnessed, or knew or suspected that others might have witnessed. The carrot which led people to testify during the grace period was the promise of lighter punishment for freely confessed transgressions, which is to say that confessions voluntarily elicited during that period constituted a kind of plea bargaining. During the early years of the Inquisition, the grace period confessions tend to exhibit a kind of artless naiveté with which the witnesses describe what they had done or seen, and try to sidestep any personal responsibility for culpable acts. These early outpourings are transparent windows through which the victims' terror and frantic maneuverings can be clearly seen. Later, when all the roles had become somewhat ritualized, and the consequences

5. Before 1492 Spanish Jews were also required to report any Judaizing activities of their converso brethren.

of too-candid speech were widely understood, the confessions exhibit a more guarded hypocrisy. As Gilman pointed out, with respect to the Fernando de Rojas family, "rigid masking of the inner self, calculated conformity, unremitting self-observation induced in these first dwellers in the shadow of the Inquisition states of extreme tension and instability. Later on, hypocrisy was to become a second nature" (85–86).

But even with these generational distinctions, a constant theme of these confessions is their concern for minimizing the potentially negative consequences of confession. In practice, three strategic considerations influenced how people told their stories. The first strategy was that the confession had to be true-seeming; that is, internally consistent, psychologically convincing, and seemingly anchored in verifiable events.[6] The semblance of verifiability was crucial, for any statement about an event to which there was more than one witness ran the risk of incurring contradiction. And the confession had to appear comprehensive and complete, for obvious gaps invited the Inquisitors to use torture to elicit a fuller confession. Second, and within the restrictions imposed by the need to project a sense of completeness and verifiability, the confession had to be strategically focused: highlighting virtuous acts, admitting to just enough sin so as to leave Inquisitors satisfied with the results of their inquiry and without whetting their appetites for more, and omitting incriminating details without seeming to do so. Third, wherever possible, responsibility for negative actions had to be shifted to third parties, either to someone they did not care about very much, or to loved ones who were already safely dead or emigrated. Let us look briefly at some of these dissimulation strategies.

On October 9, 1483, during the grace period, María González appeared before a tribunal in Ciudad Real to report about her Judaizing activities in the late 1450s, before the founding of the Inquisition that made such activities mortally dangerous. María's first strategy was to affect—as the scribe put it—an air of *gran arrepentimiento y coniración* (Beinart 1: 71). Her second was to shift as much blame as possible to her husband. She claimed that at the time they were first married, they were both observant Catholics, but that in the mid 1460s her husband began to Judaize. María claimed that she attempted to resist, but that her husband employed coercion. "Porque yo no queria seguir su camino malo quel llevara, me dio muy muchas feridas," she told Inquisitors. "Me fiso contra mi voluntad que non filase el sábado." He forced her to eat forbidden food: "non la queria comer . . . por muchas feridas que me dio, alguna ves me

---

6. For Elizabeth Bruss, this apparent verifiability, that is, the assumption on the part of the reader that the writer believes that the depicted events are "true" and at least potentially verifiable, is one of the defining characteristics of autobiography (11).

la fasia comer." The same thing happened at Passover: "me fis coser pan çençeño dos o tres veses e contra mi voluntad me lo hizo comer, por non pasar mala vida" (1:72). In her extensive confession, which went on through several interviews, she stressed her heroic resolve to remain Catholic, claiming that several times her husband left her, and then returned to try to get her to emigrate with him, but that she resisted.

But this strategy was to no avail, for enough of María González' neighbors and family members testified to her willing Judaizing activities that she was jailed, and seven weeks after her initial confession, was brought from her call to testify again. Here her first instinct was to deny everything, and to protest the injustice of the interrogation: I am not a heretic; the *fiscal* says that I was intentionally misleading in my first confession, but I was not. Everything I said was true, and I am a true Catholic.

But now María was faced with some specific accusations, building on her initial free but incomplete confession. Didn't she participate in Jewish prayer services? Never . . . Well, not frequently . . . But then even if I did, "mi marido me las faria oyr del . . . et despues de aquello me arrepenty et non las quise oyr." Didn't their children receive a Jewish education? No . . . Well, maybe . . . But if they did, "la reçeberian de su padre et non de mi, et a mas, yo gelo retraeria, et como al su padre convenga dotrinar a los fijos, paresçe, segund dicho es, que yo non seria en lo tal." When asked if she ever ate chicken during Lent, María's blame-shifting strategy took three paths: indignation ("digo que nunca Dios quiera ni mande que yo tal gallina comi en tal dia"); denial ("falso testimonio que me fue levantado"); and logic ("no es de creer que persona que discreçion e juysio toviese, en tal dia, syn grandisyma cabsa de enfermedad, lo tal atentase a faser") (1: 75). But it was all to no avail, for María was found guilty of being an accomplice to her husband's Judaizing activities, and in 1484 was burned at the stake.

These same three strategies appear over and over again in the Ciudad Real trials. Juan González Daza responded with indignation when he was accused in 1483 of praying like a Jew: "niego yo aver ydo a oyr las que dise . . . ni plega a Dios tal jamas me ouiese pasado por pesar mio" (1: 137).

In his confession during Grace, Juan de Fez tried to shift the blame for his Judaizing to his widowed mother's lover Alonso Martínez, who made her "herrar contra la Santa Fe Catolica; e que yo era de 17 años como la fiso herrar, e ella a mi, fasta que yo oue veynte e çinco años" (1: 206).

Inés de Mérida, arrested in 1513, said that she Judaized only because her mother swore at her, mistreated her and beat her: "la dicha su madre reñía a esta confesante e le daba con lo que esta confesante tenía en la mano" (3: 360). Her mother and sisters "non la dexaban salir de casa ni yr a misa, e que la llamavan loca e dezian que hera loca, e non la dexaban salir de casa" (3: 362). Inés also adduced ignorance as a defense, claiming that "no sabia esta confesante sy lo susodicho hera bueno ni malo, hasta que el señor inquisidor Mariana fue a Ciudad Real (3: 362).

Similarly Leonor de la Oliva blamed her Judaizing on coercion from her older siblings, particulary a brother who was deceased by the time of her 1523 trial: "por industria deste yo ayune algunas vezes." She protested that as a woman in a male-dominated world she did not have the free will to refuse to Judaize: "E porque en estas çerimonias como muger en ellas ynpuesta herre por yndustria deste mi hermano falesçido" (3: 680).

At this juncture it is important to be clear about the principal differences between inquisitorial and accusatorial judicial processes, and to remember that the Santo Oficio, despite its use of prosecuting and defense attorneys, was an archetypal inquisitorial process. In accusatorial processes, the accuser and judge are distinct and separate; specific charges are brought against the accused, and the prosecutor must prove the charges to the satisfaction of the judge by means of presenting independent, verifiable evidence. Proceedings are generally open. The accused is considered innocent until proven guilty. The use of torture is generally excluded, on the logical ground that employing coercion to extract a confession of guilt presupposes an assumption of that guilt. Accusatory procedure generally reaches conclusion—guilty, or innocent by virtue of exoneration or insufficiency of evidence—and is thus closed-ended.

Inquisition processes could not be more different. They are less deliberative than investigatory. The accused is the focal point of questioning, and, since confession is the goal, a variety of psychologically coercive techniques,[7] and even torture, are justified. Hearsay evidence and rumor are welcomed as aids to interrogation. Generally there are no specific charges, but rather the judicial apparatus goes fishing in order to specify and clarify the accusations. The aim is to contrive a convincing indictment, which becomes tantamount to a statement of summary judgment. Inquisitions are invariably open-ended, for there is always the possibility of more to confess (Kirschenbaum 3–5). In Spain, as we know, they were so open-ended that they transcended the grave, for finding the dead

---

7. For insights into how these techniques are still used to elicit "voluntary" confessions, see Kamisar. Talmudic law, by virtue of contrast, bans as evidence confessions of any sort, on the grounds that it is impossible to determine the degree of psychological coercion, including self-imposed coercion, that was used to elicit the confession (Kirschenbaum 17).

grandmother guilty legitimized the Inquisition's confiscating the live grandson's property.

The mere presence of the Inquisition, and the very real possibility that one might be called to account—completely—for the particulars of one's life, made every living soul a potential autobiographer. From 1480 through the next two hundred or so years, Spaniards, and particularly Spanish conversos, who were suspect by nature of their lineage, had to keep a mental notebook of everything they had done, and when, and with whom; they had to keep a mental log of the events they had witnessed, and what they might mean; of the conversations—first hand, second hand, third hand—to which they had been party. Moreover, it was imperative to keep running mental track of the implications of all of these events for their own life, and be attentive to how others might interpret their actions or their spiritual development. They became—very actively—the first reader of their life's events. If they were of a sincerely religious nature, and believed in divine judgment and retribution, they shaped those events, as they were recalling them, in the way that they believed would earn them a seat in Heaven (Catholic), or would lead them to be considered *tzadik* by the Almighty (Jewish, or crypto-Jewish).

Because they were at very least outwardly Catholic, they were required periodically to narrate those same events to their confessor. But first, of course, they mentally edited those events, because the confessor—their life's second reader—held vast power over them. This was not only the power to grant or withhold absolution, the transcendental power vested in priests by the Church, but also the power to call their deeds and thoughts to the attention of the wider public of the Holy Office, invested by the king and the papacy with control of their life and property in addition to their immortal soul.

Mentally, then, people kept at least two sets of books: the book of their life as they perceived it, and as they hoped the all-seeing divine judge would view it, and the book of their life as they hoped the temporal judges might read it, the temporal Judges being the neighbors and servants, the business acquaintances and clergy—those people whom Ferlinghetti called the "priests and other patrolmen" (88)—who might at any moment narrate their life to the Inquisition.

In this environment, at least for conversos whose Jewish background attracted attention, or whose crypto-Jewish practices courted the disaster of disclosure, paranoia made perfectly good sense. People *were* out to get them. Fear was pervasive, for any action could be misconstrued, and the watchers were everywhere.[8] The

8. The terror that awareness of the omnipresent watchers induced comes through clearly in Solomon Usque's 1553 description of converso reaction to the Portuguese Inquisition: "People are filled with such fear of this beast that they glance furtively in all

purity-of-blood statutes required people to mask their past; the Inquisition required them to be circumspect about their present. They had to write the past life that they remembered and the current life that they were living for themselves and their divine judge and for their public readers all at the same time. They had to be a private person and simultaneously wear a public persona. In Gilman's phrase, one had "constantly to observe oneself from an alien point of view, that of the watchers from without" (104).[9] They had to sit there on their own shoulder, like Long John Silver's parrot or Alonso Quijano's Cide Hamete Benengeli, and watch themselves act. They had to live and plead the case of their life simultaneously.

Thus from the 1480s over the next several generations, Spaniards had to train themselves to think autobiographically. For intellectuals, and for conversos of any rank or station or religious predilection, survival required habits of thought which prepared one to give autobiographical account on demand. The Inquisition confessions which are responses to those demands not surprisingly have a number of features in common with the autobiographical report genres which emerge during those years.

One common feature, in addition to their tendency toward first person narration,[1] is the fact that they relate the details of an individual's life to an authority of some sort, an addressee who has commissioned (or at least who is eager to receive) the report. Moreover, the reporter, the enunciator of the true facts of the case in question, invariably has an ax of some sort to grind: he or she seeks reward, or seeks to avoid punishment, or is under some sort of compulsion from a legal or spiritual authority to give account of him or herself. The narrative voice is compromised, not disinterested. The narrative is an assertion of self meant to persuade, to self-portray not merely as an expression of ego, or a compulsion to leave a presumably true record for posterity, but rather as a lobbying document, a means toward an end. The end governs those facts which are reported and those which

---

directions in the streets to see if it is nearby, and walk and stop in fear, their hearts tremulous and fluttering like the leaves of a tree, afraid that it will attack them. Whenever this animal strikes a blow, no matter how far away it is, all feel it as a blow in the pit of their stomachs" (200).

9. Moreover, as the psychiatrist R. D. Laing, has pointed out, this "dialog" between self and other is a process fundamental to the way humans define themselves "self-identity ('I' looking at 'me') is constituted not only by our looking at ourselves, but also by our looking at others looking at us and our reconstitution of an alternation of these views of others about us" (cited by Bruss 13).

1. Not all autobiographies are rendered in the first person. Since the "I" of autobiography has to an extent been objectified through the processes of recall and the imposition or narrative structure, Gunn notes that some autobiographers feel more comfortable with the third-person pronoun (6). Elbaz goes further, arguing that the act of rendering a former "persona" (or of selecting among "personne") in language by necessity relegates "self" to the status of third person, even when adopting the "I" mode of narration (12). This perspective blurs the differences between confessions to the Holy Tribunal which were recorded by scribes in the first-person and those recorded in the the third-person.

are omitted.[2] The end governs the context in which they are framed, the rhetorical palate with which they are colored, and the nuances to which, or away from which, the readers' attention is drawn.

The two commonly perceived subdivisions of the report genre are seemingly quite disparate in shape and in focus, even though in the essence of their dialog between the writer and the readers they prove to be quite similar, and in fact both have elements in common with Inquisition confessions. The first type is the report which looks outward to events (a traveler's journey to a newly discovered territory, a soldier's memorandum about the details of a conquest, an attorney's summation of the facts of a legally troubling event). Presumably the audience mainly wants to know what happened, and the reporter is mostly just the vehicle.

The second type of report looks inward to spiritual processes, what Gusdorf calls the "private face of existence" (37), and includes the many varieties of confessional literature. Here the audience is presumed to want to know how the reporter felt and understood and reacted to the internal and external stimuli in their life, and the reporter's psychological history is foregrounded as he or she struggles to depict the sequence of influences on his or her soul.

The first type tends to follow events in their chronological sequence, and to narrate and interpret them from the point of view of the witness or the participant. Their claim to the validity of truth purportedly rests on the accuracy and objectivity of the reporter, who must allow for the fact that the principal events in his narration will be verifiable by other "objective" observers of the same events. The second type, the confessional, does not rely on external verification of facts, but rather on the apparent coherence of the psychological and spiritual introspection being undertaken, and its conformity to accepted patterns of religious spirituality.

Yet in fact, both of these subgenres of the report depend for credibility on how rhetorically convincing they are, on how well they create the impression of verifiability, and how psychologically coherent they appear to be. In the final analysis, truth is identical to what seems true: verity and verisimilitude are one and the same. In this regard Augustine's confessions, Bernal Díaz' report of the conquest of Tenochtitlán, and the explanations offered on the witness stand by any accused felon are similar: they are true insofar as they seem true, insofar as the jury—that is, the reader—holds them to be true.

But the jury is in fact juries, for the stories at the heart of each of these reports are directed at a variety of readers, not all of whom

2. Even Saint Teresa acknowledges that church pressure has resulted in her omitting certain important matters from her autobiography, leading to Louis Renza's observation that her narration is really a "secondary revision, a public version of a 'life' being silently and coterminously traced in her mind" (284).

share the same agendas. And therefore the reporter's story is by necessity passed through a number of filters.

The first reader is, as we have seen, the reporter him- or herself. The reporter, from a perspective of here and now, and some degree of maturity, insight and reflection,[3] and in some cases self-delusion,[4] "reads" the assemblage of scattered past events displayed in his or her memory, and selects from them those which are judged best to tell the intended story. Even at this first level of readership, self-readership, perspectives tend to be multiplied, for even in the most straightforward of autobiographies three entities coincide and share a single name. There are significant differences between the reconstructed protagonist of the remembered events (the "Lazarillos"), the narrative voice assumed in retelling those events (the "Lázaros"), and the authorial ego (in the case of the *Lazarillo*, anonymous) standing above the stage and pulling the strings of both the protagonist and the reporter.[5]

Reporters select events with respect to a number of criteria. One is their representationality, the intensity with which they characterize a particular happenstance or character trait or motivation. Autobiography (or for that matter any biography or historical writing) depends upon synecdoche, the carefully chosen example which represents emblematically a much larger reality (Fernández 8). A second criterion is their relevance to the author's implied purpose, which, broadly, is to display the narrator to the public in the best possible light: exemplifying virtues, masking faults, side-stepping responsibility for failures and underscoring credit for successes. A third criterion is their effect on the rhetorical credibility of the narration: the verisimilitude of spiritual experience, or the degree to which the events are or seem verifiable.

As we have noted, the second reader of the autobiographical report is the person or persons to whom it is explicitly addressed: St. Teresa's confessor, the Consejo de Indias or one of the royal councils, the jury, or some other version of Lázaro's "Vuesa Merced." To a very great extent this addressee plays an active role in shaping the report itself, for the reporter's assumptions about the expectations of the second reader perforce govern the choices about what material to include, and what rhetorical slant to give it. Here are three examples. The first relates to selection of episodes: if the reporter assumes that the addressee expects him to relate the circumstances of his lineage, his birth, and his childhood education, then these will

---

3. Autobiography inevitably involves "a certain mode of self-placing in relation to the auto-biographer's past and from a particular standpoint in his or her present." (Gunn 16).

4. An autobiography, in Gusdorf's phrase, displays an individual "not as he was, not as he is, but as he believes and wishes himself to be and to have been" (45).

5. For a fuller discussion of these concepts see Eakin's "Foreword" to Lejeune; Bruss 10–11; and Paul Smith 105.

appear in his first chapter; if the Inquisitor wants instances of Sabbath observances, then this is what the confessor will report. The second impacts structure and style: if the author thinks the addressee expects dimly remembered conversations from long-ago times to be rendered as dialog, they will be. The third influences both the philosophical framework of the report and its tone; if the reporter expects the reader to have each of the narrated moral choices related to homilies of Christian doctrine, then they will be. These examples are easily multiplied, for in the broadest sense the real or hypothetical audiences' cultural codes are by necessity in constant dialog with autobiographical authors, who simultaneously "manipulate and are manipulated by their implied readers" (S. Smith 6).

One label for the product of all these expectations is genre; the generic constraints which shape an author's[6] work are his or her own preconceptions (i.e., assumptions about the audience's preferences) about what ought to be in the work, and how it ought to look. Prior literary models, too, influence every author's sense of what should go into his or her creation, and how it should be treated.[7] Generic expectations may play out in the conscious designs of the author/reporter, of course, but they may also reflect the subconsciously shared culture of beliefs and taboos prevalent in the society to which both writer and reader belong. In other words, the autobiographical reporter's conscience, as well as his or her ideological, political, aesthetic and strategic judgments, derive from the "individual's reconstruction of the community's gaze" (Fernández 22). In these ways the readers of the "relación" of a person's life are not only observers of the writer's identity, they help to shape that identity.[8]

Most Inquisition confessions are superb examples of reports shaped by the reporter's assumptions about the addressee's expectations. These narrations tend to be so much more focused than the other varieties of reportorial autobiography we are discussing, because the expectations of the interrogators were so much more explicit. The initial call to confess was documented in an Edict of Grace, which tabulated customs indicative of Judaizing in such a way as to provide Iberian crypto-Jews with not only a handbook for their

6. While generic expectations govern the writer, they have a similar effect on the reader. In Peter Dunn's formulation, "genre is that which enables us to make a provisional recognition of the thing and hence to adopt a decision as to what is the appropriate attitude of expectancy" (22).

7. Looked at from the other side, from the point of view of the reader, genre "does not tell us the style or construction of a text as much as how we should expect to 'take' that style or mode of construction—what force it should have for us" (Bruss 4).

8. In Fernández' words, "identity—be it generic or individual identity—[is] something that is invented, forged, precisely through tension and dialogue with those historical and social circumstances, those models, those third persons," and thus a repressive institution such as the Inquisition "not only represses individuals, it also plays an important role in the historical articulation of what individuals are or should be" (10–11).

own religious observances but also a guide to the sorts of behaviors
they were expected to confess to the tribunals of the Holy Office.
Should they be arrested, the first round of involuntary confession
was cued by the *monición*, a general instruction to give the particulars of one's family state (genealogy, age, domicile, profession, mar-
ital state) and to confess everything that one might have done or said
or heard said that might be construed as heretical. The followup
interrogation was guided in part by the initial confession, and in part
by a protocol of questions geared to the various categories of Judaizing customs that are so comprehensively enumerated in the Edicts
of Grace.[9]

For conversos, then, the Inquisition, the explicit "second reader"
of the report of their lives, was a controlling force that imposed the
nature of the autobiography they were required to report. The communities of crypto-Jews struggling to maintain the vestigial customs
of their Jewish ancestors, and the Inquisitors resolutely mapping the
extent and influence of crypto-Jewish culture, were dealing from the
same deck of expectations. Whether a particular behavior was
labeled belief or taboo depended on which side of the table one was
sitting on. But players on both sides tended to give preeminence to
transgressions that fit their shared pattern of expectations.[1]

In addition to the explicit addressee of the report, a third-level
audience for the majority of these reportorial autobiographies was
the broader public who would presumably experience the work when
it was published, or passed widely around.[2] The unfortunate witnesses narrating their lives to the Inquisition had little thought that
their depositions would be read by anyone outside the Holy Office;
but the soldiers, travelers, conquistadors and mystics putting the
record of their lives into words clearly anticipated a readership
broader than the officials whom they explicitly address. This third-
level audience are people like the plural readers referenced in the
prologue to *Lazarillo de Tormes* when the author writes that "no me

9. Good examples of a *monición* and a schedule of follow-up questions are given by López
   Martínez (390, 429–32). The information elicited by the *monición* coincided with that
   of the *relación* in which the writer first states the particulars of his family background
   and geographic origin before describing for the record the events of the case he is report-
   ing (González-Echeverría 112).
1. This process governed what was included or omitted in the reports; the meaning given
   to a particular set of events—as with all ethnographic observation—was inevitably influenced by the specific cultural codes of the observer. Crypto-Jews describing clandes-
   tine Passover *seders* report distributing matza, and making a blessing over wine, as
   vestigial remnants of ancient Jewish custom; summation statements in Inquisition dossiers frequently allege deliberate and malicious parody of the Christian sacraments.
2. The passage of time divides these third-level readers into two groups: the author's con-
   temporaries, whose imagined expectations influence how the author shapes his or her
   words, and ourselves, who from the perspective of history—that is, knowing or thinking we know how it all comes out—gain a certain ironic distance.

pesara que hayan parte y se huelguen con ello todos los que en ella
algún gusto hallaren, y vean que vive un hombre con tantas fortunas, peligros y adversidades" (89). The effect on the narrated text of
the generic expectations of the broader public could be similar to
those of the addressee, but there are legions of examples when they
were different.

For writers, this potential disjuncture was rich in opportunities
for satire, irony, and other sardonic rhetorical approaches. The
classic example is the *Lazarillo*, where it is precisely the difference
between what the reporter-commentator Lázaro presumably wants
Vuesa Merced to read, and what the anonymous author presumably
wants the greater public to read, that gives the book its rich ironic
dimensions.

These texts have a fourth reader as well. In Catholic Golden Age
Spain, always cognizant of the inevitability of death, final judgment
and the consequences of eternity, the implied fourth "reader" is the
divine judge, or at least the transcendental, immutable moral standards by which all acts must be evaluated.[3] Moreover, the making
of the case to put before the divine judge requires the reporter to
write from a perspective of completion and of knowledgeable reflection. The reporter says "in looking at how I was then, before my
enlightenment, before my 'conversion,' from where I am now, and
in the light of my current true understanding of immutable moral
values, the experiences of my life are to be evaluated as follows. . . ."
But of course inherent in this view of reflective self-examination are
the usual fallacies of hindsight: one tends to ascribe meanings to
incidents which, when one was living them, were either devoid of
meaning, or whose meanings were unclear. One tends to gloss over
the fact that individual events generally have multiple potential outcomes, and that only from the perspective of the present, when the
single resultant outcome is visible, do the original events cast their
aura of inevitability. In addition, as one judges the moral weight of
the outcomes in one's life, it is tempting to perceive moments when
one could have made moral choices leading to other outcomes,
even when decision points were imperceptible or unavailable to a
person at the time.

To recapitulate, then: the text that the reporter writes, or the
confessional testimony that a witness deposes, is the product of the

---

3. As Gusdorf put it, in the light of the Christian sense of the eternal, every "Christian
destiny unfolds as a dialogue of the soul with God in which, right up to the end, every
action, every initiative of thought or of conduct, can call everything back into question.
Each man is accountable for his own existence, and intentions weigh as heavily as
acts—whence a new fascination with the secret springs of personal life" (32).

narrator's assimilation of the expectations of at least four sorts of "readers." The autobiographical case, that is to say the story line of the reporter's vindication document, is first assembled in the remembering eye of the author, and is then reported to the jury of the explicit powerful addressee and to the implied broader public, which includes historical posterity, and to the ahistorical divine judge whose ultimate decisions brook no appeal. For the literary authorial voice, the disjunctures between life-when-lived in a "then" in which the writer did not fully understand the conditions of the world or of his or her acts, and life-as-reinterpreted from the point of view of a "now" in which the writer presumably has the knowledge, insights, and moral perspective to make coherent and to validate the disparate events of his or her life, are precisely what permit the writer—for example, in the picaresque[4]—to speak of the past with conscious irony, condescension, pity, or amusement (Starobinskl 83).[5]

In the Inquisition confessions themselves, we often perceive ironies where the autobiographical reporters probably did not intend them. The first-level reader of events, the authorial ego who as he or she read edited the material for broader consumption, desperately tried to shift the emphasis from the reporter as guilty party to the reporter as innocent, or as victim. The second-level addressee, seated at the Holy Office's table of judgment, tended to see the Judaizing practices as indicative of malice aforethought, or, in Gilman's phrase, to read adherence to "a traditional way of life as a conscious, intentionally perpetrated crime" (74). On the other hand we—who are part of the broad, third-level readership which is posterity—interpret the narrated life quite differently. We are likely to empathize with the reporter's struggles to escape martyrdom and financial ruin, and—depending on our assessment of the degree of conscious control the reporter exerts over the details of his report—tend to interpret his evasive techniques as strategic choices, as hypocrisy, or as self-delusion.

4. The coexistence in picaresque novels of at least two versions—in *Lazarillo de Tormes* the "relación" read by Vuesa Merced and the "Vida" read by ourselves—has been noted by several critics, most recently Peter Dunn (45). For *Lazarillo* as a parody of a classic Christian confession see Jauss (1959) and Gómez Mariana, who notes its "práctica discursiva confession de carácter jurídico" (46).

5. Contributing to this doubling of perspective is the clash between two types of what Elbaz calls "discursive space": the "dominant practices which constitute the bulk of signifying practices within a social whole (the hegemonic mode, the commonsensical, the thinkable and the sayable, in any given society)"—which is to say the habitual values and modes of expression which characterize the social world from which the author is struggling to emancipate him or herself—and the newly "emerging practices which will solidify over time and come to compose the new discursive space, thus displacing the previous dominance" (viii)—in other words, the values and modes of discourse which the author is espousing in direct opposition to the rejected, prior rhetorical codes. The fact that irony is such a potent weapon in this process may help explain its emergence as a newly dominant mode of expression in the first half of the sixteenth century, particularly among converse writers.

Almost any case drawn from the thousands in the Inquisition dossiers could illustrate these points. But the 1635 confession of the Portuguese Estevan de Ares de Fonseca in Madrid (Caro Baroja 3: 332–36) not only provides several sterling examples, it also reflects the episodic "mozo de muchos amos" structure of the picaresque. At his initial audience, inquisitors specifically admonished Ares to state "donde ha residido que ocupaciones ha tenido y a q a venido a esta corte y por orden de quien." His answer—taken down in third person by the Tribunal's scribe—made clear his crypto-Jewish activities.

Ares grew up in Pinhel and Trancoso, and was sent to study Latin in Lisbon and then several other cities. Arrested for Judaizing in the Portuguese capital, he alleged ingenuously that he confessed to minor heresies then only so that they would reconcile him and let him go: "por guardar la vida confeso en la dicha Inq.ᵒⁿ de Lisboa que era Judio, siendo la verdad que ni aun saber que los avia ni en q consistia el serlo no avia llegado a su notcia." However, he said that in jail in Lisbon he began to be courted by conversionist crypto-Jews who wanted him to join them in their beliefs. There follows a devastatingly long list of examples of Ares' Judaizing practices after his release from prison, accompanied by a series of disclaimers of the "they-made-me-do-it" sort.

At first Ares said that "no dió oydo ni condescendio" to his friends' invitations to become openly Jewish, but instead fled to Spain where for five or six years he worked in Seville, Madrid, and other Spanish cities. But because he had family connections in Bayonne he went there, where all his friends and relatives tried—he alleged unsuccessfully—to get him to renounce his Catholicism. The text of the confession makes clear that Ares was motivated mainly by economic concerns, but he casts his travels and his relationships with friends and family members in religious terms. When he asked French relatives for money to return to Spain, he said that they whisked him off to Amsterdam where they would have a better chance of persuading him to become a Jew. He claims that they promised him material help ("le darian con que pudiese pasar") in hopes that he would convert, and they even tried to persuade him to allow himself to be circumcised, "porque era hijo de madre descendiente de Israel," and since he was about to undertake a sea voyage "si moria en la mar no se podia salvar si no lo estava y que era bien llevarse la marca del Señor." Ares claims that he withstood their pressure for six months, but that when the Amsterdam Jews excommunicated him (i.e., would have nothing at all to do with him), after sixteen days he caved in, had the operation done, and took the new name David.

In the next phase of his life he traveled as a Jew to Liorno, Venice, Trapana, Salonica, Italy, Turkey, and eventually back to Amsterdam, where he lived openly as a Jew for five years. In 1633 he went to Rouen, where—he claims—at his own initiative he was reconciled with the Church, even bringing his three-year-old son Isaac in to be baptized, and then later persuading his wife to bring herself back to the Church. The way Ares tells it, the French and Dutch Jewish/crypto-Jewish communities were a constant battleground between conversionist Christians and Jews, where he himself—although sometimes weak-willed—played mainly on the Christian team: "por persuasion de este t.⁰ vino en su compañia desde las dichas sinagogas de Olanda Emanuel Valencin judio nacido en Venecia en el Gueto della y se baptizo." But then later, to find work, Ares and Valencin went to Antwerp, where (he implies) in order to receive the support of the Jewish community there they again began to Judaize, and where the Jews promised him a captaincy in the expedition to wrest Pernambuco from the Portuguese.

Ares seems to want to paint himself as a reluctant victim, a reasonable man who caved in to extreme pressure from the Jewish communities outside of Iberia only when he had no other choices. Presumably the Holy Office saw him as a relapsed heretic, a criminally deliberate renegade from the true Catholic faith. While we, his distant third-level readers, are likely to see him as a Judaizing opportunist who gave lip service to Catholicism when it was to his short-term advantage to do so, who preferred Judaism, all things being equal and whose attempts to weasel out from responsibility for his actions seem more pathetic than evil.[6]

In the ways that these confessions to the Holy Office are transparently self-serving, so too are the other *memoriales, relaciones,* spiritual autobiographies, and travelers' tales of the Spanish Golden

6. A similar example is Juan de León's confession to the Mexican tribunal in 1642. León, also known as Salomón Machorro, had been arrested some months earlier, and had been instructed to prepare himself to tell his story. On June 12, he requested an audience. He said that at the age of two his parents took him to Liorno, where they forced him to attend Hebrew school, where "nunca la aprendió de buena voluntad," and where he only went because of the "muchos azotes" which they gave him. But he alleged that as soon as he reached the age of reason "se iba inclinando a ir a la escuelen de los católicos a oír la doctrina cristiana." When his parents found out they packed him off to Izmir with an uncle, who would presumably inculcate Judaism in him in isolation from Christian influence. Later captured by pirates and imprisoned in Algiers, he attended the synagogue to "complacer a los judíos," but he swore to the Inquisitors that he had resolved that if he was ever freed he would become Christian. When at last he found himself back in Italy, he returned to his mother (still a practicing Jew) in Liorno, only to find that his father had set off for the Indies. Following him to Cádiz, where he learned that his father had died, Muchorro went to Mexico, where he was sponsored in his settling-in by a group of crypto-Jewish women. He freely admitted that he had celebrated a number of Jewish holidays with these women, and he assumed that this is why he had been arrested. However, he wanted the Tribunal to know that there were mitigating circumstances: "aunque hacía los dichos ayunos con las dichas mujeres, lo clerto es que les daba a entender que los hacía, y ellas lo entendían así, porque se lo decían, pero que este confesante comía a escondidas y en su corazón no se tenía por observante de la dicha Ley, sino como católico cristiano como lo es" (Lewin 125–28).

Age. Their authors remember selectively, and they interpret remembered events with a purpose. They direct themselves to readers of high status and great power. They are the antithesis of disinterested: they all seek some sort of reward (money, title, prestige, acceptance,[7] or else the lessening of punishment). Because their self-advocacy is frequently so transparent, its valence is reversed and it becomes ironically self-destructive. Ares de Fonseca is not the weak-willed Christian he would have his readers take him for; his Inquisitors saw him and we see him as a crypto-Jew trying quite cynically to mitigate the consequences of his behavior. This process is the *modus operandi* of the first great picaresque novel, *Lazarillo de Tormes*. To cite just one emblematic example, the protagonist's father "pacedió persecutión por justicia"; but he suffers not for the sake of justice, as an innocent victim, as Lázaro avers to Vuesa Merced, but rather as a thief at the hands of the judicial system, as the anonymous author so clearly says to his broader public.[8]

In these narrations, the *yo* whose *caso* is on the block adopts a narrative persona who portrays a protagonist who is designed to persuade the jury of Inquisitors to do that *yo* as little harm as possible. The autobiographic reporters speak to their Inquisitors as Lázaro speaks to Vuesa Merced. Each one, supplicant and desperate for approval, constructs a Lazarillo who is designed to please, cajole, and lobby. Yet we—their wider public—perceive their inconsistencies and hypocrisies in ways that produce effects radically different from those the authors intended. Whether or not autobiographic reporters were structuring their *casos* explicitly for the Inquisition, or for any of the other numerous official Vuesas Mercedes in Spanish society positioned to receive their reports, the expectations of the Holy Office so infused the psychic landscape of sixteenth-century Iberia that it provided a narrative framework, a mode of conceiving and talking about self, that influenced all of the autobiographies of that century.[9]

---

7. Stephen Spender notes how "all confessions are from subject to object, from the individual to the community or creed. Even the most shamelessly revealed inner life pleads its cause before the moral system of an outer, objective life. One of the things that the most abysmal confessions prove is the incapacity of even the most outcast creature to be alone. Indeed, the essence of the confession is that the one who feels outcast pleads with humanity to relate his isolation to its wholeness. He pleads to be forgiven, condoned, even condemned, so long as he is brought back into the wholeness of people and things" (120).

8. Zahareas, extending this paradigm to the *Buscón*, notes that the ironic contradictions of the text are purposeful; that the protagonist "Is a clever liar whereas, at the same time, the narrator or social offences is brutally honest; the narrated life-story does not hide from readers outside the text, what the narrator was hiding from others inside the text" (140).

9. Adrienne Schizzano Mandel, in her discussion of the writings of Sor María de San Jerónimo, points out that the judicial structure itself "organizes" the conceptual space which the narrating "I" inhabits. "La structure judiciaira inquisitoriale lui organise cet espace concret où le *je* de Sor María pout s'inscrire comme personnage principale, lié à ses circonstances temporelles et historiques" (163).

Works Cited

Beinart, Haim. *Records of the Trials of the Spanish Inquisition in Ciudad Real.* Vol. 1: 1483–1485. Jerusalem: Israel National Academy of Sciences and Humanities, 1974.

———. *Records of the Trials of the Spanish Inquisition in Ciudad Real.* Vol. 2: 1494–1512. Jerusalem: Israel National Academy of Sciences and Humanities, 1977.

———. *Records of the Trials of the Spanish Inquisition in Ciudad Real.* Vol. 3: 1512–1527. Jerusalem: Israel National Academy of Sciences and Humanities, 1981.

Blecua, Alberto, ed. *Lazarillo de Tormes.* Madrid: Castalia, 1974.

Bruss, Elizabeth. *Autobiographical Acts.* Baltimore: Johns Hopkins UP, 1976.

Caro Baroja, Julio. *Los judíos en la España moderna y contemporánea.* 3 vols. Madrid: Ariel, 1961.

Dunn, Peter N. *Spanish Picaresque Fiction: A New Literary History.* Ithaca: Cornell UP, 1993.

Eakin, Paul John. Foreword. *On Autobiography.* By Philippe Lejeune. Minneapolis: U of Minnesota P, 1989.

Elbaz, Robert. *The Changing Nature of Self: A Critical Study of the Autobiographic Discourse.* Iowa City: U of Iowa P, 1987.

Ferlinghetti, Lawrence. *A Coney Island of the Mind.* Norfolk, CT: New Directions, 1955.

Fernández, James D. *Apology to Apostrophe: Autobiography and the Rhetoric of Self-Representation in Spain.* Durham: Duke UP, 1992.

Gilman, Stephen. *The Spain of Fernando de Rojas: The Intellectual and Social Landscape of "La Celestina."* Princeton: Princeton UP, 1972.

Gómez Moriana, Antonio. "La subversión del discurso ritual." *Imprévue* (Montpellier: Centre d'études et de récherches sociocritiques) 2 (1980): 37–67.

González-Echevarría, Roberto. "Humanismo, retórica y las crónicas de la conquista." *Isla de su vuelo fugitiva: ensayos críticos sobre literatura hispanoamericana.* Ed. Roberto González-Echevarría. Madrid: José Porrúa Turranzas, 1983. 9–25.

———. "The Law of the Letter. Garcilaso's *Commentaries* and the Origins of the Latin American Narrative." *Yale Journal of Criticism* 1 (1987): 107–31.

Gunn, Janet Varner. *Autobiography: Toward a Poetics of Experience.* Philadelphia: U of Pennsylvania P, 1982.

Gusdorf, Georges. "Conditions and Limits of Autobiography." *Autobiography: Essays Theoretical and Critical.* Ed. James Olney. Princeton: Princeton UP, 1980. 3–27.

Jauss, Hans Robert. "Ursprung und Bedeutung der Ich-Form im *Lazarillo de Tormes.*" *Romanistisches Jahrbuch* 10 (1959): 285–92.

Kamlsar, Yale. *Police Interrogation and Confessions, Truth, and the Law.* Ann Arbor: U of Michigan P, 1980.

Kirschenbaum, Aaron, *Self-Incrimination in Jewish Law.* New York: Burning Bush P, 1970.

Levisi, Margarita. *Autobiografías dei Siglo de Oro.* Madrid: Sociedad General Española de Librería, 1984.

———. "Golden Age Autobiography: The Soldiers." *Autobiography in Early Modern Spain.* Ed. Nicholas Spadaccini and Jenaro Talens. Minneapolls: Prisma Institute, 1988, 97–118.

Lewin, Boleslao. *Singular proceso de Salamón Machorro (Juan de León), Israelite liornés condenado por la Inquisición (México, 1650).* Buenos Aires: Julio Kaufman, 1977.

López Martínez, Nicolás. *Los judaizantes castellanos y la Inquisición en liempo de Isabel la Católica.* Burgos: Seminario Metropolitano de Burgos, 1954.

Mandel, Adrienne Schizzano. "Le proces inquisitoriale comme acte autobiographique." *L'autobiographie dans le monde hispanique.* Provence: U de Provence, 1980, 155–70.

Renza, Louis A. "The Veto of the Imagination: A Theory of Autobiography." *Autobiography: Essays Theoretical and Critical.* Ed. James Olney. Princeton: Princeton UP, 1980, 268–95.

Smith, Paul. *Discerning the Subject.* Minneapolis: U of Minnesota P, 1988.

Smith, Sidonie. *A Poetics of Women's Autobiography: Marginality and the Fictions of Self-Representation.* Bloomington: Indiana UP, 1987.

Spender, Stephen. "Confessions and Autobiography," *Autobiography: Essays Theoretical and Critical.* Ed. James Olney. Princeton: Princeton UP, 1980, 115–22.

Starobinski, Jean. "The Style of Autobiography." *Autobiography: Essays Theoretical and Critical.* Ed. James Olney. Princeton: Princeton UP, 198,. 73–83.

Usque, Solomon. *Consolation for the Tribulations of Israel.* Trans. Martin A. Cohen. Philadelphia: Jewish Publication Society of America, 1965.

Zahareas, Anthony N. "The Historical Function of Picaresque Autobiographies: Toward a History of Social Offenders." *Autobiography in Early Modern Spain.* Ed. Nicholas Spadaccini and Jenaro Talens. Minneapolis: Prisma Institute, 1988, 129–62.

GABRIEL H. LOVETT

Lazarillo de Tormes in Russia[†]

The fame of Spain's first picaresque novel, the *Lazarillo de Tormes*, has not been confined to Lazarillo's homeland. The book, whose authorship is still a mystery today, has enjoyed great success outside of the Iberian peninsula. It has been translated into many languages and has been widely read. Its first French version appeared in 1560, its first English version in 1586, the first German translation dates from 1617, the first Italian from 1622 and the first Portuguese from 1838.[1] Russia, too, has seen versions of the famous novel in its own language. Of these we have had access to two, one a translation that appeared in 1893 and that is the first Russian version of the novel[2] and the other a children's version that saw the light in 1938. The first came out in two installments (November-December, 1893) in a St Petersburg journal, the *Syevernyi Vyesinik*[3] (Northern Herald) and was the work of a certain I. Glivenko.[4] It bears the title *Lazarilyo iz Tormes* (Lazarillo from Tormes) with the subtitle *I yevo udachi i neudachi* (And his fortunes and adversities). Below this appears a statement in parentheses that it is a translation from Spanish. It is devoid of illustrations. In a foreword the translator, after pointing out that Lazarillo is the forerunner of the contemporary realistic novel, mentions the fact that the book was placed on the 1559 Inquisitorial *Index Expurgaiorius* and quotes a few appreciative lines from the preface to the expurgated edition of 1573 by the historiographer of the Court, Juan López de Velasco. He concludes the foreword by noting that the book, although it appeared almost four and a half centuries ago (sic), is still full of interest today and that every reader will read it with delight.

The 1938 version is in the form of a thin, approximately 6½ by 5 in. booklet, printed on rather rough paper, which was published by the *Tzentralnyi Komitet Vsesoyuznovo Leninskovo Kommunisticheskovo*

† From Gabriel H. Lovett, "'Lazarillo de Tormes' in Russia," *The Modern Language Journal* 36.4 (1952): 166–74. Reprinted with permission of Wiley.

1. See bibliography in H. J. Chaytor, ed., *La Vida de Lazarillo de Tormes* (Manchester & London & New York, 1922).
2. *The Russkaya Entziklopediya* (Vol XI, p. 127) in a brief notice on *Lazarillo de Tormes* gives a 1897 version by the same translator as the first Russian translation, but this is nothing more than the version in book form which appeared four years after it was published in a Russian literary journal
3. Throughout this article we follow the system of transliteration used by the New York Public Library, Main Branch, 42nd St.
4. The periodical is available in the New York Public Library, Main Branch, 42nd St., Slavonic Section. The first installment can be found in the November issue (pp. 107–125) and the second in the December issue (pp. 109–124).

Soyuza Molodiozhe (Central Committee of Communist Youth Federation of the Soviet Union) in Moscow and Leningrad. It has 88 pages and contains illustrations by the French artist Maurice Leloir There are seven full-page illustrations and so many cuts distributed throughout the book, that few pages remain without illustrations The illustrations as well as the frontispiece, which bears the French legend *Lazarille de Tormès*, have been taken from the French translation of the *Lazarillo* by A. Morel-Fatio, Paris, 1886.[5] The title page states that *Ghizn Lazarilyo s Tormesa* (Life of Lazarillo from Tormes) is an old story which has been translated and adapted for children by E. Visotzkaya.[6]

The 1893 version, which for the sake of convenience we shall call A, is a straight translation, almost a literal one in a number of cases.[7] There are, to be sure, a few changes. Three, which we shall discuss later,[8] occur in the prologue. In the body of the text, a curious omission is found toward the end of the episode with the Moor, when the author states:

> No nos marauillemos de un clérigo ni frayle, porque el uno hurta de los pobres y el otro de casa para sus deuotas y para ayuda de otro tanto, quando á un pobre esclauo el amor le animaua á esto. (p. 85)

A possible explanation for the omission of these lines in the Russian text is that such a sweeping accusation against the secular and the regular clergy could not pass through Tsarist censorship. However, since the story was printed *in toto*, without any omissions in the passages dealing with the cleric and the seller of Papal bulls, it is difficult to see why these lines had to be omitted. Possibly the Tsarist censorship did not object to individual members of the clergy being presented as misers, gluttons and swindlers, but would not pass an anti-clerical statement of such a sweeping character

Other omissions by the translator of A are very few in number None of them involves any questions of censorship but only of technique In the third chapter, which deals with Lázaro's life with the squire, there is a wonderful little scene, in which the famished *hidalgo* in a heart-rending struggle with his pride uses his most

---

5. This deluxe edition is available in the Spencer collection at the New York Public Library, Main Branch, 42nd St.

6. A copy of this edition is now in the possession of Professor E. H. Hespelt of New York University, who was so kind as to let us have the text, who suggested the topic and whose valuable suggestions, as well as those of Mrs. Hespelt, have been of considerable help in the preparation of this article.

7. As a basis of comparison we have used the edition of Cejador y Frauca of 1914, as it is the most available edition.

8. See p. 152, n. 7.

delicate diplomacy to induce the boy to share his meager meal with him. As Lázaro begins to eat the squire says to him:

> Digote, Lázaro, que tienes en comer la mejor gracia, que en mi vida vi á hombre, y que nadie te lo verá hazer, que no le pongas gana, aunque no la tenga. (p. 192)

Lázaro's thought provoked by this remark does not appear in A.

> La muy buena que tu tienes, dixe yo entre mi, te haze parescer la mia hermosa. (p. 192)

Since the translator of A omits very few lines the latter were probably omitted because of the difficulty involved in rendering in Russian this veiled allusion to the word *gana*. In this case a free translation would destroy the stylistic effect created by the pouring of one abstraction (*gana*) into two personal molds and the confrontation of these two personal manifestations of the same element. On the other hand too literal a translation could hardly have any meaning in Russian.[9] The same type of difficulty probably prompted the omission of two more asides by Lazarillo in the same scene. Commenting on the *uña de vaca* that he is eating, the *hidalgo* declares "Con almodrote . . . es este singular manjar" (p. 193). Lázaro's silent answer—"Con mejor salsa lo comes tu"—does not appear in A.[1] Neither does the aside to the following statement by the squire: "Por Dios, que me ha sabido como si oy no ouiera comido bocado" (p. 193). Lázaro: "Ansi me vengan los buenos años como es ello".[2]

The translator of A has a definite tendency toward literal translating. For example, the Spanish saying "Por no echar la soga tras el caldero" (p. 86) is given as *"Chiobyi ne opusht za vedrom i veriovki,"* i.e., "in order not to lower the ropes after the pail." As in Russian the phrase has no symbolic meaning; there is immediately following an explanatory phrase in parentheses, *"Chiobyi ne poteryat vsevo,"* i.e., "in order not to lose everything" (p. 110). Another example of literal translation is found in the passage where Lázaro says that after the miserly cleric, thinking that he was finally catching up with the snake, had struck him with his stick, he had been unconscious for three days. The Spanish text is as follows:

---

9. The 1938 version has Lázaro's aside, but deviates somewhat from the original text. The squire's words are rendered thus: "You eat with such an appetite that to every one your eating seems very tasty and tempting." Lázaro's thought reads as follows: "It is not my appetite but yours which makes my eating tempting" (p. 59).
1. This remark has also been kept by the later translation, but in the following form: "Your appetite is better than any sauce" (p. 59).
2. In the 1938 version Squire: "I ate as if I had not eaten anything since morning. And this in spite of my having had a full meal." Lázaro: "May God guard me against the kind of full meals which you had today" (p. 59 f).

> De lo que sucedió en aquellos tres dias siguientes ninguna fé
> daré, porque los tuue en el vientre de la vallena. (p. 162)

A has ". . . because I spent them as it were in the belly of a whale"
(p. 102). The allusion to Jonah and the whale is clear, but the sentence thus translated sounds rather awkward in Russian.[3] Finally, at
the beginning of the third chapter we find the familiar Spanish
expression "sacar fuerças de flaqueza" (p. 165). A translates literally
and the result is another foreign sounding Russian sentence (p. 102).
In general it can be said that the translator's tendency toward literal
translating often robs his Russian of precision and of literary quality

The Soviet version of 1938 presents a marked contrast to this
earlier translation It is an interesting example of how literature is
made to serve the official ideology in post-revolutionary Russia The
highly critical view of sixteenth century society, especially of the
clergy, which is found in *Lazarillo de Tormes*, must have been very
pleasing to the Communist translator. However, an integral version,
like the pre-revolutionary one of 1893, could not be her aim, for in
the first place this was to be a children's version and a number of
passages judged as too crude for children's ears or as presenting no
interest for the youthful reader had to be omitted. Furthermore, she
had to keep in mind that the book was to serve an ideological purpose as well as an esthetic one. Children in modern Russia are
counted upon by the regime to lead Communism to new victories
both at home and abroad. That is why everything possible is done to
indoctrinate the youth to the utmost. The books that are read by the
young have a vital role in this respect. They are one of the most indispensable tools with which the state fashions the Weltanschauung
of its citizens of tomorrow.[4] Even a translation of a foreign work can
be of great use in this propaganda for the young. By additions and
freely translated passages it can acquire a coloring which is that of
the glass through which a Soviet child is made to look at the world.
Lazarillo de Tormes, too, in its Soviet version, has been made to serve
the purpose of indoctrination. A certain number of deviations from
the original text have been made and as a result the 1938 text, which
we shall call B, is a considerably condensed version and contains
many changes from the original text. Some passages have been omitted completely, either because they are not fit to be read by children, or because they are lacking in interest for the latter, or again

3. The 1938 version also translates this sentence literally, but instead of having "*as it were*
   in the belly of a whale" it has "*as though* in the belly of a whale" (p. 42), which conveys
   more strongly the idea that this is a comparison.
4. This relentless process of indoctrination is very well shown in the recently published
   book by Arthur Goodfriend, *If You Were Born In Russia* (New York: Farrar, Straus,
   1950). This abundantly illustrated volume gives the reader a vivid picture of how the
   Soviet citizen from the cradle to the grave literally breathes Communist propaganda.

because they would do disservice to the purpose of indoctrination. Other passages or lines have been changed for one or all the reasons just mentioned. In some cases the translator adds a few lines of her own in order to explain some references with which Russian readers may not be familiar. There are a number of footnotes which explain the meaning of unfamiliar words or concepts, such as *alguacil, legua, capellán,* etc. In a few instances the translator goes so far as to make additions of her own in order to give the text a definite slant.

The preface by the translator offers some interest because from it can be learned that the Spanish Civil War (1936–39) played a definite role in reviving Russian interest in Spanish literature and that that internal conflict probably was responsible for this 1938 translation of *Lazarillo de Tormes* into Russian. We therefore quote it in its entirety.

> Almost four hundred years ago—in 1554—in the Spanish town of Burgos there was published the *Life of Lazarillo de Tormes.* From the first days of its appearance this story became one of the most popular books in Spain. But it is not known who wrote it; the author did not make himself known. He probably feared persecution, for the story was too truthful an account of how difficult life was for the common people.
>
> For many years scholars tried to determine who was the author of *Lazarillo.* Some supposed that it was Diego de Mendoza, a famous poet of the period. But that possibility must be ruled out, for Diego de Mendoza who wrote verse and treatises for the Spanish nobility and the Spanish Court could not write two lines in prose without a Latin quotation.
>
> Others thought that the *Life of Lazarillo* was written by the monk Juan de Ortega, the superior of the Order of St. Jerome. Somebody even claimed that in his cell was found the draft of that book.
>
> Such a hypothesis is not very plausible. It is doubtful whether the superior of a monastic order could have written so boldly and so ironically about his brethren.
>
> The dispute concerning the identity of the author has lasted for centuries, and meanwhile there have been countless editions of the work in its original form as well as of reworked versions. Seventy years after the publication of the story, the poet[!] De Luna added a lengthy second part. But the author of the first part has remained unknown. It may be that it was not even a

---

The theater for children in Soviet Russia is another weapon for political education. In an article entitled "Teatro Soviético Para Niños" written for the Mexican journal *El Reproductor Campechano* (Campeche, Mex, 1950), the author Mipail Dolgopolov states (p. 73), "Educar a la joven generación en el espíntu comunista he ahí la base ideológica fundamental del arte teatral."

writer but some wandering student who collected and wrote down a number of stories circulating among the people, stories about beggars, vagabonds, clever servants and greedy masters.

At present, the country through which Lazarillo once wandered is undergoing a cruel war. The heroic Spanish people are fighting for their freedom. Today more than ever we are keenly interested in anything that acquaints us with Spain, its literature, its history.

We hope that this little book will help the reader to learn something of the past of Spain.

Among minor changes in the Soviet version we may mention the frequent use of dialogue in passages where the original uses narrative. As a result the translator succeeds at times in making the story even more lively than the original and in giving it a dramatic quality. Furthermore, B does not have Lázaro address the reader as is the case in the Spanish text. This method must have been considered too archaic, but even if the translator had kept this method, she certainly would not have kept the formula *Vuestra Merced* (translated as *Vasha Milost* in A), for although it does appear in the Soviet text, it would have been highly objectionable if used as a form of address to the Soviet reader. Another term generally omitted in B is the word *gospodin* (lord, master). While A translates *señor* as *gospodin*, B prefers to use the Spanish title itself when Lazarillo addresses the squire and otherwise refers to him as *dvoryanin* (aristocrat) or as *khozyain* (employer, boss). The use of the word *dvoryanin* shows that the translator stresses the class to which the squire belongs. Thus the traits that are ridiculed in the squire—his exaggerated sense of honor, his idleness—are more directly linked to the social sphere which he represents

In a few cases B seems to follow the original text more closely than A. We have already seen[5] that B translates some remarks which A omits. Two more cases where B is more faithful to the Spanish than A are found in the prologue to the *Lazarillo*. While A states that writers desire *not only* money but also the attention of their readers, B follows the original and says that an author does *not* expect a money reward, but rather hopes that his work will be seen and read.[6] B also keeps the remark—omitted by A—that the story starts with the very beginning of the author's life instead of with the middle in order that the reader may have the complete life story of the author. Otherwise the prologue appears completely reworked and made much shorter in B. It does not mention Pliny's statement to the effect that in each work there is something valuable. It does not

5. Cf. p. 4.
6. P. 72 in the Cejador y Frauca edition.

mention Cicero's name, but translates his remark to the effect that praise fosters art. However, it does not proceed with the examples given by the original.[7] It does follow the original text in declaring that he is not more of a saint than anyone else and that he hopes that his awkwardly-written story will find an interested reader somewhere.

Among the passages which are omitted entirely in B are the description of the first years of Lazarillo's life, his father's unpleasantness with justice, and his mother's relationship with the Moor. We learn only that Lazarillo was born at the river Tormes and that his father died in a crusade against the Moors. A younger brother is mentioned, but it is not specified that he was colored As the book was edited for children, the translator probably avoided references to the extra-marital relationship of Lazarillo's mother for reasons of a moral nature. As for the omission of the references to his father, the translator again must have deemed it improper to introduce the hero to young readers as the son of a thief. Probably as a matter of good taste the references to the blind man's advice to pregnant women and to women who want to recover the love of their husbands (p. 93 in Cej) are also omitted. Another omission on the part of B which must have been based on moral considerations is found in the third chapter, that is, the one that deals with Lázaro's experiences with the squire. In the translation most of the scene between the *hidalgo* and the two "ladies" of easy virtue (p. 184 ff in Cej) has been suppressed All we find are three lines which state that the squire "was walking in the garden with two well-dressed ladies and was probably telling them some compliments" (p. 55). The same considerations probably prompted the translator to eliminate the final passage, in which Lázaro recounts the fact of his marriage to the maid servant of an archpriest, and the gossip about her relations with her former master B merely has Lázaro tell about his responsibilities in his function as the official town crier of Toledo and has him declare that he is happy in his new office (p. 88). The reference to the convocation of the imperial Cortes in Toledo is also omitted[8] and B ends with the sentence "I hope that I have not taken so much time that I have bored my readers with my story about my fortunes and adversities." As B omits the passage concerning the marriage of Lázaro as well as that which relates his experience with the *alguacil* and since the experiences with the other masters besides the seller of Papal bulls—the friar, the painter and the chaplain—are treated only in summary fashion in the original text, all of Lázaro's life after the third chapter has been compressed into one chapter.

---

7. Of the three examples given by the original (p. 72 f), A omits the lines in which a gentleman gives a coat of arms to a flatterer.
8. Also omitted in A.

Thus, instead of the seven chapters of the original text, we have only four chapters[9] in the Soviet version and as a result the translation seems more balanced than the original, in which the last four chapters are considerably shorter than the first three.

While these passages have been omitted almost totally or in their entirety by the Soviet translator, others the same translator has seen fit to modify in one way or another. For example, whereas in the original story the meeting between the blind man and Lázaro is given in very summary fashion and merely states that the blind man asked Lazarillo's mother to give him her son as a guide (p. 87 in Cej), the Soviet version explains that the blind man was one of those who went around, singing, from chapel to chapel and from castle to castle. It adds that the blind man was old and that he took a liking to Lázaro after he sent him for a pitcher of water and after he realized how prompt the boy was (p. 8). This type of additional background material is found elsewhere in B. It serves the double purpose of making certain passages more lifelike and of providing additional information without which Russian children might lose some of the meaning contained in a number of passages. Another example is found also in chapter I, when the translator wrestles with the rendering in Russian of the word *jengonça* (p. 91 in Cej). Whereas A merely calls it "his language" (p. 111), B calls it *tarabarski* (incomprehensible) and explains that it is "the language spoken by beggars and vagabonds" (p. 9). When some of the habits of the blind man are described by the author, mention is made of the prayers that he would offer to say for his almsgivers. But whereas in the original text all that is given is one sentence, "Mandan rezar tal y tal oracion?" (p. 98 in Cej), in B this is expanded to a number of lines, "Devout lady, have me pray to the Holy Virgin![1] . . . to the Christ Child . . . to St. Jerome . . . to St. Magdalene . . ." (p. 12). Not only are these lines explanatory in nature, but they also serve to inject into the text a certain derogatory attitude toward religion, since the names of the Virgin, Jesus, St. Jerome, etc., when pronounced by such a rascally fellow as Lázaro's blind master, cannot fail but give the whole passage a burlesque quality. We shall deal with the anti-religious attitude of the translator later.

B finds it necessary to explain what a boy could do to help in Church services. While the original merely states that Lazarillo was taught by his first master to be helpful during Mass (p. 126 in Cej), B explains what this help consists of: "Handing [to the deacon] the censers, the candles, making the rounds among worshipers with a copper plate" (p. 24). To make Lazarillo's hunger and his hopes for

9. B calls each chapter *rasskas* or story, which is close to the Spanish *tratado*. A has *glava* or chapter.
1. Not capitalized.

a speedy meal more vivid to the minds of children, B contains the following additions in the passage where the Spanish text, after describing the meeting between Lazarillo and the *hidalgo*, reads "Passauamos por las plaças donde se vendia pan y otras prouisiones" (p. 167 in Cej) ". . . where were being sold bread, meat, tripe, liver, hot *piroshki* (Russian meatpies), pears, pumpkins, oranges" (p. 45). Another addition inserted by B for the sake of vividness is found toward the end of the episode with the indulgence seller. In the original, Lazarillo's discovery of the complicity of his master and the *alguacil* is given barely four lines:

> mas con ver despues la risa y burla, que mi amo y el alguazil lleuaban y hazian del negocio, conosci como auia sido industri-ado por el industrioso é inuentiuo de mi amo. (p. 242 in Cej)

However, B reads as follows:

> On one occasion, waking up in the middle of the night in the inn, I saw my boss and the *alguacil*. They were sitting at a table under the light of a candle and were dividing money. I pretended to be asleep and I heard their conversation. Laughing, they were recalling how well they had managed to fool the people in the church and to sell the Papal bulls. (p. 86)

As we have seen, some passages have been omitted by the Soviet translator for reasons of propriety. The same reasons caused the changes that have been made in the amusing episode of the turnip, which Lázaro substitutes for the sausage of his blind master (p. 111 ff in Cej). The original version was probably judged too realistic and too crude for children. Instead of eating the whole sausage and vomiting it into the face of the blind man, when the latter smells Lázaro's breath, as is the case in the original, Lazarillo does not eat up the whole sausage, but keeps one half of it in his mouth. The blind man smells it and pulls it out from between his young guide's teeth (p. 18).

After having examined changes which are made out of regard for the age of the readers we now come to a most meaningful type of change, one which is the result of the political system and the offi-cial ideology of the country in which the book was published. Since religion is frowned upon in modern Russia, it is not surprising to see that the mention of God is avoided whenever the Soviet transla-tor sees fit or that the references to God are replaced by phrases which for her have approximately the same meaning or which con-stitute an appropriate substitute. For instance, in the leave-taking scene between Lázaro and his mother, the original text quotes the mother as saying "Dios te guie" (p. 89 in Cej). The Soviet text says instead "Be an honest servant, try to please your master" (p. 9). In the second chapter, where the miserly priest is called a *Pope* (Russian priest)[2] Lázaro, who is hungrier than ever, declares, "Vime claramente yr á la sepultura, si Dios y mi saber no me remediaran" (p. 133 in C) B has ". . . only luck and my astuteness" (p. 26). Still in the second chapter, Lázaro tells of his praying for the speedy death of as many people as possible, as this provides his only chance to get something to eat (during the wake following each death). In the course of this passage he twice begs God for forgiveness (p. 136 ff in C). There is no such expression of repentance in B. However, the translator does include the line in which he prays to God that He take the dying—i.e., his only hope for food—out of this sinful world (p. 27). But here the name of God[3] is associated with a rather shocking attitude on the part of the boy and is therefore robbed of much of its positive value. Hence the translator did not find it necessary to omit the phrase. For approximately the same reason the name of God appears in B in connection with the remarks of passersby who are shocked at the beatings the blind man administers to his young guide. When the blind man tells of the incident of the straw, which Lazarillo had used to drink the blind man's wine, the strangers change their tune and advise him to keep on punishing Lazarillo (p. 103 in C). As the name of God in this instance is associated with the idea of punishment, B has "Punish him, punish him, God will reward you a hundredfold" (p. 14). When Lázaro is on the verge of dying of hunger in the service of the avaricious cleric, he is pleasantly surprised one day when a locksmith happens to pass by. The latter will be able to open the chest in which lies the coveted bread and Lázaro will be able to still his hunger. The original states that the locksmith seemed to Lázaro "angel embiado . . . por la mano de Dios" (p. 140 in C). The latter part of the sentence is characteristically omitted in B (p. 28). But again, when God is called upon to do evil, as is the case a little later in the same chapter, the translator sees no objection to render the phrase. Thus "Nueuas malas te dé Dios!" (p. 144 C) is faithfully translated in B (p. 30). Because the name of God is juxtaposed with the mention of human suffering the next sentence is also given in B. "O Señor mio!, dixe yo entonces, á quanta miseria y fortuna y desastres estamos puestos los nascidos y quán poco turan los plazeres de esta nuestra trabajosa vidai!" (p. 148 C).

We shall cite a few other changes in B with respect to the name of God:

> C (Cejador) "Plega á Dios que no me muerda, dezia yo (p. 157).

2. A uses the word *klerik* (cleric).
3. Never capitalized in B.

B "I hope the snake will not bite me" (p. 38).

C Bendito seays vos, Señor, quedé yo diziendo . . ." (p. 182).

B How strangely the world is made (p. 54).

C O Señor, y quántos de auqestos deueys vos tener por el mundo derramados, que padescen por la negra que llaman honrra, lo que por vos no suffririan! (p. 183).

B And how many people there are who are willing to suffer anything in the name of their foolish honor (p. 55).

C Toma, Lázaro, que Dios ya va abnendo su mano (p. 203).

B Look how rich we have become (p. 63).

The systematic elimination of or substitution for the word God, excepting the cases where the translator has seen fit to let it stand,[4] is calculated to remove from the characters much of the manifestation of the latter's devotion to the Lord. Other passages in the book, dealing with religion or the clergy, are changed so as to render these two as either ridiculous or odious to the reader The impression must be conveyed that religion is mere humbug and that the clergy is altogether corrupt. In most cases the groundwork had already been laid by the author, so that the translator only had to retouch the text slightly in order to achieve her aim. For instance, where the Spanish text indicates that Lazarillo's blind master prayed for an almsgiver only as long as the latter was within hearing distance (p. 97 C), B adds to the whole passage a concrete element by saying that the blind man would pray twice as much for a *blanca* coin as for a half *blanca* (p. 12). Thus the relationship between praying and money is strongly underlined and the burlesque character of the blind man's prayer, which is already present in the original, stands out all the more in the translation

The whole second chapter with its repulsive cleric is of course grist for the Soviet mill. As the character of the priest is odious enough the way he is presented in the original, we do not find any significant changes in the second chapter of the Soviet version.

Shortly after meeting his third master, Lazarillo accompanies the latter to church. There "muy deuotamente" he sees him "oyr missa y los otros officios diuinos . . ." (p. 168 C). However, B changes the text to read "My *dvoryanin* patiently stood there throughout the whole service" (p. 46), conveying the impression that a service in church is necessarily something tiresome When referring to canons and to "señores de la yglesia" the *hidalgo* declares that they are "gente tan limitada, que no los sacaran de su paso todo el mundo" (p. 213). B is blunter and has the hidalgo state flatly "The holy fathers are so stingy!" (p. 68).

---

4. Occasionally expressions with the word *God* that have a popular flavor are kept. An example is *klyanus tebe bogom* (p. 66), the translation of *votote ha Dios* (p. 210 C).

Lazarillo's fifth master is a *fraile de la Merced* and although
this episode is treated in very summary fashion in the Spanish
text (pp. 225–26 C) it contains anticlerical barbs which have been
sharpened in the Russian text. The latter omits the remark that
Lázaro was guided to the friar by some women who called him
pariente (p. 225 C), and instead begins the chapter with a play on
the word *milost* (mercy-merced), saying that although Lázaro did
not know exactly what religious order it was, he owed it to the
milost (mercy) of the friar that he received shoes for the first time
in his life (p. 74). The variations in B concerning the rest of the
episode are significant; they are shown at the top of p. 158. It is
interesting to see how the Soviet translator, using the original text
as a starting point, has inserted the necessary additional details
which give the friar a sharper silhouette and at the same time
injected into the passage a more marked anticlerical flavor than
that which can be found in the original text. We have underscored
the words "this man of God," for their sarcasm clearly shows the
attitude of the translator and the impression that she has tried to
convey to the reader.

The whole episode with the seller of indulgences must have
been a sort of *pièce de résistance* for the Soviet translator, for
there one finds much material that fits Soviet anti-religious doctrines like a glove. What can be more effective for Communist
anti-religious propaganda than the description of this fraud perpetrated by a rascally seller of papal bulls and an unscrupulous
alguacil upon the simpleminded folk of a town? It is not surprising to see that the Soviet translator has made the most of this
chapter.

First, the Russian text had to explain to the young readers the
meaning and purpose of indulgences, a term with which Russians,
not to mention present-day children, are probably for the most part
unfamiliar Indulgences (in Russian *gramotyi*, i.e., letters, credentials)
are explained as being *papskie bumashki s olpushcheniem grekhov*
or slips of papal papers for the remission of sins. The translator has
added the following passage:

> Well informed ladies and poor peasant women, merchants
> and soldiers, bakers and money-changers, without bargaining,
> would pay for those slips of paper four silver blancas, hoping
> that each slip would cleanse them of dozens of voluntary and
> involuntary sins. None of those credulous people suspected that
> those papers had been issued by the deceased pope thirty years
> before and that they promised the pardoning of sins only to
> those who would take part in the campaigns against the unbe-
> lievers, which had ceased long before. (p. 75)

Spanish text

> Gran enemigo del coro y de comer en el conuento, perdido por
> andar fuera, amicissimo de negocios seglares y visitar Tanto,
> que pienso que rompia él mas çapatos, que todo el conuento.
> Este me dió los primeros çapatos, que rompi en mi vida, mas
> no me duraron ocho dias. Ni yo pude con su trote durar mas. Y
> por esto y por otras cosillas, que no digo, sali dél. (p. 226)

In other words the whole episode is presented to the reader not
merely as the sale of valid documents through fraudulent methods,
as is the case in the original text, but as the sale of *valueless* papers
by means of trickery. In both the original text and in B the *alguacil*
accuses the pardoner of selling fake indulgences, but whereas in the
Spanish text these accusations are without foundation and are only
a part of a clever plan, in the Soviet version the same accusations
are part of the same plan, but at the same time are true in themselves. The indulgences are false not because they were forged by
Lázaro's master, but because they are official documents which have
lost all value. The people are therefore presented as being the victims
of a double fraud. On the one hand they are tricked by the *alguacil* and
on the other they are made to buy valueless papers. What the translator is really getting at with this subtle variation is the whole principle
of indulgence selling. The impression that the reader of the Soviet
version is bound to carry away is that this fraud was a common practice at the time and that the people of the time were being shamelessly deceived and robbed by representatives of the Pope.

The climax of the whole episode takes place in a church. There
the *alguacil*, after having publicly accused the pardoner of selling
falsified indulgences, feigns a sort of epileptic fit in order to have
the *buldero* "revive" him miraculously with a papal bull that is placed
on his head As a result the sale of the indulgences is a tremendous
success. In that scene the name of the Lord is used several times and
since the prayers involved are an essential part of the whole incident,
B had to keep one or two of them and also had to render the name of
God several times. But this could not be particularly embarrassing to
the Soviet translator, for soon afterward the reader discovers that it
all has been nothing but a trick and the prayers thus lose all their
value and, in retrospect, only add to the caricaturesque quality of the
whole scene. Here and there, however, one line or more is omitted.
Before the *buldero* places the papal bull on the head of his accomplice
he pronounces a prayer of which the original text reads as follows:

> comiença una oracion no menos larga que deuota, con la qual
> hizo llorar á toda la gente, como suelen hazer en los sermones

Russian text

But I wore them [the shoes] out in one week. My master himself
liked to go visiting and would take me with him. Although he
wore the cassock of a monk, he preferred the gossip of the
town to prayers and a gay meal in a tavern to the meagre pittance in the monastery. *This man of God*[5] had his poor servant
run all over town day and night. I was to find out for him where
there would be a rich wedding, or a baptism, or where there was
to be a wake, where he could enjoy a fine meal and where he
could drink to his heart's content. Neither my shoes nor I could
endure such errands. I took leave of the monk. (p. 74 f)

---

de passion, de predicador y auditorio deuoto, suplicando á
nuestro Señor, pues no queria la muerte del peccador, sino su
vida y arrepentimiento, que aquel encaminado por el demonio y
persuadido de la muerte y peccado le quisiesse perdonar y dar
vida y salud, para que se arrepintiesse y confessasse sus peccados. (p. 241 C)

This must have sounded too religious to Soviet ears and B merely
states that the *buldero* "pronounced the words of the indulgence"
(p. 83).

In the Spanish text the indulgence seller is called on three occasions, *señor commissario* (pp. 230, 232, 239). This title happens to fit
Soviet terminology like a glove and it is not surprising to see the
words *papski komissar* (commissar of the Pope) in the Russian text
The Spanish text says that once in church the *buldero*

se subió al pulpito y comiença su sermon y á animar la gente á
que no quedassen sin tanto bien é indulgencia como la sancta
bulla traya. (p. 232 C)

To make the whole scene more vivid the translator has put it in direct
discourse, thus bringing out more forcefully the knavery of the
"Pope's commissar" and weaving around the word *gramolyi* (indulgences) an atmosphere of fraud and deceit:

"Do not deprive yourselves, good Christians, of the blessing of
our Church"[6] he exclaimed with a clear, solemn voice "Remove
the burden of your sins. Buy the saving bulls of his Holiness the
Pope[7] of Rome." And he began to explain to the people that by
buying one of those bulls one could at once cleanse oneself of a
number of sins. (p. 79)

5. Not capitalized.
6. Not capitalized.
7. Not capitalized.

The reader will note the particular significance acquired by their presence in this text by the words Christians, Church, his Holiness the Pope of Rome. The Soviet translator has taken full advantage of this episode and has imparted to it a tone which cannot fail to make an impression on the malleable minds of young readers.

Summarizing our findings on these two Russian translations of *Lazarillo de Tormes*, we may say that the 1893 version follows the original text very closely and at times even too literally, a fact which prevents it from rising to the level of a superior translation, i.e., one which would remain as faithful to the original text as possible, but which at the same time would adapt itself to the vital cultural background of the other language. As for the Soviet translation, it is a considerably condensed version as well as a very free one At the same time it must be regarded as an ideological weapon in the relentless communist indoctrination of the future citizens of the Soviet Union. In the Spanish text the translator found a terrain easy to exploit and she did not hesitate to introduce a number of changes and additions which would give the Russian text a definite orientation. The end product is a curious little book which does not lack artistic qualities and which fits neatly into Soviet Weltanschauung.

E. HERMAN HESPELT

The First German Translation
of *Lazarillo de Tormes*†

Until 1919 it was quite generally believed that the earliest German translation of the *Lazarillo* was the one published at Augsburg in 1617 in a volume which contained also Cervantes' *Rinconete y Cortadillo* done into German by Niclas Ulenhart. To Ulenhart were ascribed both of the "Zwo kurtzweilige, lustige und lächerliche Historien" making up the volume and this *Lazarillo* translation is listed in all handbooks of literature as the "Ulenhart translation." In 1919 the *Sitzungsberichte*[1] of the Prussian Academy of Sciences, which was engaged in inventorying the German manuscripts of the Middle Ages, listed among its finds the following item:

> 1614 wurde eine deutsche Übersetzung der Lebensbe-
> schreibung des Lazarillo de Tormes geschrieben (Nr. 33); die Hs.

† From E. Herman Hespelt, "The First German Translation of *Lazarillo de Tormes*," *Hispanic Review* 4.2 (1936): 170–75. Reprinted by permission of the publisher, University of Pennsylvania Press.

1. *Sitzungsberichte der preussischen Akademis der Wissenschaften*, 1919, p. 63.

ist also älter als der erste Augsburger Druck der Ulenhartschen
Übersetzung.

No further mention was made of the manuscript until ten years
later when an article by Richard Alewyn appeared in the *Zeitschrift
für deutsche Philologie*[2] on "Die ersten deutschen Uebersetzer des
Don Quixote und des *Lazarillo de Tormes*." Alewyn limited his discussion of the *Lazarillo* to proving that Ulenhart was not the author
of the 1617 Augsburg translation, concerning which work he adds:

> Sie ist nicht die erste deutsche Übersetzung des *Lazarillo*
> überhaupt. Auf der Breslauer Dombibliothek befindet sich
> die Handschrift einer Übersetzung aus dem Jahre 1614. . . .
> Nähere Untersuchungen darüber wären sehr erwünscht.

He quotes the reference in the *Sitzungsberichte der preussischen
Akademie*, mentioned above, as the source of his information.

The manuscript[3] of this translation of 1614, which is in the possession of the Cathedral library at Breslau, consists of 31 folios which
contain 59 pages of closely written text in German script with a fairly
wide margin at the outer edge and bottom of each page. The average size of the written page is 257×183 mm. The title page reads:

> Leben und Wandel / Lazaril von Tormes: / Und beschreibung, /
> wass / derselbe fur unglück und wider, / wertigkeitt aussgestan-
> den hat. / Verdeutscht 1614

The text is made up of the author's prologue, the seven chapters
which originally formed the Spanish first part and an eighth chapter containing the adventure with the Germans in Toledo which was
originally Chapter I of the anonymous Spanish second part. The
Alcalá interpolations have not been included.

These few facts are not enough to identify positively the text which
our translator had before him, but they do enable us to limit the
number of editions from which we must guess. The division of the
story so as to include the eighth chapter in the first part appeared
first in the French translation of 1560. Between that date and 1614,
the date of the manuscript, the same arrangement was followed in
two Spanish versions (the Antwerp edition of 1595 and its reprint
of 1602), in at least one additional French version (that of 1561), and
in two bilingual versions (those published in Spanish and French in
Paris in 1601 and 1609).

---

2. Richard Alewyn, "Die ersten deutschen Uebersetzer des *Don Quixote* und des *Lazarillo
de Tormes*," *Zeitschrift für deutsche Philologie*, 1929, LIV, 203–216.
3. I have not had access to the manuscript itself. The photostats indicate that the whole
forms a notebook. The folios containing the title page and the text are numbered, apparently in pencil, in the upper right hand corner from 6 through 36.

It seems highly probable that the translator worked directly from a Spanish text. The translation follows the original very faithfully. Nothing is omitted. All proper names in the translation, with one exception, are given either in their correct Spanish form or in the proper German equivalent. (The exception is "Vagliadolid" instead of Valladolid.) Titles of functionaries, such as "commisarius" and "commendator" show no traces of having been derived from the French. There are comparatively few other words of foreign origin and among these few there seem to be none outside the regular vocabulary of early 17th century German to indicate a direct and immediate French influence on the translation. Most of the words from the French used by the translator—turnier, proviant, vexiren, curiren, etc.—are still accepted as good German usage. On the other hand, we find a few words which look as if they had come directly from the Spanish,—"real" and "guarda roba,"[4] for example. The author is acquainted, moreover, with the value of Spanish coins; he explains "einen real" as "acht kreutzer" and "200,000 anderthalben" (this is his word for "maravedis") as "sechshundert Reichsthaler."

If we admit the value of this evidence, we may reduce the number of editions which may have been used by our translator to the four containing the Spanish text, i.e. the two Antwerp editions and the Paris editions of 1601 and 1609.

In the very first paragraph of Chapter I there occurs a peculiar translation which makes it possible further to eliminate one of these four editions. The phrases in which Lázaro describes his birth as having taken place "dentro del rio Tormes" and "en el rio" our translator renders literally, though illogically, "in dem Flusse drinnen" . . . "in dem Fluss." The author of the 1617 Augsburg translation and his German successors wrote instead "auff dem Fluss," and all the early French translators, "sur la rivière," except "P. B. Parisien," the author of the French version in the bilingual edition of 1601, who writes also "Je suis né dedans la rivière de Tormes" . . . "en la rivière." We may therefore conclude that if our translator had had the French version of 1609 before him he would have been emboldened to use the more logical "auf." Since he did not, the original of his text was probably either one of the Antwerp editions or the Paris edition of 1601. More definite identification must wait until a more detailed collation of the translation with these editions can be made.

As to the identity of the translator himself, we know only what we may infer from his work. His language shows that he must have come from somewhere in Middle Germany—perhaps Saxony. He writes indiscriminately *ü* for *ie*; *d* for *t*; *t* for *d*; initial *p* for *b*; initial

---

4. The letters b and p were used interchangeably in the author's dialect.

s for z; etc. He was probably not a scholar for he never uses the learned style. His language is vigorous and alive. He is fond of homely, vulgar expressions which are very much in keeping with the tone of the story. He outdoes the Spanish Lázaro in the names he calls his masters. "El mísero de mi amo" becomes "Mein Herr, der Dürrkäse" (i.e., "the old cheese"); "el mezquino amo" becomes "der lausichte Herr"; the stingy priest is variously dubbed "der elende Geitzhals," "der karge Filtz und Druckenpfennig," and "der elende kahle Kerle undt laussiger filtz." He uses with relish other phrases which are more at home in the mouths of peasants than in literature. When the blind man bites into the turnip and the Spanish author tells us "hallóse en frio con el frio nabo," the German says even more expressively "da lieff ihm die lauss über die leber." When Lázaro in the squire's empty house thinks back on the lucky days when he could unlock the priest's chest and eat as much as he would, he says "ich meynete es hette mich ein Hase gelecket." When he makes his decision at last to stay with his wife and let the German soldiers go on without him, he does so by reminding himself of the saying "Es bleibe einer nur auf seinem Mist."

As has already been said, our translator avoids words of foreign origin—a surprising fact when we consider that his work was written at a time when their almost universal use was becoming a menace to the language. Three years later the first of the German societies for the purification and enrichment of the mother-tongue, the "Fruchtbringende Gesellschaft," was formed to combat this evil. Our translator anticipates also another of the Society's principles by creating new words from old German stems when he wishes to produce a comic effect. Thus "comer" becomes "schnabeliren"; "el comer," "Schnabelweyt"; and "nariz," "Löschhorn."[5] We are therefore justified in declaring that if he did not later become a member of the Society he at least deserved election.

He has one pronounced stylistic peculiarity which amounts almost to a mannerism. Whenever a Spanish word or phrase occurs which has no exact German equivalent, and many times when such an equivalent is at hand, he uses two German words or phrases in the translation. On one specimen page of the manuscript, chosen at random, the following synonyms translate single Spanish expressions:

> *artes*—fündlin und kunststücklin
> *contraminava*—zu untergraben und heimlich beyzukommen
> *argolla de hierro y su candado*—Anwürfflin oder
>   Vorlegeschlösslin

---

5. This word may not be the invention of the translator. It was certainly used elsewhere, for it is listed in Götze's *Frühneuhochdeutches Glossar*. It is typical, however, of the words introduced into the language by the Sprachgesellschaften.

  una migaja—ein bröcklin oder geringstes Bisslin
  cerrava el candado—das schloss vorgeleget und
   zugeschlossen.

 His interpolations are very few. They are almost always in the form of a parenthetical explanation of some word. Thus, "triperia" is translated "Kuttelhofe" and the translator explains "wo man kuttelfleck und derogleichen sachen feyle hat"; "un señor de título" is translated "einem grossen ansehnlichen Herren" and explained as "fürsten oder Marggrafen." Concerning the service of such a person the translator adds—possibly from his own experience—"obgleich auch Elend genug darbey ist." He adds also his surname to St. Thomas Aquinas when he speaks of him and he calls the emperor "Carol." The other interpolations are negligible.

 His mistranslations are likewise comparatively few in number. Most of them occur in passages containing some unusual Spanish idiom or some obscure reference. Some are interesting as throwing light on possible differences between Spanish and German customs. One of these may be found in the first chapter where Lázaro describes the punishment dealt out to his mother: ". . . a mi madre pusieron pena por justicia, sobre el acostumbrado centenario, que en casa del sobredicho Comendador no entrase. . . ." The translator does not understand "centenario," wrongly associates it with "Zentner" and writes:

  . . . die Mutter aber musste den grossen Stein, der einen Centner wieget, auffm platz, nach altem brauch, herümb tragen, und über dieses legten sie ihr die Straffe auff, dass sie nicht mehr in des obgedachten Commendators Hauss kommen dürffe.

Another occurs in the third chapter: Lázaro goes down to the river in the morning and finds his master, the squire, making gallant remarks to "dos reboçadas mugeres." The translator represents the fastidious gentleman as talking with "zweyen Weibern, die da gar schlotterich und schmutzig hereingingen." On the whole, it may be justly said, however, that the translation is remarkably faithful both to the letter and to the spirit of the original.

 He would be a bold critic who, on the evidence of these characteristics of language and style, would venture to guess the identity of the author. I can suggest only one name which might deserve further study: it is that of the first translator into German of the *Quijote*, Pahsch Bastel von der Sohle. The *Lazarillo* translation observes all the rules for the translator's art laid down by Pahsch Bastel in his prologue to the *Quijote*, except one advocating the Germanization of Spanish names, which would not have the same significance here as in Cervantes' work. A work, he says, should read as if it were composed in the language into which it has been translated; more attention should be paid to sense than to literal accuracy; when necessary to make the meaning clear two German words or phrases should be used for one Spanish word or phrase; words of foreign origin should be avoided.

A direct comparison of the language and style of the two translations fails to yield conclusive evidence on the question. In the first place the enormous difference in style in the two original works makes inevitable a great difference in style in the translations. Both works are full of inconsistencies in the spelling of the same words—inconsistencies characteristic of 17th century German before the influence of the Sprachgesellschaften was felt. The *Quijote*, moreover, has gone through the hands of the printer, who may have eliminated some orthographical peculiarities.[6] I wish only to suggest that it is not out of the question that the two translators may have been one and the same person.

At least three different opinions have been expressed as to who Pahsch Bastel actually was. Hermann Tiemann,[7] who, in 1928, edited the reprint of the first German translation of the *Quijote*, identifies him as Hans Ludwig Knoche, a member of the Fruchtbringende Gesellschaft, born about 1610. If this identification is right, of course, the *Lazarillo* is not his work. Richard Alewyn[8] takes issue with Tiemann and suggests that Pahsch Bastel was the Freiherr Matthias von Wolzogen, likewise in his later years associated with the Fruchtbringende Gesellschaft, who was born 1588 in Niederösterreich, and travelled in 1613 through Spain, England and France. He believes that the same author under the pseudonym of Caesar von Joachimsthal published in 1628 a translation from the Italian called *Die Regierkunst* dedicated to Count Anton Günther of Oldenburg to whose court he had come when exiled from home for his Protestant activities. Eduard Schröder[9] does not venture to give Pahsch Bastel's right name, but believes that he came from Upper Saxony, perhaps from Anhalt, and that he was associated with the Fruchtbringende Gesselschaft. If he is right, or if Alewyn is right, it is still possible that the first German *Lazarillo* and the first German *Quijote* both owe their existence to the labors of the same accomplished but modest translator.

---

6. One consistent peculiarity of spelling in the *Lazarillo* translation is the insertion of *h* before, instead of after, a long *a* or *u*; e.g., *jhar*, *rhum* etc.
7. "Nachwort" to *Don Kichote de la Manizscha, Das ist: Juncker Harnisch auss Fleckenland* [Reprint of the Frankfurt, 1648 edition], pp. 401–418.
8. *Op. cit.*, pp. 207–210.
9. *Göttingsche Gelehrte Anzeigen*, 1929, pp. 77–82.

JANE W. ALBRECHT

Family Economics/Family Dynamics: Mother and Son in the *Lazarillo de Tormes* (1554)[†]

Lazarillo de Tormes and his mother have been called a lot of things. As with her son, who is alternately perceived as an innocent victim or a scam artist and wolf in sheep's clothing, critics are of two minds about Antona, who is variously seen as a bad mother and helpless widow. Antona is a miller's wife, concubine, thief, prostitute and inn-servant, all of which tar her with the brush of promiscuity and immorality.[1] She is also a hardworking wife, widow, mother, cook, washerwoman and "la triste," which taken together tag her as a woman whose sexual involvements are not the result of lasciviousness, but poverty.[2] Often, the characterizations of the mother reflect on the son, and vice versa. For example, in Redondo's words, "'Hideputa' . . . define exactamente lo que es Antona Pérez, por el oficio que ejerce," but while directed at her son, the insult defines her as a marginal woman ("Molineras" 89). At the same time, the depiction of Lazarillo as an inverted Doncel del Mar or young Moses renders his mother an ironic princess. Importantly, her desire to "arrimarse a los buenos" seeps into Lazarillo's consciousness and orients his life, and he ends up married to "tan buena mujer como vive dentro de las puertas de Toledo." In a few short paragraphs, "one of the most effective authors of all time" (Morreale 28) manages to conjure Antona and Lazarillo from a variety of sources, folklore and the oral tradition, literary texts and sixteenth-century social reality while, as elsewhere in the novel, also deploying irony, parody, satire and sarcasm in the narrator's manipulation of point of view.[3]

[†] From Jane W. Albrecht, "Family Economics/Family Dynamics: Mother and Son in the *Lazarillo de Tormes* (1554)," *The Hispanic Journal* 33.2 (2012): 11–22. Reprinted by permission of the publisher.

1. These characterizations appear in both the novel and the criticism it has inspired. In general, the novel describes women (Antona, the "mujercillas" of the third *Tratado* and Lazarillo's wife) as either sexually active, pregnant or giving birth, a reflection of the contemporary view of woman as disordered and unruly, controlled by her uterus, which must be kept occupied in case it take over her mind and senses. See Davis, 124–25. In her important article on the role of women in the *Lazarillo*, Cruz observes that Antona is the foremost example of the social and textual repression of women's actions and words. Antona's image as a mother is so debased as to cast a long shadow over all women in the text while, at the same time, it is "the narrative's shadowy female figures" who not only condition the *picaro*'s relations with males in the patriarchal society in which he must survive, but whose "metaphorical presence successfully resists rejection within the narrative" ("Abjected" 100–02).

2. Lazarillo calls her "la triste" (20). All quotes are from the edition by Rico. In Márquez Villanueva's estimation, her husband's departure and demise and the unavailability of charity throw Antona into prostitution in the inn (111–12). El Saffar saw Antona Pérez's trajectory as going from wife to concubine to prostitute. Antona had to sacrifice her children "para llegar a ser instrumento ilegitimo de los deseos libidinosos de los que tienen poder" (271).

3. On the *Lazarillo*'s creation of different horizons of expectations based on the reader's response to certain kinds of texts, see Dunn.

The various labels and descriptions, such as those cited above, reflect the two characters' multiple origins and roles, comment on their interdependence and underscore their socio-economic standing. What is more, as many critics have stressed, the *Lazarillo* frequently portrays individuals as commodities and human relationships as an exchange of goods and services, and Lazarillo and Antona are often implicated. This motif comes as no surprise in a novel of survival, whose characters scrape, skim and scam their way through life by performing manual labor or trickery, committing petty thievery, trading sexual favors or serving at mass. The commodity and exchange pattern is set with the representation of Lazarillo's parents and repeated in the depiction of other characters and connections, but little has been said of the mother-son relationship. Although the question of the economic incentives and disincentives inherent in Lazarillo's bond with his mother seems fundamental, it has not been elucidated entirely. I propose to review the commodity and exchange design in the text's rendering of important characters, then, examine the historical circumstances of widows and children and, finally, discuss the nature of Lazarillo's and Antona's relationship.

To pay his debt to society for stealing grain from clients, Lazarillo's father is sent into exile to serve a nobleman in war.[4] Lazarillo's mother, "sin marido y sin abrigo," begins her work life earning what she can cooking for students and washing laundry for stable boys. She starts frequenting the stables and becomes involved with Zaide. (What she earned cooking and washing could not have amounted to much, as Lazarillo suffered hunger and cold before Zaide arrived on the scene). Some years ago, Sieber portrayed their union in terms of a transaction for profit, and remarked how the language of the novel reflects certain values and economic behaviors:

> Antona Pérez, Lazarillo's mother . . . becomes the provider. She provides [Lazarillo] not only with material goods—shelter and food—but also with a language and a domestic situation that are defined in terms of honor and profit. More importantly, she substitutes Zaide as the father in a relationship whose contractual nature implies mutual profit. Sex becomes a commodity, a currency, to be exchanged for material security and comfort. (3)

Zaide's presence in the family is associated with the things he brings into the household, but he, too, is an object. He has been bought and sold. His punishment by law is to be "pringado," a word that reappears later in the first treatise when Lazarillo relates that the blind man eats the "pringadas" of a sausage that "había pringado," which Lazarillo then switches for a turnip. Through the repetition of "pringado / pringadas" the man, Zaide, is equated with the

---

4. On the folkloric associations between "molinero" and "ladrón," see Redondo, "Folklore."

commodity, meat, and both represent defeated male sexuality.[5] After
Lazarillo's mother and Zaide are forced apart,[6] she continues earning what she can by serving in the Inn of the Solana. Lazarillo's
mother began a "molinera," then was "amancebada" to Zaide and,
the last we hear, becomes a "criada de meson." Both "molineras" and
"criadas de mesón" are women who perform sex acts in addition to
their regular labors.[7] Antona Pérez has sex for money and goods.

From an early age Lazarillo is involved in others' commerce and
trafficking. He helps Zaide and his mother fence stolen property:
"hasta ciertas herraduras que por mandado de mi madre a un herrero vendí." Later, the boy starts serving in the inn, again taking
orders from adults, now not his family members, but the strangers
who are his first masters. From the blind man Lazarillo learns that
the church is a "marketplace of spiritual values," in which he and
his master trade a service for a place: "El pobre tenía . . . algo que
ofrecer al poderoso o simplemente, al que tenía un buen pasar: la
oración. ¿Acaso no era la mercancía que una y otra vez ofrecía aquel
ciego . . . ? . . . Y así Lázaro nos lo describirá con esta frase admira-
tiva: 'En su oficio era un águila. Ciento y tantas oraciones sabía de
coro'" (Fernández Álvarez 155). In the fourth chapter, Lazarillo is
implicated in the sex life of a worldly Mercedarian friar, who himself could have abused him, or sold or traded the services of the boy
to other adults.[8] Lazarillo has become the goods.[9]

The last chapter reveals an economic arrangement between
the Archpriest, Lazarillo's wife and Lazarillo himself, a relationship which may feature homosexual sex, as may any triangle (El
Saffar 263). In exchange for used clothing, meals and firewood, Lazarillo's wife takes care of the Archpriest and his house. The words
"provecho" and "provechoso" appear four times in the space of a few
paragraphs, underscoring the pecuniary nature of Lazarillo's mar-
ital relationship: "[j]ob and marriage are intertwined, and Lázaro
accepts the assets and liabilites of a 'profit-sharing agreement' that
makes cuckoldry profitable" (Maiorino 5). Niceties like upholding
sacred vows do not measure up against having sufficient food,

5. García de la Concha writes of the novel's "personificaciones y cosificaciones" as an
example of its humor (230–32). On the sexual symbolism of the sausage and turnip, see
Herrero, "Great" 14–15.

6. In Salamanca, as elsewhere, one hundred lashes was the customary corporal punishment for any woman who violated one of the many laws by which prostitution was regu-
lated. See Villar y Macías 155–56. He cites "De mancebia y mugeres públicas,"
Chapter 35, Book Five of the Ordenanzas of the city of Salamanca "que reproduce las
de Sevilla, que Felipe II hizo extensivas á toda Castilla."

7. See Redondo, "Folklore" and "Molineras," who points to the roots of the figure of Lazarillo's mother in folklore, as a miller's wife, and a maid in an inn, both women who
have sex in exchange for cash, food or clothing.

8. For interpretations of the sexual connotations of the phrase "otras cosillas que no
digo," see Shipley, "Otras," and Thompson and Walsh. Shipley interprets Lazarillo's work
with the master tambourine-painter of the sixth treatise as pandering (see "Case").

9. In Cruz's words, "what the young boy vividly learns . . . through his apprenticeship to
his teachers are the ruthless economic lessons of exchange value" (Discourses 34).

clothing and firewood. Even the clergy break their vows and pass on to the faithful the cost of maintaining their illicit love affairs and illegitimate children: "[no] nos maravillemos de un clérigo ni fraile porque el uno hurta de los pobres y el otro de casa para sus devotas y para ayuda de otro tanto, cuando a un pobre esclavo el amor le animaba a esto" (19), as Lazarillo earlier observed of Zaide's devotion to his family. Thus, the text colors human relationships as some sort of transaction—no one gets something for nothing, and love is a luxury one can ill afford, or, perhaps only afford by doing ill.

Individually, mother and son are presented as merchandise. The question is, does their relationship resemble the other human ties depicted in the Lazarillo, a type of transaction based on exchange value, and profit and loss? To address this, a review of the economic situation of widows and their children is in order. The historical setting can tell us what life was like for widows and their children in sixteenth-century Castile, and what to expect of them. By placing Antona and Lazarillo in that context we can then consider how they may conform to, and diverge from, their real-life counterparts.

A widow such as Lazarillo's mother was one of the legitimate poor who elicited a measure of sympathy and charity in society.[1] In Zamora, reforms designed to keep the poor from begging allowed each man twelve maravedís [mrs.] per day, woman, ten mrs., and child, six mrs.[2] What those sums purchased can be understood in the context of a budget that Álvarez de Toledo drew up in 1596 to illustrate the typical expenditures of a very poor person. The budget excludes housing but is in other ways quite specific regarding food, fuel, taxes, and clothing. According to his breakdown, "un contribuyente muy pobre" spends thirty-two and a half mrs. per day on:

> carne, 4; vino, 4; tocino, 1; aceite, 1; vinagre, .5; verdura, .5; fruta, 1; pan–libra y media–, 4; calzones–ropilla, ferreruelo y polainas, al año, 5; tres pares de medias al año, 1; tres pares de zapatos al año, .5; un sombrero al año, .5; un jubón, con dos pares de mangas, al año, 1; tres camisas, una sábana y tres valonas al año, 1.5; leña o carbón, 2; jabón, 1; impuestos–alcabalas y millones–, 4. (Reglà 375)

Alvarez de Toledo figures taxes apart from food, fuel, textile and clothing costs and he does not include an amount for housing at all. Therefore, the very poor person he had in mind was either homeless, or lived as a servant in a house or stable, or, as in the case of

---

1. Márquez Villanueva, Ricapito (Intro. 58–63) and others have underscored the Erasmist thrust of the novel and its treatment of the theme of "viudas desamparadas." We are mindful, as well, that this fits with Lázaro-narrator's project to simultaneously create sympathy for himself as a victim of circumstances.

2. Martz reckons that other towns in Castile, including Valladolid, Toledo, Salamanca, and Madrid, initiated poor laws similar to those of Zamora.

Lazarillo's mother, an inn. The funds, derived from church poor boxes and weekly collections, were never sufficient to meet the needs of the deserving poor (Martz 22). Although, as a widow, Antona was legitimately poor and qualified to receive charity, even if that support were forthcoming, ten mrs. per day for herself and six for Lazarillo would hardly keep the wolves from their door. If we look at the typical expenditures above, when Antona Pérez tried to spend that hypothetical charitable donation, taxes alone would have devoured a hefty portion of what she might have received from charity,[3] reducing the buying power of their combined sixteen mrs. to, say, fourteen. With that sum, a widow and her boy could buy little more than a daily ration of bread and maybe some meat or "tocino," olive oil or fruit, and try to keep clothes on their backs.

The scenario in which a widowed mother like Antona Pérez delivers a young child into the hands of a stranger was not an unusual one. The death of one parent often precipitated the abandonment of the couple's child or children. Across Europe, the act of parents separating from children was repeated daily, whether those parents farmed their offspring out into near-slavery to work for others, apprenticed their young children, deposited infants on cathedral doorsteps, passed them through a hospital turnstile or otherwise "exposed" them, or surrendered them to childless couples.[4]

In Salamanca, infants were customarily left at the Puerta del Perdón of the Old Cathedral by mothers who were poor, widowed, unwed, or who already had two children with their husband (Fernández Álvarez 164).[5] Like other cities in Spain, Salamanca had institutions to care for foundlings. The confraternity of San Joseph y Nuestra Señora de la Piedad was dedicated to the rescue, baptism and care of abandoned infants, an average of 72 per year in Salamanca (population 20,000) between 1590–96, the years for which documents still exist. The confraternity procured paid wet-nurses who raised the foundlings until they reached age six or seven. For this service, the women received six ducats (2,250 mrs.) annually, or six mrs. per day, which figure coincides with the one from Zamora, above, the charity allocation for a needy child. More than half of the children died or disappeared under the care of the wet-nurses, or en route to them (Fernández Álvarez 163–66; 170).[6] Of

3. "Alcabalas" were long-standing taxes of 10% levied on transported goods; the "millones," sales taxes on food, were not established until 1590. Given the high sales tax on food after 1590, after that time it would have made more sense for the poor to beg, or trade sex or other services, for food and clothing, than to buy them. But that is too late for this novel.
4. See Boswell, Fernández Álvarez, Martz and Terpstra.
5. The economic breaking point for many poor couples came with the arrival of their third child (Hufton 301).
6. Fernández Álvarez cites the Libro del recibo y gastos de los niños expósitos de la Cofradía de San José y Nuestra Señora de la Piedad (Archivo Municipal de Salamanca). In Madrid between 1650 and 1700, the figure is higher: 70.23% of abandoned children sent to be raised by a wet-nurse died before age seven (Larquié 73).

those who survived to age seven, a few were given in adoption but, more frequently, they were indentured (Martz 231).[7]

Beggars were legion in the towns and cities of Spain and the rest of Europe. The existence of poor laws promulgated in the 1540s to curtail begging in Castile indicates that it was practiced to such a degree that it was a public nuisance.[8] Castilian poor laws of the 1540s (the novel was written between 1525 and 1554), ordered that children like Lazarillo be placed with a master or turned over to the Colegio de los Niños de la Doctrina, one of the institutions in Castile whose purpose was to help destitute women and children. Underwritten by tax revenues and run by civil authorities in a number of municipalities, the Doctrinos were founded to care for and educate children, with an emphasis on Christian doctrine, and eventually place them as apprentices or send them on for more schooling.[9] By 1598 Pérez de Herrera's *Amparo de pobres* criticizes the Doctrinos for sending children out begging instead of fulfilling their original purpose of schooling and placing them in a trade (96). Whether the result of corruption among city and school officials, as Pérez de Herrera sustained, or of there being too few situations available in which to place all of the needy children from the schools, a number apparently ended up begging.

In 1551, at age nine, Juan de Yepes, the future San Juan de la Cruz, tried his hand at many jobs in Medina del Campo before his widowed mother succeeded in getting him into the Colegio de los Niños de la Doctrina in that city. At ten years old, Lazarillo would have been expected to work, too.[1] A boy of that age was thought "mayorcito" and able to earn a subsistence living. Even under the best of circumstances—that is, with both parents alive and able and the father regularly employed—it was necessary for poor children to go into the world as beggars, laborers, apprentices or servants.

7. One school for orphan boys in Salamanca, the Colegio de la Purisima Concepción (or de los Huérfanos) later became the Hospital de Dementes, and is presently part of the Facultad de Educación of the University of Salamanca. According to Vidal y Díaz, the school was founded by Francisco Solís Quiñónes y Montenegro in 1545 (304); Villar y Macías gives the year as 1549, when Solís returned to Salamanca (332). He states that in the sixteenth century orphans were essentially cloistered within its confines.
8. On the growing spectacle and fear of beggars in towns, see Maravall, especially 192–93. Carlos V issued a *Pragmática* against begging in 1540.
9. See Martz 223, Bennassar 445 and Vidal y Díaz 305–06. Villar y Macías describes the school's founding and mission (346). An example of the way schools were funded comes from Toledo, where in 1586 the contribution from tax revenues to the Colegio de los Doctrinos was 400 ducats (150,000 mrs.) per annum; a commission suggested raising that to 500 ducats (Martz 146–47 cites the Archivo Municipal de Toledo, *Autos de los Pobres*, Memorial and letters, 1586).
1. According to Lazarillo, he was eight when his father was arrested. If his mother carried his half-brother to full term, and he grew to the age when he could walk, then eighteen months to two years have elapsed, meaning Lazarillo is nine and a half or ten when he is sent off with his first master.

Lazarillo and Juan had few options in life when their fathers, the primary breadwinners, died and their mothers had to move to town to find work. Juan was luckier than Lazarillo. His mother, perhaps sharper and more persistent than the fictional Antona Pérez, managed to get him into the Doctrinos in Medina del Campo. In truth, in Salamanca, that school was not founded until 1577, so, regardless of the ease or difficulty with which a parent could place a boy there, it was not an option that Lazarillo's mother could exercise (Vidal y Díaz 305–06).[2]

The historical circumstances are a vital part of the textual equation that yields the figures of Antona and her son, and provide a background against which we can interpret their actions and interactions. For a widow in her circumstances, Antona Pérez seems to have kept both children with her as long as she could. Alegre has pointed out that she, an unmarried parent of a biracial child, could have wed Zaide and kept the baby, or aborted, committed infanticide or abandoned him (30–31), as poor parents across Europe did. (The author tells us that Lazarillo's own wife "parió tres veces," and those children are nowhere to be seen).[3] What lies ahead for Zaide's child when he is too old to be nursed and has to be fed and clothed? Would the biracial son of a slave and a woman forced to trade sexual favors live even a decade, to Lazarillo's age? Lazarillo himself survived infancy in a two-parent household, and his mother kept him and raised him to the age of ten. Lazarillo was working around the inn, so he had worth to someone at some level,[4] but at that age he was a drain on his mother who, besides sustaining herself, had, in Lazarillo's "hermanico," another mouth to feed and another body to clothe and shelter. An eight or ten year old was to be placed with a master or in a school. As a male, Lazarillo would not have elicited any special sympathy or attention from societal institutions, all of which were underfunded, and which, given their scant resources, favored rescuing impoverished girls to keep them from prostitution. His mother could have kept Lazarillo and sent him out to beg, which was, apparently, the practice of enough parents in Castile to prompt the drafting of poor laws in the 1540s that, among other strictures, expressly forbade using children for that purpose. Had Antona sent him out begging on the streets of Salamanca, she would have run

2. Presumably, the enactment of poor laws in Castile prompted the founding of these schools in the 1540s–1570s.

3. There are commonalities between Antona Pérez and Lazarillo's wife, but one big difference: Antona Pérez held onto her children as long as she could, in spite of the fact that she was on her own.

4. Boswell's observation about ancient and medieval Europe surely applies to the sixteenth century: "it would require extraordinary circumstances—for example, a great oversupply of workers and a very high cost of food—to render children valueless to anyone in such a society" (429).

afoul of societal norms, perhaps already written into law if the novel were composed in the 1540s. This would have amounted to her third transgression, first for stealing or receiving stolen goods, second for consorting with a black man,[5] and, lastly, for violating poor laws.

But, more significantly, had Antona made Lazarillo, an unemployed ten-year-old male, try his hand at begging in Salamanca, he would not have been counted among the deserving poor and would not have been successful. Pérez de Herrera recommended that, at the age of seven or eight, "que es el tiempo que han menester para criarse" (104), able-bodied poor boys be placed in a seminary, or in the Doctrinos, or with a master, or be put to work, and that girls of that age be set up as servants in monasteries (104). "De siete años abajo" poor children might be permitted to beg (55), but at age eight, it was incumbent on society to "ocupar los niños en oficios mecánicos" (238). For that reason, although Lazarillo's mother tried to keep her ten-year-old occupied at the inn, apparently he was not busy enough to be considered worthy of staying on, or able to contribute anything to his mother's and little brother's keep.

The blind man, become aware of the boy at work in the inn, and, in Lazarillo's words, "paresciéndole que yo sería para adestralle," asks Antona Pérez for her son. For him to have taken notice of the boy, Lazarillo either had personal interaction with him, perhaps waiting on him in some capacity, or Lazarillo happened to fit the bill when he asked around for a boy. In other words, Lazarillo may have seemed particularly able and industrious, or may just have been available at the right time. Could Lazarillo's mother have sold him to the blind man? She may have taken something if he offered but, because boys like Lazarillo were common in Salamanca, it is unlikely that she either asked for or received payment. The blind man accepts the child "as his son." His use of kin-language reflects the social reality of poor parents who relied on others, their extended family, the Church, a guild, municipal authorities, or a master, to help their young ones to survive childhood and have the possibility of reaching adolescence and adulthood (Terpstra 2–4). In this context, giving up her child is not something Antona Pérez did to Lazarillo, but for him and herself. Antona did not approach the blind beggar, but, at the same time, she must have known—everyone knew—that it was time to part from her son who, like any other ten-year-old boy, was expected to earn his daily bread and keep himself clothed. She had to sever her relationship with her son to give him, and herself and second child, the chance to survive. With the blind man, who could legitimately live off the public purse, Lazarillo could beg.

5. On the crime of sleeping with an infidel, see García de la Concha (130), who cites Titulo XXIX of the *Novisima recopilación* [*de las leyes de España*, Madrid, 1807], Ley I, p. 426, a.

Their parting moment—when Lazarillo "leaves the world of love
and enters a new one" (Herrero, "Renaissance" 881)—is wrenching:
"yo fui a ver a mi madre, y, ambos llorando, me dio su bendición y
dijo: Hijo, ya sé que no te veré más. Procura de ser bueno, y Dios te
guíe. Criado te he y con buen amo te he puesto; válete por ti" (22).
First, as a Christian parent, she gives him her blessing, which means
essentially invoking God's blessing, as in Genesis 27. She calls on
God to watch over her child, words we do not hear but that are
reflected in the phrase "Dios te guíe." Where, in fact, life later leads
him renders this mother's prayer ironic, as does the repetition of
"bueno," but it comes across as heart-felt at the same time. Her
instruction, "válete por ti," simultaneously acknowledges Lazarillo's
intrinsic value and refers to the fact that he is on his own, effectively negating the view of his "buen amo" as a surrogate parent, and
suggesting that he will need to step lively and make himself useful.
"Válete por ti" announces Lazarillo's release onto the marketplace.

Antona's act may be considered both altruistic—she gives Lazarillo away in the hope of a better life for her son—and eminently
practical—abandoning him provides her a way to survive and be able
to raise her second child to the age of nine or ten when he, too, is
old enough to go his own way, and she has only to find the means to
feed, clothe and shelter herself. In spite of the "mil importunidades"
she undergoes while working in the inn, Antona does not abandon,
sell, or prostitute her children, or send them out to beg or steal.[6] The
words, "con buen amo te he puesto," indicate that she considers the
blind man a master with whom she has placed her son. A real-
life Antona Pérez may have looked for months without success to
apprentice her son with a master in a trade in Salamanca. Sending
Lazarillo out of the home made life less arduous for Antona. The
practical act, precipitated by extreme hardship, benefited Antona's
struggle for survival.

Lazarillo and Antona, each a rich amalgam of folkloric, literary
and social types, expose many of the ills of the poor in sixteenth-
century Spain. The mother-son tie, although strong, is inevitably
frayed and severed by economic forces, "the trial by market everything must come to."[7] An approach to the *Lazarillo* that takes into
account the historical reality of poor widows and children treats the
characters in human, terms, and reveals the author's understanding of the life of a poor family.

---

6. Child-selling, child slavery and human trafficking were common across Europe. Of the
ancient and medieval practice of child-selling, Boswell explains that "If sale was the best
hope for the child's survival, it was little different from drastic measures any parent
would take to save a child" (430).
7. From Robert Frost's "Christmas Trees" (1920).

Works Cited

Alegre, José María. "Las mujeres en el *Lazarillo de Tormes*." *Arbor* 117 (1984): 23–35. Reprint from *Revue Romane* 16 (1981): 3–21. Print.

Bennassar, Bartolomé. *Valladolid au siècle d'or: une ville de Castille et sa campagne au xvie siècle*. Paris: Mouton, 1967. Print.

Boswell, John. *Kindness of Strangers: The Abandonment of Children in Western Europe from Late Antiquity to the Renaissance*. New York: Random House, 1990. Print.

Cruz, Anne J. "The Abjected Feminine in the *Lazarillo de Tormes*." *Crítica hispánica* 19.1–2 (1997): 99–109. Print.

———. *Discourses of Poverty: Social Reform and the Picaresque Novel in Early Modern Spain*. Toronto: U Toronto P, 1999. Print.

Davis, Natalie Zemon. *Society and Culture in Early Modern France*. Stanford: Stanford UP, 1975. Print.

Dunn, Peter N. "Reading the Text of *Lazarillo de Tormes*." *Studies in Honor of Bruce W. Wardropper*. Ed. Dian Fox, Harry Sieber and Robert Ter Horst. Newark, DE: Juan de la Cuesta, 1989. 91–104. Print.

El Saffar, Ruth. "La literatura y la polaridad masculino / femenino. II. Entre poder y deseo: Lázaro como hombre nuevo." *Teorías literarias en la actualidad*. Ed. Graciela Reyes. Madrid: El Arquero, 1989. 259–84. Impreso.

Fernández Álvarez, Manuel. *La sociedad española del Renacimiento*. Salamanca: Anaya, 1970. Impreso.

García de la Concha, Victor. *Nueva lectura del "Lazarillo": El deleite de la perspectiva*. Madrid: Castalia, 1981. Impreso.

Herrero, Javier. "The Great Icons of the *Lazarillo*: The Bull, the Wine, the Sausage and the Turnip." *Ideologies and Literature* 1.5 (1978): 3–18. Print.

———. "Renaissance Poverty and Lazarillo's Family: The Birth of the Picaresque Genre." *PMLA* 94.5 (1979): 876–86. Print.

Hufton, Olwen. "Life and Death among the Very Poor." *The Eighteenth Century: Europe in the Age of Enlightenment*. Ed. Alfred Cobban. New York: McGraw Hill, 1969. 293–310. Print.

Larquié, Claude. "El niño abandonado en Madrid durante el siglo XVII: Balance y perspectivas." *Familia y sociedad en el mediterráneo occidental, siglos XV-XIX*. Ed. Francisco Chacón Jiménez. Murcia: U Murcia, 1987. 69–91. Impreso.

Maiorino, Giancarlo. *At the Margins of the Renaissance: "Lazarillo de Tormes" and the Picaresque Art of Survival*. University Park: Penn St UP, 2003. Print.

Maravall, José Antonio. *La literatura picaresca desde la historia social (Siglos XVI y XVII)*. Madrid: Taurus, 1986. Impreso.

Márquez Villanueva, Francisco. "La actitud espiritual del *Lazarillo*." *Espiritualidad y literatura en el siglo XVI*. Madrid: Alfaguara, 1968. 69–137. Impreso.

Martz, Linda. *Poverty and Welfare in Habsburg Spain: The Example of Toledo*. Cambridge: Cambridge UP, 1983. Print.

Morreale, Margarita. "Reflejos de la vida española en el *Lazarillo*." *Clavileño* 5 (1955): 28–31. Impreso.

Pérez de Herrera, Cristóbal. *Discurso del amparo de los legítimos pobres*. Ed. Michel Cavillac. Madrid: Espasa-Calpe, 1975. Impreso.

Redondo, Augustín. "De molinos, molineros y molineras. Tradiciones folklóricas y literatura en la España del Siglo de Oro." *Literatura y folklore: Problemas de intertextualidad*. Ed. J.-L. Alonso-Hernández. Salamanca and Groningen: U de Salamanca P, 1983. 101–15. Impreso.

———. "Folklore y literatura en *Lazarillo de Tormes*: Un planteamiento nuevo (El 'caso' de los tres primeros tratados)." *Mitos, folklore y literatura*. Ed. J. Cueto and A. Egido. Zaragoza: Caja de Ahorros y Monte de Piedad, 1987. 81–110. Impreso.

Reglà, Juan. *Historia de España y América*. Dir. by Juan Vicens Vives. 2nd ed. Vol. 3. Barcelona: Editorial Vicens Vives, 1971. Impreso.

Ricapito, Joseph V., ed. Introduction. *Lazarillo de Tormes*. Madrid: Cátedra, 1979. 11–85. Impreso.

Rico, Francisco, ed. *Lazarillo de Tormes*. Madrid: Cátedra, 1987. Impreso.

Shipley, George A. "A Case of Functional Obscurity: The Master Tambourine-Painter of *Lazarillo, Tratado VI*." *Modern Language Notes* 97 (1982): 225–53. Print.

———. "'Otras cosillas que no digo': *Lazarillo's* Dirty Sex." *The Picaresque: Tradition and Displacement*. Ed. Giancarlo Maiorino. Minneapolis: U Minnesota P, 1996. 40–65. Print.

Sieber, Harry. *Language and Society in "La vida de Lazarillo de Tormes."* Baltimore: Johns Hopkins UP, 1978. Print.

Terpstra, Nicholas. *Abandoned Children of the Italian Renaissance: Orphan Care in Florence and Bologna*. Baltimore: Johns Hopkins UP, 2005. Print.

Thompson, B. Bussell, and J. K. Walsh. "The Mercedarian's Shoes (Perambulations on the fourth *tratado* of *Lazarillo de Tormes*." *Modern Language Notes* 103.2 (1988): 440–48. Print.

Vidal y Díaz, Alejandro. *Memoria história de la Universidad de Salamanca*. N.p.: Oliva y Hermano, 1869. Impreso.

Villar y Macías, Manuel. *Historia de Salamanca*. Vol. 2. Salamanca: Francisco Núñez Izquierdo, 1887. Impreso.

Selected Bibliography

• indicates works included or excerpted in this Norton Critical Edition.

• Albrecht, Jane W. "Family Economics/Family Dynamics: Mother and Son in the *Lazarillo de Tormes* (1554)." *Hispanic Journal* 33.2 (2012).

Alemán, Mateo. *Aventuras y vida de Guzmán de Alfarache*. Ed. Benito Brancaforte. Madrid: Cátedra, 1979.

Alpert, Michael, trans. *Lazarillo de Tormes* and *The Swindler: Two Spanish Picaresque Novels*. London: Penguin, 1969.

Alter, Robert. *Rogue's Progress: Studies in the Picaresque Novel*. Cambridge: Havard University Press, 1964.

Appelbaum, Stanley, trans. *Lazarillo de Tormes*. Bilingual ed. Mineola, NY: Dover, 2001.

• Ávila, Teresa de. *The Way of Perfection*. Trans. Abraham Woodhead. Ed. A. R. Waller. London: J. M. Dent, 1902.

Ávila, Teresa de. *The Way of Perfection*. Trans. E. Allison Peers. Colorado Springs, CO: Image Books, 1991.

Bataillon, Marcel. *El sentido del* Lazarillo de Tormes. Paris: Editions Espagnoles, 1954.

Bennassar, Bartolomé. *The Spanish Character: Attitudes and Mentalities from the Sixteenth to the Nineteenth Century*. Trans. Benjamin Keen. Berkeley: University of California Press, 1979.

———. *La España del Siglo de Oro*. Barcelona: Crítica, 1990.

Bjornson, Richard. *The Picaresque Hero in European Fiction*. Madison: University of Wisconsin Press, 1977.

Blackburn, Alexander. *The Myth of the Pícaro: Continuity and Transformation of the Picaresque Novel, 1554–1954*. Chapel Hill, NC: University of North Carolina Press, 1979.

Castillo, David B. *(A)Wry Views: Anamorphosis, Cervantes, and the Early Picaresque*. West Lafayette, IN: Purdue University Press, 2001.

Castro, Américo. "El Lazarillo de Tormes." *Hacia Cervantes*. Madrid: Taurus, 1957.

• Cervantes, Miguel de. *Don Quijote: A Norton Critical Edition*. Trans. Burton Raffel. Ed. Diana de Armas Wilson. New York: Norton, 1999.

Cooley, Jennifer. *Courtiers, Courtesans, Pícaros, and Prostitutes: The Art and Artifice of Selling One's Self in Golden Age Spain*. New Orleans: University Press of the South, 2002.

de Onís, Harriet, trans. *The Life of Lazarillo de Tormes: His Fortunes and Adversities*. Great Neck, NY: Barron's Educational Series, 1959.

Dunn, Peter N. *Spanish Picaresque Fiction: A New Literary History*. Ithaca, NY: Cornell University Press, 1993.

Fernández Ardavín, César, dir. *Lazarillo de Tormes*. Hesperia Productions, Spain, 1959. Film.

Friedman, Edward H. *The Antiheroine's Voice: Narrative Discourse and Transformations of the Picaresque*. Columbia, MO: University of Missouri Press, 1987.

———. "From the Inside Out: The Poetics of *Lazarillo de Tormes*." *Philological Quarterly* 89.1 (2010).

González-Echevarría, Roberto. *Celestina's Brood: Continuities of the Baroque in Spanish and Latin American Literature*. Durham, NC: Duke University Press, 1993.

• Gitliz, David. "Inquisition Confessions and *Lazarillo de Tormes*." *Hispanic Review* 68.1 (2000).

Guillén, Claudio. *Anatomies of Roguery: A Comparative Study of the Origins and Nature of Picaresque Literature*. New York: Garland, 1987.

• Hespelt, E. Herman. "The First German Translation of *Lazarillo de Tormes*." *Hispanic Review* 4.2 (1936).

Kagan, Richard L., with Abigail Dyer, eds. and trans. *Inquisitional Inquiries: Brief Lives of Secret Jews and Other Heretics*. Baltimore, MD: Johns Hopkins University Press, 2013.

Kamen, Henry. *Inquisition and Society in Spain in the Sixteenth and Seventeenth Centuries*. Bloomington, IN: Indiana University Press, 1985.

Lazarillo de Tormes. Ed. Francisco Rico. Madrid: Cátedra, 1992; reprinted, Madrid: Real Academia Española, 2011.

Lázaro Carreter, Fernando. *Lazarillo de Tormes en la Picaresca*. Barcelona: Ariel, 1983.

• León, Fray Luis de. "The Night Serene." *Hispanic Anthology: Poems Translated from the Spanish by English and North American Poets*. Collected and arranged by Thomas Walsh. New York: Putnam, 1920.

• *The Life of Lazarillo of Tormes, His Fortunes and Misfortunes As Told by Himself*, with sequel by Juan de Luna. Trans. Robert S. Rudder with Carmen Criado de Rodríguez Puértolas. New York: Frederick Ungar, 1973.

López, Kimberle S. *New World Rogues: Transculturation and Identity in the Latin American Picaresque*. Diss. University of California, Berkeley, 1994.

• Lovett, Gabriel H. "*Lazarillo de Tormes* in Russia." *Modern Language Journal* 36.4 (1952).

• Mancing, Howard. "The Deceptiveness of *Lazarillo de Tormes*." *PMLA* 90.3 (1975).

Markley, J. Gerald, trans. *The Life of Lazarillo of Tormes*. New York: Bobbs Merril, 1954.

Matorino, Giancarlo. *At the Margins of the Renaissance: Lazarillo de Tormes and the Picaresque Art of Survival*. University Park, PA: Pennsylvania State University, 2003.

Merwin, W. S., trans. *The Life of Lazarillo de Tormes*. New York: New York Review of Books, 2005.

• Pérez, Louis C. "On Laughter in the 'Lazarillo de Tormes.'" *Hispania* 43.4 (1960).

• Perry, Anthony T. "Biblical Symbolism in the *Lazarillo de Tormes*." *Studies in Philology* 67.2 (1970).

Quevedo y Villegas, Francisco de. *La vida del Buscón*. Ed. F. Cabo Aseguinolaza. Barcelona: Crítica, 1993.

Riggan, William. *Pícaros, Madmen, Naifs, and Clowns: The Unreliable First-Person Narrator*. Norman, OK: University of Oklahoma Press, 1981.

Sánchez, Francisco. J. *Early Bourgeois Literature in Early Modern Spain: Lazarillo de Tormes, Guzmán de Alfarache, and Baltasar Gracián*. Chapel Hill, NC: University of North Carolina Press, 2003.

Sieber, Harry. *Language and Society in La vida de Lazarillo de Tormes*. Baltimore, MD: Johns Hopkins University Press, 1978.

Smith, Paul Julian. *Writing in the Margins: Spanish Literature in the Golden Age*. Oxford: Calendon, 2001.

Stavans, Ilan. *Quixote: The Novel and the World*. New York: Norton, 2015.

Tierno Galván, Enrique. *Sobre la novela picaresca y otros ensayos*. Madrid: Tecnos, 1974.

Vogeley, Nancy. *Lizardi and the Birth of the Novel in Spanish America*. Gainesville, FL: University Press of Florida, 2001.

Whitlock, Keith, ed. *The Life of Lazarillo de Tormes*. Trans. David Rowland. Warminster, UK: Aris, 2000.

Zimic, Stanislav. *Apuntes sobre la estructura paródica y satírica del Lazarillo de Tormes*. Madrid: Iberoamericana, 2000.